Life in Prairie Land

Life in Prairie Land

BY ELIZA W. FARNHAM

Introduction by John Hallwas

"Dear Nature is the kindest mother still."—Childe Harold

University of Illinois Press

Urbana and Chicago

Paperback reissued, 2003

© 1988 by the Board of Trustees of the University of Illinois
Manufactured in the United States of America
P 5 4 3 2 1

This book is printed on acid-free paper.

Library of Congress Cataloging-in-Publication Data

Farnham, Eliza Woodson Burhans, 1815-1864.
   Life in prairie land / Eliza W. Farnham ; introduction by John
Hallwas.
      p. cm.—(Prairie State books)
   Reprint. Originally published: New York : Harper, 1846.
   ISBN 0-252-06039-3 (alk. paper)
   1. Illinois—Description and travel—To 1865. 2. Illinois—Social
life and customs. 3. Farnham, Eliza Woodson Burhans, 1815-1864.
4. Illinois—Biography. 5. Pioneers—Illinois—Biography. 6. Women
pioneers—Illinois—Biography. I. Title. II. Series.
F545.F23 1988
977.3'03'0924—dc19   88-14369
[B]   CIP

CONTENTS

PART II

INTRODUCTION

To Eliza Farnham the Illinois frontier was an educational adventure. In 1836 she was a young woman with remarkable intellectual gifts who had educated herself despite a traumatic and deprived childhood, and she wanted to broaden her knowledge of the human condition. Unlike most settlers, she was not motivated by a desire for material success, although her background had been poor enough. She came west to live with her sister, to be courted by a young lawyer, to view American society at its formative edge, and to discover, perhaps, how she could make a difference. By the time she left four and a half years later, the West had made a difference in her. She had seen the wild beauty of the prairies and had studied the peculiar character of the pioneers. She had enjoyed the freedom of a less restrictive society and had experienced the satisfaction of purposeful struggle. She had known love and death. And she had begun to formulate her views on the importance of women to American social development.

Farnham's Illinois experience became the subject of *Life in Prairie Land* (1846). The book combines the descriptive variety of travel writing, the self-characterization of autobiography, and the analytical depth of the extended essay. It also includes one lengthy narrative with the aesthetic qualities of fiction. A miscellany of frontier sketches, akin to Caroline Kirkland's *A New Home — Who'll Follow?* (1839) and *Forest Life* (1842), the work is nevertheless held together by the unique personality of the author. It also provides an engaging account of human interaction with the environment on the rapidly changing frontier. Uneven in quality but fascinating in texture, *Life in Prairie Land* is a significant depiction of the early Midwest and a revealing self-portrait by a remarkable woman.

I

The story of Farnham's life is as interesting as her book, and it provides a helpful context for reading *Life in Prairie Land*.[1] Eliza Wood Burhans was born at Rensselaerville, New York, on November 17, 1815. She was the fourth of five children born to Cornelius and Mary (Wood) Burhans. Her mother was a member of the Society of Friends, so Quaker values, including a strong commitment to helping others, probably had some impact on the family. Mary Burhans died in 1820, and two years later her children were separated. Eliza was sent to live with her atheistic aunt and alcoholic uncle at Maple Springs, in the western part of the state. They lived on a small farm, and the precocious, dark-haired girl soon learned to do her share of the chores. Eliza resided with them for nine years, receiving harsh treatment from her domineering aunt. Although she was not allowed to attend school, Eliza read widely, eventually developing her own religious skepticism. During that time her father remarried and subsequently died.

The emotional deprivation of her family life was compensated by her experiences with nature, as she indicates in the partially fictionalized account of her childhood, *My Early Days* (1859), which was later re-titled *Eliza Woodson* (1864): "I was repulsed [by her aunt], and my thoughts and emotions . . . flowed out upon the objects about me, and found expression in soliloquy—in talks with trees, with the waters, with contemplative cows and thoughtful-looking sheep. I longed for human tenderness and help, but nature never failed me when, lacking these, I turned to her."[2] She developed a remarkable sensitivity to nature as a result of such childhood experiences, so it is not surprising that *Life in Prairie Land* contains many fine passages on her response to the Illinois landscape. In fact, the title page of the book displays a quotation from Byron's *Childe Harold's Pilgrimage* which relates the volume to her childhood situation: "Dear Nature is the kindest mother still."

Eliza was eventually reunited with her brothers and sisters at Palmyra, New York, in 1831. Her sister Mary describes their reunion in *Life in Prairie Land*, remarking that Eliza had spent the period at Maple Springs "not only in a natural but moral wilderness, away from society, away from schools, away from everything but the tyranny of a selfish, passionate woman, and . . . that woman an Atheist . . ." (p. 150). She was appalled at Eliza's lack of religious belief—her acquaintance with "the works of Paine, Volney, Voltaire, and nearly the whole school of infidel writers" and her "im-

pious reasoning, made up the boldest conceptions and most unshrinking conclusions." It is apparent that the period of time Eliza
spent at Maple Springs, no matter how unfortunate in other ways,
helped to produce the independence of mind that is evident in her
books. After the reunion, she obtained a year of formal education
at a Quaker boarding school, through the assistance of her brother
Kelly, and then she supported herself by teaching.

Another event took place in 1831 that was also to have an important impact on Eliza's life. Her sister married and moved to a
homestead near Groveland in Tazewell County, Illinois, several
miles east of Pekin. (Eliza includes Mary's story of her early life,
her marriage, and her trip west to Illinois in *Life in Prairie Land*,
pp. 146-54.) That area later became the most important location
for Eliza's observations of life in the West. Mary's husband was
John M. Roberts, a former teacher from New York who was later
active in the Underground Railroad. The Roberts homestead, called
Prairie Lodge, was located in section eighteen of Morton Township,
about a mile west of where the town of Morton was later established
and three miles northeast of Groveland.[3]

Eliza came west to live with John and Mary in the spring of 1836.
During the previous year, her brother Kelly had sent her to study
at the Albany Female Academy, but she had collapsed from exhaustion after her first examinations. Hence, the move west may
have been recommended for health reasons. But while in Albany
she had also become acquainted with — and probably attached to —
Thomas Jefferson Farnham, a young lawyer from Vermont who
was planning to move to the Groveland area, so she undoubtedly
also intended to see him, as well as visit her sister. In the summer
of 1835 Thomas had purchased property a couple of miles west
of Groveland, in sections twenty-one, twenty-eight, and twenty-
nine of Groveland Township, so he was evidently residing there
when she arrived the following spring. Of course, the trip west
also represented an opportunity for further learning at a time when
Eliza was deeply committed to educating herself. The early chapters
of *Life in Prairie Land* record some of her initial observations, when
"the peculiarities of the people" provided her with amusement and
"themes for speculation" (p. 72). She kept diaries, which suggests
that she may have planned to write about her experience in Illinois.

On July 12, 1836, she married Thomas, who later became a
noted western explorer and travel writer.[4] They resided for almost
three years in the nearby village of Tremont — which, although

unnamed, is described in the book (pp. 92-93; 98-99). They probably settled there because the county seat was moved from Pekin
to Tremont during that year, and lawyers must have been in demand to handle land transactions during the boom period of the
mid-1830s. Eliza returned to the Roberts homestead during the
summer of 1837, and during the next spring and summer as well,
to nurse her ailing sister. Mary finally died in late July of 1838 (p.
161). Two weeks later, Eliza's first-born child also died (p. 163)—
the victim of an epidemic that accompanied a severe drought. In
a moving part of the book, she describes those tragedies and the
period of spiritual struggle afterward, when her own sorrow was
amplified by the drought and disease that continued to ravage the
countryside. She eventually overcame her grief and even attained
"a religious state of mind" (p. 168) with regard to those two deaths.

There is a break in the rather vague chronology of the book at
this point—the end of Part I—and Part II is largely devoted to
Eliza's travels while her husband was away on an exploratory trip
to Oregon in 1839 and 1840. The Farnhams remained in Tremont
until the spring of 1839, when Thomas organized the expedition.
His interest in that area had been kindled by Reverend Jason Lee,
superintendent of the Oregon mission of the Methodist Church,
who had stopped in nearby Peoria on a lecture tour. The group
of nineteen men departed from that town in early May, carrying
a flag upon which Eliza had embroidered their motto: "Oregon or
the Grave."[5] The expedition encountered severe hardships while
crossing the Great Plains, and most of the men rejected Farnham's
leadership, but he continued on to Oregon with four of them.

While her husband was away, Eliza probably lived with her brother
Kelly, who had purchased land from the Farnhams and settled near
Groveland. She may also have stayed briefly with her younger
brother Henry (or Hal), who had moved to Peoria. However, she
traveled much of the time. In the summer of 1839 she made an
extensive visit to the Rock River country near Como, and that was
followed by various trips to other locations in Illinois, including
Springfield and Alton. Some of her traveling was done in the
company of Kelly, but she also traveled alone. Her husband came
back from the West Coast in August of 1840, and a few months
later she returned with him to New York, by way of the Illinois
River and the Great Lakes, and never saw the Mississippi Valley
again.

The Farnhams settled near Poughkeepsie at a place called Wash-
ington Hollow. It was there that Thomas Farnham published *Travels*

in the Great Western Prairies (1841), an account of his Oregon expedition. The book was soon reprinted in New York and London, and his success as a travel writer undoubtedly encouraged his wife to write *Life in Prairie Land*.

Meanwhile, Eliza had become involved in various controversies and was especially outspoken on the role of women in society and the treatment of prison inmates. In 1843 she wrote articles for the magazine *Brother Jonathan*, arguing that women should not seek political power but, rather, should strive to elevate society as mothers and homemakers. That view not only conflicted with the perspective of Susan B. Anthony, Elizabeth Cady Stanton, and other feminist leaders, it increasingly conflicted with the social activism and personal independence of Farnham herself.

In 1844 she became matron of the female division of Sing Sing Prison at Mount Pleasant, New York, where she instituted many reforms. Farnham had been influenced by the pseudoscience of phrenology, which related human character to the organization of the brain (as evident in the conformation of the skull) and regarded criminal behavior as treatable through moral improvement. Historian of penology W. David Lewis has described the impact of her leadership at Sing Sing: "Mrs. Farnham began a program of sweeping change aimed at rehabilitation instead of repression. Inmates who had formerly been restricted to their cells after working hours were now allowed to gather for group instruction in such subjects as history, geography, astronomy, arithmetic, physiology, and personal hygiene. The gloomy atmosphere of the prison was brightened with flowers and music, holidays were celebrated with candy and special meals, inmates were encouraged to pursue arts and crafts, and prizes were given for good behavior."[6] In 1846 Farnham illustrated and wrote a preface to *Rationale of Crime and Its Appropriate Treatment*, a treatise by British phrenologist Marmaduke Blake Sampson. Without doubt, she regarded herself as a clinician who was applying his recommendations at the prison.

Farnham's work at Sing Sing broadened her intellectual contacts and made her a controversial figure. In 1845 she hired Georgiana Bruce (later Kirby) as one of her assistants.[7] Bruce had been a member of the Brook Farm Community, and she shared Farnham's interests in phrenology, women's rights, abolitionism, and other causes. Also, John Bigelow became Farnham's chief supporter. A lawyer, writer, and journalist, he was an influential member of the prison board. Despite the help of such people, she was forced to leave her position in 1848, having been criticized as an infidel and a destroyer of prison discipline by those who opposed her reforms.

By that time Farnham had given birth to two more sons, Charles and Edward, and her husband had left for the West, settling first in Alton, Illinois, and then in San Francisco. He may have been seeking to restore his health, but it is also possible that their marriage was not a happy one. Certainly husband and wife moved in different directions and endured—or enjoyed—long separations. Eliza's career may have been a problem: her growing independence and notoriety would have been difficult for most men of that era to adjust to. There is no evidence of martial discord, however, so they may have simply allowed each other to seek fulfillment individually.

During the 1840s Eliza became acquainted with various other writers. She met William Cullen Bryant, probably through Bigelow, who was not only Bryant's friend but later his biographer. And she was often present at Anne Charlotte Lynch's literary salon, which was frequented by Bigelow, Bryant, and many of their friends and was visited by writers like Edgar Allan Poe, Margaret Fuller, Caroline Kirkland, and Richard Henry Stoddard.[8] Although the exact nature of Bryant's influence on Farnham is hard to determine, she shared his romantic sensibility, love of nature, and knowledge of the Illinois River Valley. In *Life in Prairie Land* she refers to "the magic pen of Bryant" (p. 47). She may also have been influenced or inspired by Kirkland's achievement. Indeed, the title of Farnham's book suggests that she may have intended *Life in Prairie Land* to complement *Forest Life*, expressing the prairie culture of frontier Illinois in the same way that Kirkland's book expressed the forest culture of early Michigan. In any case, since her preface is dated March, 1846, Farnham probably did most of her work on the book during the previous year or two, while she was employed at Sing Sing and in contact with the eastern literati.

Her next post was at the Perkins Institute for the Blind in Boston, where she assisted Dr. Samuel Gridley Howe with his most famous pupil, Laura Bridgman, the first known deaf-blind person to be educated. Farnham's work was cut short in 1848, when she was informed that her husband had died in San Francisco. She had maintained an interest in the frontier, and now there was an estate to settle as well. She made plans to sail around Cape Horn to California with her two sons.

She also attempted to get a large number of single women to come to the West Coast with her, in the belief that marriageable women of good character were sorely needed to shape society on the mining frontier. Although the plan was announced in the newspapers and was endorsed by such figures as Henry Ward Beecher, William Cullen Bryant, Horace Greeley, and Caroline Kirkland, few women sailed with her. The proposal had aroused much controversy, and Farnham had been ill for two months prior to embarkation. Nevertheless, she remained convinced that women were needed in California. The first letter that she wrote to friends in New York after reaching her destination was widely reprinted in the newspapers. It includes a description of the great shortage of women in San Francisco, along with Farnham's assertion that "the best of all missionaries to such a population [of morally degenerated men] are resolute, virtuous, intelligent women."[9]

Her feminist activism was based on a romantic conception of woman as man's moral superior—a Rousseauistic child of nature who possessed inherent purity, sensitivity, and integrity. Because of their virtue, women were essential to the elevation of society, but they needed freedom to realize their potential. Of course, the frontier provided that freedom, as she had discovered in Illinois, but women could also degenerate there because of the harsh conditions that surrounded them, so they had to possess strength of spirit.[10] That was the ideal which Farnham herself exemplified in California.

With the female emigration plan behind her, she operated a 200-acre farm, El Rancho la Libertad, in Santa Cruz County for five years. During that time, she plowed and planted, built her own house, mended fences, practiced homeopathic medicine, and rode horseback to San Francisco and the nearby mining country. Furthermore, she wore pants—a kind of bloomers that she made from an old gymnastics suit—which no doubt drew much attention from the other settlers. She was determined to demonstrate that a woman could manage a farm. Fortunately, she soon had the help and companionship of her former assistant at Sing Sing, Georgiana Bruce, with whom she discussed phrenology, prison reform, antislavery agitation, the role of women, and other matters dear to both of them.[11]

After two years of hardship and struggle, Farnham married an Irishman named William Fitzpatrick in nearby Soquel, on March 23, 1852. They had a daughter, Mary, but the match was a quarrelsome affair. Evidently he abused her. To make matters worse, her daughter died in 1854 and her son Eddie died the following year. But despite a frustrating and tragic personal life, she accomplished much—teaching school at Santa Cruz, writing occasional articles for the newspapers, recommending reforms for San Quentin Prison, and lecturing on spiritualism, womanhood, slavery, vigilantism, and contemporary civilization, as well as working on her next book.[12]

In 1856 she got a divorce—the first in Santa Cruz County. Because of that, her two children's deaths, and her inability to keep much of her property under California law, she returned to New York. Later that year she published *California, In-doors and Out*, a cultural-autobiographical work similar to *Life in Prairie Land*. As one might expect, it emphasizes the importance of women in a pioneer society. It was not, however, as popular as her Illinois book.

During the next two years Farnham studied medicine, and she continued to lecture and write, especially about woman's potential for improving society. In 1858 she spoke at the national Woman's Rights Convention in New York. Her topic was "The Superiority of Woman." The speech was later summarized by Elizabeth Cady Stanton, Susan B. Anthony, and Matilda Joslyn Gage in their *History of Woman Suffrage* (1881): "She presented a series of resolutions, recognizing the right of man in the primary era, in his physical and cerebral structure, to be the conqueror, the mechanic, the inventor, the clearer of forests, the pioneer of civilization, but she looked to the dawning of a higher era, when woman should assume her true position, in harmony with her superior organism, her delicacy of structure, her beauty of person, her great powers of endurance, and thus prove herself not only man's equal in influence and power but his superior in many of the noblest virtues."[13] By that time she was bolstering her theory of woman's moral superiority by arguing that the female sex was biologically more advanced than the male—a controversial view, even among ardent feminists.[14]

Farnham's autobiographical account, *My Early Years*, appeared the following year. She presented herself as a sensitive, deprived youngster with a yearning for education, whose difficult childhood experience prompted an interest in human welfare. She dedicated the book to "G.B.K."—her great friend Georgiana Bruce, who had married a man named Kirby and had remained in Santa Cruz County.

The closing years of Farnham's life were filled with activities for various causes. Between 1859 and 1862 she was in California again, visiting with Georgiana, lecturing on the role of women, and working as matron of the female division of the Stockton Insane Asylum.

She then came back to the East, where she was active in the Woman's Loyal National League, which petitioned Congress for a constitutional amendment to abolish slavery. In 1863 she was a volunteer nurse at Gettysburg, and while there she contracted tuberculosis, which eventually led to her death. Eliza Farnham died on December 15, 1864, in New York City and was buried in the Quaker cemetery at Milton-on-Hudson, New York.

During the late 1850s and early 1860s, she had worked on *Woman and Her Era* (1864), a lengthy study which was published just before she died. Like her speech at the 1858 convention, it propounds the superiority of the female sex. As she points out in the book, woman is the chief agent of human improvement—through her moral influence within the home—but for her to fulfill that role, she needs "absolute freedom": "Woman must become universal in her development. All portals must part at her approach—all fields be open to her. . . . Experience must be hers. No arbitrary or conventional lines must be drawn around her. Going whither she pleases, she will never go widely or long astray. For as soon as Nature's laws in her are read, faithfulness to them will be seen and felt to be her freedom."[15] That perspective had its origin in Illinois, where she was deeply impressed by the physical and social freedom of the frontier and where her observations convinced her that women, by fulfilling their natural potential as wives and mothers, were the key to social improvement.

Another book written during the 1860s, *The Ideal Attained*, was published posthumously in 1865. A fictional presentation of her views on manhood and womanhood, it centers on a lovely young widow with strong opinions on the role of woman in society, who sails to California and eventually marries a man of the right character. An imaginative revision of her California experience, it provided literary fulfillment of her lifelong quest for self-realization as a woman and a moral leader.

II

Life in Prairie Land is the best of Farnham's books. It is a significant depiction of frontier Illinois from the perspective of an eastern emigrant. In the 1830s the Prairie State was the edge of the Far West.[16] The opening of the Erie Canal in 1825 and the coming of steamboat travel on the western rivers a few years later facilitated immigration into the state, and between 1830 and 1840 the population of Illinois grew from 157,000 to 476,000. Towns and settlements sprang up by the hundreds. In particular, the land rush that followed the Black Hawk War of 1832 brought many settlers from New England and New York. Those easterners, or "Yankees," were better educated and frequently more industrious than the southern upland frontier people they encountered. They were readers, writers, and organizers, as well as moral crusaders. Hence, they were apt to be involved in temperance and anti-salvery agitation, and they sympathized with the recently displaced Indians. It is, then, not surprising that Farnham expresses disgust at the filthy, unimproved homestead of a nearby Kentucky woman (pp. 39-40), depicts the degeneration and death of a settler who frequented a local tavern (pp. 113-16), and laments the fate of the Indians while visiting a Sauk burial ground (pp. 224-27).

But *Life in Prairie Land* is an important book because it reflects the unique vision of Eliza Farnham. That is evident from the very beginning, as she describes her trip from St. Louis up the Mississippi and Illinois rivers aboard *The Banner*. For example, she does not miss the contrast between the broken-down boat, with its grotesque crew members, and the pompous captain, "a soft-voiced, red-haired gentleman, in white silk hose, and French pumps, unbrageous ruffles, and a light satin cravat; who had strangely enough been transferred from his natural profession of lounging in the Broadway of some western town, to the command of this antediluvian piece of water craft" (p. 4). Nor does she fail to note the mismatch between a "raw Hoosier girl" who was "astonished at the poverty and filth about her" (p. 6) and her husband, an uncouth prairie settler several years her senior who had gone back to Indiana to get a wife to help him on the farm. This tendency toward displaying contrasts is no minor aspect of Farnham's approach to her subject matter; it is central to her literary art.

Already interested in the position of women in society, she deliberately engages the farmer in a discussion about his plans for wedded life on the frontier. Her view of marriage is, of course, very enlightened: "Marriage is a moral contract. . . . The parties promise to study each other's happiness, and endeavor to promote it" (p. 20). The farmer's outlook could not be more opposed: "I reckon women are some like horses and oxen; the biggest can do the most work, and that's what I want one for." Farnham's conclusion: "He was hopelessly benighted and brutified" (p. 22).

While Farnham is describing her acquaintance with the farmer and his new bride, she introduces a theme which receives considerable emphasis later in the book—freedom. In this case, however, it is the young woman's lack of freedom that impresses the author. As she says, "There was no hope for her but to settle into her slavery, and wear the shackles, if possible, without chafing under them. She had not character enough to redeem herself, and the brutal treatment to which she was doomed would tend every day to diminish the little that she had, and reduce her to the condition of a mere machine" (p. 23). The ignorant, virtually enslaved Hoosier girl strongly contrasts with someone else in the book— Eliza Farnham. The author was dedicated to the expression of her own individuality, the maintenance of her spiritual freedom. The very name of her later homestead in California, El Rancho la Libertad, conveys that about her. The Hoosier girl is, in fact, a sort of anti-type of the cultured, capable, perceptive, and spiritually emancipated young woman who emerges in the pages of *Life in Prairie Land*.

The texture of the book becomes richer and more complex once Farnham reaches her sister's home east of Pekin (referred to as "Pokerton" in the book). Shortly after she is reunited with Mary, who is as clean and capable a homemaker as one could wish for, she visits another residence nearby and meets a fat, pipe-smoking woman from "Kaintucky" who is a "perfect picture of self-satisfaction" (p. 39) amidst a cabin of utter filth. The contrast between the two neighboring homes is striking, and in Farnham's view it reveals a "disgusting indifference to the common comforts of a more civilized condition" (p. 40).

As this suggests, the author's observations convinced her that women were the key to cultural improvement, for where a "degraded condition" was apparent in a frontier homestead, "the credit was due in nearly every one to the females" (p. 39). Hence, she realized that although women could elevate society, they could also degenerate under the influence of harsh conditions and fail to fulfill their social potential. What she was reacting to, of course, was cultural regression on the frontier, which clashed with her eastern values.

Despite her effort to depict the reality of frontier life, Farnham also reflects the mythic view of Illinois as the garden of the wilderness, where vast Edenic prairies were waiting to nourish the American dream.[17] William Cullen Bryant had already presented that mythic perception in "The Prairies" (1833), which became a kind of signature poem for the state, and others had done so as well. Farnham reflects the garden myth in Chapter 21, where she asserts that passage through the area by water reveals an immense

Edenic landscape, with a vast potential for supporting humanity (p. 133). But she also recognizes that the paradisiacal prairie landscape concealed a horrible potential for causing destruction and death. That complex perspective emerges when she tells the story behind a tomb on the prairie—a fictionalized account that was based on a local tragedy.

At the outset, she describes the coming of a settler and his family to "these beautiful gardens"—the prairies of Tazewell County—where "the rifle of the father brought down abundant supplies of deer and grouse, and the smaller members of the family could trap the quail, gather berries and plums, and beat the hazel and nut trees" (p. 176). Their Edenic life ends in tragedy, however, when the father and his eldest son go to a settlement many miles away for supplies, and a prairie fire sweeps toward the cabin: "It was an unbroken line of flame, wide as the eye could reach, mounting, roaring, crackling, and sending up columns of black smoke . . ." (p. 179). Hence, she emphasizes how quickly the benevolent natural world could become destructive. The cabin burns to the ground, the family suffers from hunger and exposure, the pregnant mother gives birth to a stillborn child, and after her husband finally returns, she dies. Thus, in a sentimentalized but still powerful story, Farnham portrays the prairie landscape as both Edenic garden and inhospitable wasteland.

In Chapter 21 she provides yet another contrast, between the Old World and the New—the one burdened with "exquisite products of human energy" and offering a "spectacle of warning," and the other laden with "exquisite forms and hues of beauty" inviting people to an "untrodden empire of nature" (p. 134). Her statement of preference for the latter is couched in religious terms that recall Emerson's *Nature* (1836): "The lofty edifices which art, directed by the religious feelings, has wrought and piled, may waken devotion in others, but my cathedral should be the overhanging cliff, my temple the eloquent shades. My worship is kindled by these into far more intense life than by the displays of human power. Living much with nature makes me wiser, better, purer, and therefore, happier!" (p. 134). In fact, this entire chapter, including a remarkable opening section that illustrates the process and value of nature appreciation (pp. 129-30), was apparently influenced by Emerson's famous essay.

Bryant's poems had an impact on her view of nature as well, and his romantic celebration of the natural world is probably the most important aspect of that influence.[18] But his constant themes of transience and death are unimportant to her, whereas the process of the nature appreciation and its value for self-development are concerns that unite her with Emerson. To put it another way, the latter says in *Nature* that "man is the dwarf of himself"—"a god in ruins"—but that "nature is made to conspire with spirit to emancipate us."[19] In the same way, Farnham refers (in her preface) to "the endwarfed, debased mind of man" and declares that nature's influences on the human spirit "are purifying, ennobling, and elevating" (p. xxxiii). To her, unspoiled nature in the West offers the same kind of spiritual "emancipation" (p. xxxiv) that Emerson mentions.

She probably came into contact with Emersonian transcendentalism through Georgiana Bruce, who had been a worker and a student at the Brook Farm Community from 1841 to 1844. While there she had met Bronson Alcott, Orestes Brownson, and Emerson, and she had become a close friend of Margaret Fuller, editor of *The Dial*. Directly after leaving the community, Bruce met Farnham and became her assistant at Sing Sing, but she kept in touch with Fuller and induced her to lecture at the prison. That was during the period when *Life in Prairie Land* was being written. Farnham did not publicly espouse transcendentalism, but the writings of Emerson and his associates may have encouraged her to express her own passionate individualism, heightened sensitivity to nature, and sense of spiritual emancipation. Her immersion in phrenology would have made her very receptive to that influence, for phrenology was not just a means of analyzing behavior. It was a social philosophy that emphasized freedom, individualism, and human perfectibility—values that the transcendentalists also espoused.[20]

At any rate, Farnham's interest in people and the landscape in Illinois extended beyond the present into a sympathetic understanding of the Indians' relationship to the land in the past. Clearly, they embodied her belief that living in close, sensitive contact with unspoiled nature ennobled the human spirit. Hence, she deplores what the whites had done to the Indians, referring to them late in her book as "a race that has dwindled from power and the strong majesty of freedom, to humility and wasting feebleness" (p. 226). At the same time, she believes that the march of civilization was inevitable and, in a sense, right, although it proceeded in a regrettable way and with tragic results: "A fair land abounding in all that would contribute to the highest condition of civilized life, was the lawful estate of civilized man; and when he came to claim

it, it was not the office of the savage to dispute his right. I mourn
not so much the fate of the Indian, as the indecent, the fraudulent
precipitancy with which it was consummated by our selfishness. . . . We have chosen our own time to bid them disappear from
a heritage around which the very fibres of their hearts were twined
in love and reverence for the dead who were sleeping there, and
for the living beauty and majesty that overspread it" (pp. 226-27).
Her appreciation of the perspectives of both races is one of the
most appealing aspects of *Life in Prairie Land*.

In the final chapter of the book, Farnham considers the past and
the future of "prairie land," depicting the advance of civilization
in Illinois. In doing so, she presents her own deeply felt opposing
views on the question of development in the region. On the one
hand, she idealizes the trappers and missionaries who first came
into the area, viewing them as "wild and free" like the Indians,
living "in unison with the world-wide peace and joy of nature" (p.
265). And she identifies with the early settlers, for whom population
increase meant a radical change in quality of life. A little before
her time, a few pioneers enjoyed alone all the blessings of the
wilderness landscape—"its grandeur, its freedom, its wondrous
fertility" (p. 267)—but many other, very different people—"earnest men, with hard hands and severe, calculating faces"—soon
wanted those things too. These later settlers, by their very presence,
ruined the landscape that the pioneers had enjoyed. In other words,
Farnham views the earliest settlers as having an appreciation for
the wilderness much like her own, so she recognizes the disadvantages of economic and cultural development, which would greatly
change the natural environment.

At the same time, she is glad to know that people are coming
to the area because of her convictions about the influence of such
a wilderness upon one's spiritual self. To Farnham the West was a
gigantic Walden, an unspoiled natural area conducive to the spiritual emancipation of those who withdrew from established society
to settle there. No wonder she closes her book with a vision of the
future in which the self-governing residents of prairie land have
built a great society, "free from want, from oppression, from ignorance, from fear" (p. 268). As that final section reveals, Eliza
Farnham was a prophet of the American dream.

The vast motif of people and the landscape is, then, central to
the author's achievement in *Life in Prairie Land*. This is not only
developed as a personal matter, an expression of her sensitivity to
the natural world in Illinois, but as a means of assessing the present,

past, and future of midwestern culture. Farnham realizes that if nature in the wild is spectacular and abundant, it is also unaccommodating and even destructive. She finds that people can live in harmony with the land, like the Indians and early pioneers, or disfigure its beauty while drawing upon its abundance, like many settlers. And she knows that some men and women "degenerate" on the frontier, while others are "set free." Thus, she asserts not only the influence of people upon the landscape but of the landscape upon people, and she realizes that from this reciprocal relationship the destiny of the West will be forged. For the expression of this motif alone, *Life in Prairie Land* deserves a position of importance in early midwestern literary history.

NOTES

1. There are several significant sources of information about Farnham's life: Samuel Burhans, Jr., *Burhans Genealogy* (New York: privately printed, 1894), pp. 180, 193; "Eliza Woodson Burhans Farnham," *Dictionary of American Biography*, VI, 282; W. David Lewis, "Eliza Wood Burhans Farnham," in *Notable American Women 1607-1950)*, ed. Edward T. James et al. (Cambridge, Mass.: Harvard University Press, 1971), I, 598-600; Madeleine B. Stern, "Introduction," *California, In-doors and Out* (Nieuwkoop, Netherlands: B. De Graaf, 1972), pp. vii-xlii; Madeleine B. Stern, "Introduction," *Life in Prairie Land* (Nieuwkoop, Netherlands: B. De Graaf, 1972), pp. vii-xxxii; Pamela Herr, "Reformer," in *The Women Who Made the West*, by the Western Writers of America (Garden City, N.Y.: Doubleday, 1980), pp. 205-19; and John E. Hallwas, "Eliza Farnham's *Life in Prairie Land*," *The Old Northwest* 7 (1981-82), 295-324. The present Introduction is partially based on the last of these, with the permission of the journal's publisher, Miami University.

2. *Eliza Woodson; or, The Early Days of One of the World's Workers*, 2d ed. (New York: A. J. Davis, 1864), p. 29.

3. For information on John Roberts and the location of Prairie Lodge, see the *History of Tazewell County, Illinois* (Chicago: Charles C. Chapman, 1879), p. 541. Also helpful for locating the Roberts land, as well as property owned by the Farnhams and Kelly Burhans, is the *Atlas Map of Tazewell County, Illinois* (Davenport, Iowa: Andreas, Lyter, 1873), pp. 140, 144, which is useful in conjunction with information from the Tazewell County land-deed records.

4. See "Thomas Jefferson Farnham," *Dictionary of American Biography*, VI, 283. For a list of his books, see Hallwas, p. 323, note 7.

5. Reuben Gold Thwaites, "Introduction," *Early Western Travels 1748-1846* (Cleveland: Arthur H. Clark, 1906), XXVII, 10. Farnham's *Travels*

in the Great Western Prairies is reprinted in volumes XXVIII and XIX of this series.

6. "Eliza Farnham and Phrenological Contributions to American Penology," in Marmaduke Blake Sampson, *Rationale of Crime and Its Appropriate Treatment,* ed. Eliza W. Farnham (1846; reprint, Montclair, N.J.: Patterson Smith, 1973), pp. xx-xxi. See also John Davies, *Phrenology, Fad and Science* (New Haven, Conn.: Yale University Press, 1955), pp. 102-3, and W. David Lewis, *From Newgate to Dannemora: The Rise of the Penitentiary in New York, 1776-1848)* (Ithaca, N.Y.: Cornell University Press, 1965), pp. 177, 237-50.

7. Kirby describes her association with Farnham at the prison in *Years of Experience: An Autobiographical Narrative* (New York: G. P. Putnam's, 1887), pp. 190-226.

8. Charles H. Brown, *William Cullen Bryant* (New York: Charles Scribner's Sons, 1971), p. 338.

9. "Mrs. Farnham in California," *Sangamo Journal* (Springfield, Illinois) February 27, 1850, p. 2.

10. See *California, In-doors and Out* (New York: Dix and Edwards, 1856), pp. 156, 222-24, 255, 275, 293-94, 297. See also Julie Roy Jeffrey, *Frontier Women: The Trans-Mississippi West* (New York: Hill and Wang, 1979), pp. 109-10, 140.

11. Two additional sources on the Farnham-Bruce (Kirby) relationship in California are these short articles by Madeleine B. Stern: "Two Letters from the Sophisticates of Santa Cruz," *The Book Club of California Quarterly NewsLetter* 33 (Summer, 1968), 51-62 and "A Feminist Association," *Manuscripts* 35 (1983), 113-17.

12. The following local history materials in the Special Collections unit of the University Library at the University of California, Santa Cruz, were useful in reconstructing Farnham's years in California: Meyrick Henry, *Santa Cruz and Monterey Illustrated Handbook* (San Francisco: San Francisco News Publishing, 1880), cover and p. 25; Leon Rowland Scrapbook, pp. 35, 41, 54, 59, 74, 141, 156, and 170; Jeannette Rowland, "Eliza W. Farnham," *News and Notes from the Santa Cruz Historical Society,* February, 1963, pp. 1-2; Frank McCrary and Carolyn Swift, "The Feminist Farmer, Eliza Farnham," in *Big Creek Lumber and Building Supplies 1982 Catalog and Price Guide* (n.p., 1982), pp. 42-43.

13. *History of Woman Suffrage* (New York: Fowler and Wells, 1881), I, 669.

14. For a discussion of Farnham's theory of female superiority and its biological underpinnings, see Helen Beal Woodward, "Biology Triumphant: Eliza Woodson Farnham," *The Bold Women* (New York: Farrar, Straus, and Young, 1953), pp. 337-56.

15. *Woman and Her Era* (New York: C. W. Plumb, 1865), II, 418.

16. For descriptions of Illinois during the 1830s, see John Mason Peck, *A Gazetteer of Illinois,* 2d ed. (Philadelphia: Grigg and Elliott, 1837), and

A. D. Jones, *Illinois and the West* (Boston: Jordan, 1838). The latter is especially interesting because Chapter 7 includes a description of Tremont at the time Farnham lived there. Many historical works deal with Illinois in the 1830s. The best overview of the period is Robert P. Howard, *Illinois: A History of the Prairie State* (Grand Rapids, Mich.: William B. Eerdmans, 1972), chapters 7-9.

17. For discussions of the Edenic perspective in the book, see Hallwas, pp. 309-14, and Annette Kolodny, "Mary Austin Holley and Eliza Farnham: Promoting the Prairies," *The Land before Her: Fantasy and Experience of the American Frontiers 1630-1860* (Chapel Hill: University of North Carolina Press, 1984), pp. 93-111.

18. The apparent influence of Bryant on *Life in Prairie Land* is discussed by Hallwas, pp. 312, 315, 316, and 319.

19. *Nature*, in *The Collected Works of Ralph Waldo Emerson*, ed. Alfred R. Ferguson and Robert E. Spiller (Cambridge, Mass.: Harvard University Press, 1971), pp. 30, 42.

20. See Davies, pp. 166-68.

PREFACE

The following work was commenced with the intention of writing one or two brief sketches descriptive of Life at the West. And until some hundred and fifty pages were written, I never contemplated the possibility of extending them to a volume. At that point, I was so far from having said all I felt, that I very willingly resigned myself to the current of my feelings and wrote on.

To those who read the volume first, and afterward, in some idle moment, turn back to the preface, I need not say that I have been impelled in every step by love of my theme. That will have been apparent enough to them, without any such declaration. I have loved the West, and it still claims my preference over all other portions of the earth. Its magnitude, its fertility, the kindliness of its climate, the variety and excellence of its productions are unrivaled in our own country, if not on the globe.

In these characteristics, it presents itself to my mind in the light of a strong and generous parent, whose arms are spread to extend protection, happiness, and life to throngs who seek them from other and less friendly climes. Setting a high value upon these resources, I rejoice to hear of emigration to the country possessing them— not alone because those who go will find there abundance for the supply of their natural wants, but because the influences with which it will address their spiritual natures are purifying, ennobling, and elevating. If nature ever taught a lesson which the endwarfed, debased mind of man could study with profit, it is in these regions of her benignest dispensations. The burden of her teaching here, is too palpable to be wholly rejected by any. Even vulgar minds do not altogether escape its influence. Their perceptions become more vivid, their desires more exalted, their feelings purer, and all their intellectual action more expanded.

The magnificence, freedom, and beauty of the country form, as it were, a common element, in which all varieties of character, education, and prejudice are resolved into simple and harmonious relation. Living near to nature, artificial distinctions lose much of their force. Humanity is valued mainly for its intrinsic worth— not for its appurtenances or outward belongings.

It must not be forgotten, however, that a large class of minds have no adaptation to the conditions of life in the West. This is more especially true of my own sex. Very many ladies are so unfortunate as to have had their minds thoroughly distorted from all true and natural modes of action by an artificial and pernicious course of education, or the influence of a false social position. They cannot endure the sudden and complete transition which is forced upon them by emigration to the West. Hence a class may always be found who dislike the country; who see and feel only its disadvantages; who endure the self-denial it imposes without enjoying any of the freedom it confers; who suffer the loss of artificial luxuries, but never appreciate what is offered in exchange for them. Persons so constituted ought never to entertain for a moment the project of emigration. They destroy their own happiness, and materially diminish that of others. Their discontent and pining are tolerated with much impatience, because those who do not sympathize with them, see so much to enjoy and so little to endure, that their griefs command little or no respect.

I had no such experience, for I loved the country, and when compelled to return to the crowded and dusty marts of the East, I did so with many and deep regrets; and these still linger and mingle largely with the emotions of my life. The writing of these sketches has, therefore, been a labor of love. While engaged upon them, I have lived again in the land of my heart. I have seen the grasses wave, and felt the winds, and listened to the birds, and watched the springing flowers, and exulted in something of the old sense of freedom which these conferred upon me. Visions, prophetic of the glory and greatness which are to be developed here, have dwelt in my mind and exalted it above the narrow personal cares of life.

It is the enjoyment afforded by this kind of emancipation which so endears the Western country to those who have resided in it. It steals upon the heart like what it is, the very witchery of nature; so that those who are susceptible to it, feel the charm but not the inconvenience through which it is invoked. Such persons delight in the perfection and beauty of the natural, and these suffice them.

After what has been said, it would be superfluous to add that of this latter class I am an humble member; that no deprivation or suffering incident to the country could sever my attachment to it, and that any portraiture of its life which I should draw would, therefore, abound in gay and cheerful colors. The sombre tints would not dwell in my heart, and I cannot reproduce them. This may make my picture appear to be a partial one, but to me and those who are of like spirit it will be honest.

Conscious of the intent to make it so, I shall dismiss it without care in that regard, and leave it to tell its own story of the great and generous land whose name it bears.

E. W. F.

Mount Pleasant, N. Y.
March, 1846.

PART I

LIFE IN PRAIRIE LAND

CHAPTER I

On the morning of one of the last days of April, 18——, there was a small party of persons collected in the cabin of a steamboat which had just arrived at St. Louis from Louisville, discussing some topic which seemed to possess for them an engrossing interest. This party consisted of six persons, four ladies and two gentlemen, all evidently travelers. The question was how and when they should prosecute the remainder of their voyage up the principal eastern tributary which the father of waters receives above the Ohio. One of the gentlemen had explored the forest of steamboats which crowded the wharf of this growing city, and reported that there was but one advertised "For the Illinois this evening, without fail," that he could not get on board of her, but thought her appearance extremely unpromising. It was near the close of the week, and as the other gentleman was a clergyman, and he and his party had moreover no dear friends from whom they had been separated seven long years, awaiting their arrival, they concluded to stop till the succeeding one. They accordingly went on shore, and the writer and her companion set out, accompanied by a cartman and sundry trunks, chests, et cet., to find the *elegant, fast-sailing, high-pressure* boat that was going "up the Illinois this evening, without fail."

We had traveled far enough on the western waters already, to have learned that the "this evening" of the bills might possibly be adjourned twenty-four or even thirty-six hours; but faith is no less requisite on western steamboats than elsewhere, and summoning all ours, we embarked ourselves and our baggage on board the "Banner." We soon found the faith which led us on board was a mere rush-light to that necessary to keep us there. If steamboats had been running on the Illinois at the time when Noah explored the summit of Ararat, one would have affirmed that this very "Banner" was the pioneer of that period. But there is a story to be told, by and by, of the first craft of this kind that ever went up the Illinois, and its effect on the settlers, which unfortunately conflicts with this supposition, and drives the antiquarian to a period

3

comparatively modern, as that which gave birth to the Banner. She was not a very large boat, but what she wanted in size was amply compensated in filth. One flight of stairs between the cabins was carpeted, and sundry small patches still remained on the floor of that in which we ate, being too firmly fastened by mingled grease and clay to be easily removed. It is not perhaps generally known, that these articles, properly compounded, make a paste which is quite firm and nearly insoluble in cold water. I mention it for the benefit of the unenlightened, and can bear ample testimony to its virtues, having seen them repeatedly demonstrated in various ways at the west. The floors were broken, the stairs dilapidated; there was no linen for the berths, the hurricane deck leaked, and its edge was hung with delicate filaments of tar, which the warmth of the sun often drew to an inconvenient length and sometimes quite severed, irrespective of the welfare of those passing beneath. The waste of the steam was so great that the wheels effected only about four revolutions a minute, and the boat had a strange habit which I could not then fully comprehend, but which has since been satisfactorily explained by a scientific friend, of occasionally running twice or thrice her length with considerable rapidity, and then suddenly lurching so as to throw every thing to the larboard. She averaged five of these spasms a day. There was a one-handed chambermaid on board, a one-eyed cook, and a three-fingered boy to wait at table. But all these imperfections were more than compensated by the exquisite finish and perfection of the captain. He was a soft-voiced, red-haired gentleman, in white silk hose, and French pumps, umbrageous ruffles, and a light satin cravat; who had strangely enough been transferred from his natural profession of lounging in the Broadway of some western town, to the command of this antediluvian piece of water craft. One could draw his portrait this day, by adding a thatch of red bristles over the mouth, and substituting for the silken hose gaiters of the neatest fit and finish. On deck he wore lemon-colored gloves. The first polish of the laundress was taken off his snowy linen pantaloons when I first saw him, and the plaits of his ruffle had relaxed a little from their precise angles, but the satin cravat, the pumps and hose, were unexceptionable. He walked with a mincing, uneasy gait through the little hall which led to the ladies' cabin, and presented himself before my astonished eyes—one delicate glove drawn on, and the other straightened in his hand—with a bow that would have graced the drawing-room of St. James.

"It's a ver-ry-warm day, miss." I looked my astonishment, and was about informing him that the gentlemen's cabin was in some other part of the boat, when he laid his white hand on one of the filthy chairs and placing it near the door, seated himself upon it with such an at-home sort of air, looking at the same time so familiar with the filth and disorder about, that I felt convinced he must be a part of the establishment. He must either be the captain or clerk, for the cook is black, and none of the hands would dare undertake a prank of this kind. These thoughts passed rapidly through my mind, while the object of them was adjusting his cravat, arranging his hair, and passing his cambric handkerchief slowly over his moist forehead, so that, notwithstanding my deliberation, I replied, before he was enitrely prepared to continue the conversation, that so far as the temperature was concerned, I was happy to be able to coincide with him.

"You are going up the Illinois, miss?"

"I am delighted with your sagicity, sir," I replied; "that forms a part of my present expectation."

"Have you ever been up?"

"Never, sir."

"Then you have a delightful trip before you."

"I admire your taste," I replied, glancing at the naked floor, the mutilated chairs, and the greasy berths.

"How far up do you go, miss?"

"I am not informed, sir, as to the exact distance."

"You have recently arrived in this region, I presume?"

"I have, sir."

"I shall have great pleasure in carrying so *intelligible* a young lady into the country."

"You flatter me."

"O no, miss, I believe I speak truth."

"Your sagicity, sir is beyond praise."

Before he had time to reply, a young chap in a red calico shirt, with a face dirtier than I can describe, presented himself at the door and bawled out, "Cappen, please to come *hyur*.* John's dead done with whiskey, the new ingineer's gone off on a spree, and th' ain't nobody to keep the fire up." Herupon the "cappen" rose and departed, with a pompous solicitation that I would excuse his absence.

* It is difficult to convey by any written combination of letters the sound of this word as uttered by the natives of these regions. It is more like *yur* preceded by *h* sharply aspirated, than anything else to which I can liken it.

He had been gone but a very few moments when the one-handed chambermaid entered, directing in a raw Hooshier girl who had been our fellow passenger from Louisville. Poor child! even her eyes, trained as they were to rude sights, looked astonished at the poverty and filth about her. I did not wonder that she started with an exclamation of delight and said, "I'm right glad to see you!" though we had never exchanged a word before. She was a tall, dark featured person, with a head of fine black hair that flowed to her feet when the horn comb was withdrawn from it. Her stature was large, her hands and feet proportionably so. She was accompanied by a man whose relation to her had excited a good deal of speculation among us. He was several years her senior; had lost three of his front teeth, wore a red flannel shirt with a standing collar of the same, supported by a cotton pocket-handkerchief, a fur cap, and the thickest of all possible boots, the tops of which were just invaded by the bottoms of a pair of jean pantaloons. His attentions to his traveling companion were so peculiar that we had been in a delightful state of uncertainty all the way as to what this relation could be. They were authoritative enough for those of a father, but then their age forbade the supposition. He might have been an uncle, but she never called him so; possibly a cousin, but no woman ever so prized the attention of a mere cousin. He could scarcely have been a brother, because there was not the faintest resemblance between them. What then could he be? We had examined and rejected every supposition but that of his being her husband; but nobody would listen to that, because supported by no probabilities. The riddle was turned over to me for solution. It cannot be wondered at, that in such desperate circumstances, I looked upon their entrance as quite a providence, and reciprocated the self-gratulation expressed by my fellow-passenger.

She seated herself on one chair, deposited her bundle on another, and, laughing the while, exclaimed, "This *hyur* boat ain't set out so smart by a heap as t'other. I 'lowed we shouldn't have such a fine place to be in all the way."

"Why," said I, "had you been told that the boats up the Illinois were so poorly furnished?"

"No, I never heern nothin about 'em, but 'tain't in natur to have such carpets, and cheers, and glasses everywhere; it costs a heap to have 'em."

Poor child! the spendors of a comfortable cabin had been to her like the show of regal magnificence to a peasant; and she could say with poor Hinda, though not in language so sentimental, "I knew, I knew it could not last!"

In a few minutes her companion made his appearance, and announced that he had *toted* the plunder aboard, and as the boat wa'n't goin to start till after night, he was goin up to see the place. He gave her no invitation to accompany him, nor did she seem to expect it. I did not wish to broach *the* question at once, so we had a few words on indifferent topics, till Hal (I believe I have forgotten to say that my traveling companion bore that convenient *soubriquet*) entered and asked me if I would like to stroll an hour or two over the western city.

"Most gladly," I replied; "a wilderness and motion were preferable to this tedious place."

"Have you seen the captain?" was his next question.

"Yes, he has paid his respects formally."

"Well, he's a character, isn't he, to finish off such a boat as this? but we'll have some fun out of him before we part."

We sallied forth, and my heart really ached as I left the solitary girl sitting there, robbed of all the splendor that had so delighted her senses for the last few days, and alone. She looked sad, and I made an interrogative sign to Hal about asking her to accompany us, with all the oddities of her person and apparel, but he shook his head. When we were out, I asked why he had refused my request.

"Why," said he, "Mr. Red-flannel may prefer to escort his wife himself, and his preference might be expressed rather strongly if he found me doing it without his consent. We don't know how these Hooshiers will receive any civilities to which they are not accustomed; and you have heard enough of the modes in which they express their displeasure, to be aware that it is no slight thing to awaken it. You see that clump of trees yonder in the skirt of the city?"

"Yes, but what have they to do with the resentment of insult or wrong?"

"Much. There is a heap of ashes under one of them with which this pleasant wind is playing, as if they were not the most revolting object that could be found on the face of this republic."

"And what, pray, renders them such? Your face tells a tale of horror."

"And well it may; for last night, only last night, a man, an unfortunate and guilty one it may be, but still a man, and a citizen of this proud state, was tied to that tree and burned alive!"

"Merciful heaven, it cannot be!"

"Yes, it is even so, and a crowd of people were gathered around to witness the fearful spectacle."

"And was there no heart during all that period of agony to relent and turn the tide of fury into pity and tenderness? A word uttered in the spirit of human love must have done it, methinks, and made the most violent ready to bear their suffering victim away in their arms."

"It remained unspoken, then; for the damning fact is recorded on earth as well as in Heaven."

"It surely must blast the peace of every person who had any knowledge of it and did not interpose to prevent it. But what was his offence? Surely it must have been very aggravated to have awakened such awful vengeance."

"I have not learned the precise circumstances, but rumor (and that from those who approved, or at least suffered the disgraceful event to take place, would, we may suppose, attribute to him his full measure of iniquity) says that he had led a desperate sort of life on the river and in its vicinity. His final offence was stabbing an officer who attempted to arrest him for some recent crime."

"Did the wound produce instant death?"

"No. I believe the man is still living, or at least survived some hours. I have understood that he was very much esteemed, and had a family of small children. But these are less than feather weights in the scale that will balance the guilt of his murderers."

"These things are awful truly, and disgraceful too, if we consider the boasted supremacy and efficiency of our laws. I trust the like does not occur so often that the city is not agitated by it."

"No, such extreme cases do not; but this is only an extreme one of a class of public offences that are frequent here. Individual or associated feeling often assumes the prerogative of law in the infliction of lesser punishments."

"Well, it is not perhaps, on reflection, so extraordinary as it seems at first sight to us. We come from a region comparatively old, where time has defined right and interest, and developed more fully the power of law, and established rules of action. Here all is new. Passion may break forth and do its fatal misdeeds, before the slower majesty of law is perceived by the turbulent actors to be sufficient for their purposes. Such scenes must exhibit clearly to every reflecting mind the necessity of framing in our seasons of entire self-possession rules by which we will abide when these have passed away. Fanatical liberalists may term them shackles to restrain our future freedom, but I would that every one of such might stand beside that funeral dust. Before the awful truth taught there, his ravings for large liberty would shrink into their true insignificance."

"But if such lessons are not learned from the pages of history, black with the records of fouler violence than this, how shall the shallow minds which reject them there, imbibe them here?"

"True: but we are wandering far, and your horrible recital has been so painful that I am less disposed to walk than before I heard it. Let us return."

CHAPTER II

On reaching the wharf, we found things wearing a very busy appearance. The engine was wheezing like an asthmatic, some rough-looking men were *toting* plunder on board, the captain stood upon the guard with both gloves drawn on and buttoned, the hands were moving about as if intent on business, and things began to wear quite the aspect of departure. This was encouraging.

"Will you start to-night captain?" said Hal.

"Certainly, sir," taking out his repeater. "Ring the bell, Jack. That's our first bell; we shall be off in an hour."

"Really," said I, as we walked up the street, "this affair has some creditable points, its punctuality for instance."

"Yes, you'll learn the value of that when our friends who wait here till Monday pass us halfway up the Illinois."

"Now out upon your croaking, and let's put a cheerful face on the attempt, since we have made it."

The hour extended from one o'clock to six. We left the wharf just as the sun was setting, and if the reader escapes a commonplace description of spires gilded by his last rays, of windows blazing with crimson and golden light, of trees shaking their small foliage in the evening wind, and of the dying hum of the city, stealing fainter and fainter on our ears as the muddy waters parted slowly before our prow, he may thank the Banner and her peerless captain. Either were sufficient to have put to flight the sentimentality of a legion of school-misses, — both together quite routed mine; not to mention our red-flanneled Hooshier, or his long-haired bride. Everything about me was so thoroughly uncomfortable, that I felt no disposition to rest in any anticipation short of that which pictured the home and faces we so longed to see. Three days of this dismal journeying were reported to lie between us and them, and it re-

quired under such circumstances some heroism in man or woman
to look forward through their tedious length.

I was fatigued, and requested the chambermaid to prepare my
berth as early as possible. She offered me a very disinterested piece
of advice in reference to it, which I shall give here for the benefit
of such as may be similarly situated, without the like kindness to
direct their choice. It was, that I had better abandon the little pen,
otherwise state-room, which I had chosen beside the cabin, and
take my berth in the latter apartment, "'Kase," to use her own
elegant language, "the bugs ain't a touch in *hyur* to what they be
in y*ander.*" Here was another volume of misery opened to my
already oppressed senses. Seeing my consternation, she added, "O,
you needn't dread 'em so powerful; I broomed the berths to-day,
and shook the 'trasses, so they won't be so mighty bad."

"Make my berth where you think best," I said.

"There ain't no clean sheets, but I can tear off a pair, and you
can sleep in 'em, you know, if they ain't hemmed, and I'll give you
my pillow."

"No, thank you," I replied; "just tear off a third sheet, and I'll
make a pillow-case of it for myself."

At last the berth was prepared, and the vermin made a night of
it. They had evidently not been treated for some time, and brought
vigorous appetites to my reception. After a contest of four or five
hours, I was fain to yield possession to them. Making such limited
ablution as the place allowed, I dressed myself and sat down on
the stern of the boat to wait the coming day, and speculate on the
distance we had made. When the light came up over the heavy
forest which clothed the eastern bank of the river, I saw that the
waters were still muddy, and knew, therefore, that we could not
have passed the mouth of the Missouri. Nine hours' running had
brought us twenty-two miles!—a dismal augury for the 240 that
yet remained. As the daylight gained, I saw that the current under
the eastern shore was dark and clear, and a few minutes after the
scattered town of Alton began to peer up from among its beautiful
bluffs, just touched with the first tender hue of spring.

And now the waters widened on the west, and opened up inland
a broad, eddying, plunging sea of mud. On the spine of a sand-
bar which was just visible between the two streams, the currents
met, and the waters of the Missouri rose into a circling wave which
toppled an instant and ran on, eager to mingle with the purer
element that glittered and danced beyond. But the Mississippi, as
if disdaining the foul alliance thus tumultuously sought, stole angrily

away beneath the dark forest on the opposite shore, and preserved her identity a long way down, in a narrow transparent vein, growing more slender, till at length its bed was wholly usurped by the muddy monster.

This, then, was the junction of these two streams! The point where the mighty son of the mountains meets the clear-eyed daughter of the lakes—majestic union of powers whose feeble birth is in the deep wilderness and the untrodden solitude, whose maturity makes the ocean tremble. Nothing could be more impressive. When the child's geography had first been put in my hands, I read of these great rivers and put my feeble powers to their utmost task to conceive them. I had followed the insignificant red and green lines which represent them, and explored the echoing mountains whence one plunges to the plain below, and the gushing springs and softly chiming lakes whence the other rises and winds; till fancy, wearied with the effort, drooped her pinion, and left me on the rough bench in the little brown school-house, sick and disgusted with the narrowness and coarseness of the world to which I was confined. I had taken the eagle's wing, and, perched upon the mountain pine, had seen the little rivulets

> —— "leap and gush
> O'er channeled rock and broken bush,"

bending towards each other, and swelling as they united, till their march became resistless. I had followed them where the dim wood and towering cliff reëchoed to their tread, and where they cut the verdant bosom of the sunny plain like threads of molten silver. Vast, illimitable journey! And here, beneath my eye, these messengers from the unvexed solitudes, thousands of miles away, met and pursued their path together. It seemed like a union of strength to thread the more dangerous territory inhabited by man. Both streams at this time were swollen to their fullest capacities by the spring floods. The gigantic Missouri poured out his turbid waters with a force that made his feeble neighbor recoil and leave a chasm between the transverse muddy wall, and the clear dark stream that glided timidly by on the other side.

While I was contemplating this scene, wrapt in silence, a little window close beside me opened, and a hand was thrust forth which I immediately recognized to be the solitary member belonging to the body of our chambermaid. She drew back with a scream, and an exclamation not of the most feminine character; but the next moment her eyes relieved her trepidation, and after muttering some apology, she expressed her opinion that I "must feel *right peart* to be out that *airly*." I had no little difficulty in convincing her that there was sufficient activity in my nerves of sensation to render the insects that shared my berth somewhat troublesome.

"I reckon," said she, "thar must have been a mighty small chance of the varmints about you, 'kase I swep up about a pint of 'em yesterday and throw'd 'em overboard; so it's impossible you could ha had a great many."

I yielded the point, and afterwards observed that whenever they were alluded to on board this boat, it was by measure!

We reached Alton at 8 o'clock. The bell rang when we were within 100 yards of the shore, and the boat was in one of her spasms, which the captain calculated would lay him alongside in gallant style. But alas! spasmodic action is no more to be relied on in boat nature than human. On we came, the waters quite whitening in our wake, and making, as the delighted Mrs. Raddle observed on another occasion, "*acterally* more noise" than if we had come in a better boat, for the engine creaked and hissed at every joint, and the escape-pipe disgorged itself about thrice a minute with a dismal hollow sound, as if its vitals were breaking up. We nearly touched the shore; the captain stood in his ruffles, silk hose, pumps and gloves, the passengers waited, valises and trunks in hand, ready to jump ashore, and two or three were gathered at the waterside shaking hands with their friends, and exchanging the usual ceremonies, when, oh, most inglorious spectacle! the spasm ended, the boat rolled over on the other side, threw the captain across a stool, and the passengers among barrels, et cet., and lay motionless for several moments.

" 'That was the unkindest cut of all,' was it not?" cried Hal, maliciously, to the prostrate captain. "To play you such a trick here, before the town, just as were on the eve of such a bold approach; but never mind. She'll hardly have another fit before you can bring her up."

The bell rang, the wheels revolved backward, and all the numerous mysteries were duly performed again, but now the boat refused to approach the shore. She would come up obediently to within a few feet, but the nicest calculation and the most delicate persuasion could take her no nearer. At each failure she was obliged to turn quite round, and each evolution took her half-way across the stream, and consumed nearly half an hour. No petted child ever conducted herself in a more refractory manner before company, than she before the astonished eyes of the goodly citizens of

Alton. Every prank deepened the tint of our captain's hair, whiskers, and face, and was made the occasion of as many jokes as could be uttered till another followed.

"She shows off admirably, captain; nothing could be more fortunate."

"If you could throw her into a fit just before she backs water, she'd be sure to come up."

"If she refuses again, you may as well go on; may be she'll come to her temper at the next landing."

"The wood will be out soon, and then she'll certainly float ashore somewhere."

In the midst of this scene our red-flanneled Hooshier made his appearance. His arms were inserted in his pockets, nigh to the elbow, the fur cap tipped over the left eye, and the thick boots projected more than ever as he leaned against the side of the cabin, raised his upper lip by way of adapting his eyes to the strong sunlight, and inquired with a loud voice into the meaning "of all these *hyur* turnins." He was informed by Hal that the captain had thought of landing at Alton, but had changed his mind and was now merely showing his boat to the citizens.

"Look *hyur*, stranger," said he, "do I look as if I could be gummed that easy? I've seed too many boats in my day to believe your story; but if he's trying to land *thar*, this one takes the rag off them all. I say, cappen, what'll you give me to jump over and put my shoulder under the starn, and shove her up for you? I calculate there wouldn't be much difficulty in doin it, if you'd stop that infarnal old ingine that's whizzin and bustin, below thar. It's about half man-power, I reckon, when it don't leak."

The poor captain became more and more perplexed every moment, and actually went so far as to remove one of his gloves. The people on shore cheered the last two evolutions, and the whole thing had reached the climax of the ridiculous, when, by a fortunate guess on the part of some one, the boat was at last brought alongside the shore, just one hour and a half from the time of the first attempt. Everything had been brought up to the boiling point by the long suspense and severe effort. The perspiration stood in drops on the brow of the agonized captain; the boilers had contracted the rage, and thrown off more steam than had brought us from St. Louis; the very tar had been warmed into greater freedom, and threw itself more fearlessly on the luckless by-passers. Our Hooshier had not duly considered this circumstance, and, in the excitement of the moment, he planted himself directly beneath one of these thin filaments. It spun out in a beautiful thread of dark amber, and then, unluckily, parting above, deposited a large lump on the very edge of his cap, and shot off, in a fine stream, to the immaculate bosom of red flannel below.

"Look *hyur*, now," said the wrathful Hooshier, doubling his fists; "if anybody wants to throw tar on me, he may do it as long as he can stand, after I've had two or three good licks at him. I'm a better steamboat than this when I'm set a-goin, and 'twon't take much such combustible as that aar to fire me up."

The bystanders were greatly amused, but kept themselves at a safe distance, for his arms were swinging about in a manner rather inconvenient to those on the narrow guard.

"Easy, friend, easy," said Hal; "you cannot suppose that any gentlemen would throw tar upon you: if you look up, you will see where the insult came from."

"Yes, I see it's the infarnal old boat. I could lick out twenty-four just like her; but there'd be more sense in giving that ruffled carrot yonder a taste of a live man's fists."

A little persuasion, however, cooled his wrath. Our old passengers sprang gladly ashore, and the new ones set their feet upon the plank rather doubtingly, but some one on the fire-deck settled the question by calling out "There won't be another boat till Tuesday."

CHAPTER III

We got under weigh again after several starts and backings, and ran slowly along under the magnificent bluffs that tower above the Mississippi on the Illinois side. In a short time Hal came to me, his face drawn into one of its heartiest expressions of humor, and said, "Jersey is here; who could have dreamed of the good luck?"

But as the reader doesn't know Jersey, he will hardly participate in our pleasure till he is introduced. The brief appellation by which he is here distinguished was given him on the first day of his appearance among us, in honor of the declaration which he then made, that he "was born in Jarsey, and had never been out of it till that day." He wore a suit of coarse snuff-colored homespun, a large bell-crowned white hat, and a cravat of blue ground, dotted with large oval figures of copperas color. He had lost a front tooth, and had an awkward habit of grinning, which made it manifest at every word he uttered. Though much older than Hal, the latter had kindly offered to be his Mentor on first meeting him, and many were the waggish tricks he had played upon him, and the roars of laughter which the performances of Jersey, under his direction, had elicited. The simple, credulous face of the one, and the grave, imperturbable honesty of the other, in the height of Jersey's most ridiculous exhibitions, had been an inexhaustible fund of amusement among the gentlemen during the weary hours of our journey. Jersey had left home under the auspices of the celebrated Marion City colony, but had been separated from them at Columbia, Penn., by getting on board the wrong boat. It was there that he first joined us. He traveled economically: that is, he found his own supplies, and slept on the floor of the cabin. His ignorance exposed him to every sort of imposition, against which Hal was in truth his protector. But for the honest care which he exercised over his worldly concerns, he repaid himself by letting out upon him the whole strength of his trick-loving disposition. A party of gentlemen were about leaving the packet, on the second day, for a walk. Hal suggested that Jersey had better accompany them, as his health might suffer from the long confinement. But there was a difficulty in the case. He had just purchased two large cards of gingerbread,—and what should he do with them? To leave them on his box he thought would be dangerous, and this opinion was fully concurred in by his adviser. To eat them at so short notice, was out of the question; to put them in his pocket impossible.

"There is but one way in which you can dispose of them in safety," said Hal, "and that is to tie them up in your handkerchief and take them under your arm."

This was accordingly done, and they set forth. But Jersey's handkerchief gaped and revealed the secret. It was no choice herbarium, as his friend had asserted to the company when they joined them, but a pair of luscious brown sheets of gingerbread, which he had purchased at a Dutch farm-house just back; none of your shop compounds made of dirty lard, vinegar, and salæratus, but a dainty mixture of golden butter, pure butter-milk, and superfine flour. A league was entered into at once; two of the party engaged Jersey in familiar elbow conversation, and at a rough place in the road stumbled against him, while a third at the same moment dexterously abstracted about a third of one of the loaves. The foremost rogues begged his pardon, and the walk was resumed, Jersey replacing the handkerchief, which had settled a little in the shock he received. Another stumble was soon made, and the part of the other loaf which projected behind his arm was withdrawn. After a long walk there was a short run to gain a bridge from which to let themselves down on the boat. Jersey seated himself on the railing beside Hal, and as the boat came up, the latter began to swing his arms and go through the various motions preparatory to a leap. These were continued till the moment of jumping, when at a word they all found themselves upon deck, but Jersey's bell crown was lying on the bridge. Astonished and alarmed beyond measure, he looked about with the most ludicrous terror in his countenance, and exclaimed "My hat's lost!"

"No, it isn't," said his grave friend, who had knocked it off. "There, the steersman is throwing the boat up to the shore. I'll take care of your gingerbread while you run and get it."

But Jersey preferred to keep the gingerbread under his own protection, and leaping ashore with it, soon returned with the favorite chapeau elevated to its old position. He now seated himself to examine his stores, and great was his consternation to find that more than a third of each cake had disappeared. A thousand ways of accounting for its loss were immediately suggested by the innocent youths about him. But Jersey evidently rejected them all, and from that hour, his confidence in Hal and his companions waned. When he reached Louisville, he took another boat, and came on to St. Louis alone. But if he had enjoyed greater freedom from jokes, he had been imposed on in more serious matters, and seemed rather glad than otherwise to meet his grave friend. I had never seen him yet, except in the heat of his performances, but now Hal was very desirous that I should have the pleasure of hearing him converse awhile. An opportunity soon offered.

We were passing a little wooded island three or four miles above Alton, when one of *the spasms* came on, and was succeeded by a lurch more violent than any previous one, and an immediate settling of the whole craft. She had sprung a leak. The captain made his appearance, this time without the gloves, and ordered her to be run on the island instantly. The goods were all taken out, the hands set at work, while the passengers went strolling through the woods.

The island was small and uninhabited. There was nothing of interest upon it, save two or three little glades in which the early spring flowers were just unfolding their petals. We spent three or four hours in the checkered wood, admiring the various arts by which nature ushers her tender and beautiful train into being, and were about returning for some books, when the sound of approaching footsteps arrested us. In a few minutes Jersey broke through a thick copse near us. "Stop," said Hal, "this fellow will be richer than any printed book." Accordingly we waited, and

Jersey was introduced in due form. He had in some confidential moment intimated to Hal that he was more brilliant in the society of ladies than gentlemen, and I saw at once that he needed no patronage. He prided himself on his political acumen, and, considering this his forte, plunged at once into a discussion of the various prominent men who were likely to claim the suffrages of the people in the ensuing presidential canvass. His opinion of them was delivered with a simplicity and brevity, which quite surprised me.

First of all, he thought "Mr. Clay capable, honest, and fittin." Mr. Van Buren he guessed was capable, but dishonester than Mr. Calhoun, who would be all right if he wasn't a nullifier. I asked about Mr. Webster. "Oh, Webster," said he, "is a capable man, but he ain't fittin." On proposing a word or two of the leading doctrines of these statesmen, I found him utterly ignorant of them. Nullification, for aught he knew, meant the annexation of Texas. Bank and anti-bank were the same to him. He only knew of banks in general, that they were places where people put their spare funds for safety. He seemed not to have become acquainted with that more modern feature, by the introduction of which they have become forced loans for the accommodation of gentlemen who wish to travel in Europe, Texas, or other "foreign parts." The tariff was in some way connected with trade, but whether trade between the mechanics and farmers of our own country or between us and the Indians, of which he understood there was "considerable" carried on in the west, he could not tell. In short, Jersey was one of the few Americans who, having a moderate share of sense, have grown up without travel or books, and while they have not the weakness of idiocy, have the ignorance of the most unfavored peasant. I have rarely met in a citizen of the republic a like absence of all-acquired knowledge, except among some of the miserable emigrants from the mountains of North Carolina.

Having finished his political discourse, this illustrious son of "the Jarseys" was pleased to deliver himself of some rambling thoughts on travel. On this topic his style was more discursive. In general he thought people had better stay "to hum and mind their business, than to be licking it through the country, the way they do now in steamboats and on rail-roads. He thought they'd make more by it. Besides, when he went, he preferred going in *conveyances to traveling*. He didn't think it was a pleasant thing to be carried along as if you had a whirlwind wrapped around you; and then you met so many sorts of folks. No doubt," he added, "a good many of 'em is honest as anybody, but there's a good many more that'll cheat you out of your eyes, if they can make sixpence on 'em, and some that'll steal your bread and meat and throw it away, if they don't want it themselves." These remarks *werged*, as Mr. Weller would say, on the personal, but the ringing of the bell left no time for explanation. We hurried to the boat. It was much later than we thought, before the summons called our attention to the hour. When we arrived, the last of the barrels, boxes, &c., were going on board, the steam was up, and we were just ready to be off. Supper was soon laid, and we left the pleasant island while at table.

CHAPTER IV

The night brought on another general engagement between the passengers and the vermin. The latter held the berths by prior occupancy and could not be routed, but they were more than willing to enter into a treaty for joint tenancy with certain privileges in their favor. It was these privileges that made all the mischief. Like most questions in diplomacy, they were exceedingly difficult to settle; one party claimed and exercised them on all opportunities, the other denied them, and rarely failed to offer the most violent opposition to their use, even to the taking of life. It is due to the weaker party, however, to say that they gained by industry and perseverance what they never could by strength—the partial exercise of the prerogatives they claimed, and, in general, the final rout of their more powerful opponents.

They at any rate were productive of much merriment below, but it was a heavy affair in our quarter. I had few books which were accessible and the long-haired bride had fewer ideas. She possessed little of that strength of mind and bold thought, which characterize most of those rudely-bred women. I thought the magnificent garniture of her head had taken the place of more valuable properties inside, as is often the case among more cultivated females. The strange character of the feeling manifested by her husband, made me very desirous of drawing him into an expression of it in words before he left us, and as their landing place would probably be reached on the third morning, I availed myself of a chance meeting on the shady guard in the afternoon, to engage him in conversation. A few words about the height of the water, the timber, and the prairies, served the purpose.

"You are going to become a prairie farmer?" I said.

"No, I've been one afore, I've got a farm up the river *hyur* that I've *crapped* twice a'ready; there's a good cabin on it, and it's about as good a place, I reckon, as can be found in these diggins."

"Then you built a cage," I said, "and went back for your bird to put in it?"

He looked at me, and his face underwent a contortion, of which words will convey but a faint idea. It was mingled expression of pride and contempt, faintly disguised by a smile that was intended to hide them.

"Why, I don't know what you Yankees call a bird," he replied, "but I call her a woman. I shouldn't make much account of havin a bird in my cabin, but a good, stout woman I should calculate was worth somethin. She can pay her way, and do a handsome thing besides, helpin me on the farm."

Think of that, ye belles and fair-handed maidens! How was my sentiment rebuked!

"Well, we'll call her a woman, which is, in truth, much the more rational appellation. You intend to make her useful as well as ornamental to your home?"

"Why, yes; I calculate 'tain't of much account to have a woman if she ain't of no use. I lived up *hyur* two year, and had to have another man's woman do all my washin and mendin and so on, and at last I got tired *o'totin* my plunder back and forth, and thought I might as well get a woman of my own. There's a heap of things beside these, that she'll do better than I can, I reckon; every man ought to have a woman to do his cookin and such like, 'kase it's easier for them than it is for us. They take to it kind o' naturally."

I could scarcely believe that there was no more human vein in the animal, and determined to sound him a little deeper.

"And this bride of yours is the one, I suppose, that you thought of all the while you were making your farm and building your cabin? You have, I dare say, made a little garden, or set out a tree, or done something of the kind to please her alone?"

"No, I never allowed to get a woman till I found my neighbors went ahead of me with 'em, and then I should a got one right thar, but there wasn't any stout ones in our settlement, and it takes so long to make up to a *stranger*, that I allowed I mought as well go back and see the old folks, and git somebody that I know'd thar to come with me."

"And had you no choice made among your acquaintances? was there no one person of whom you thought more than another?" said I.

"Yas, there was a gal I used to know that was stouter and bigger than this one. I should a got her if I could, but she'd got married and gone off over the *Massissippi*, somewhar."

The cold-hearted fellow! it was a perfectly business matter with him.

"Did you select this one solely on account of her size?" said I.

"Why, pretty much," he replied; "I reckon women are some like horses and oxen, the biggest can do the most work, and that's what I want one for."

"And is that all?" I asked, more disgusted at every word. "Do you care nothing about a pleasant face to meet you when you go home from the field, or a soft voice to speak kind words when you are sick, or a gentle friend to converse with you in your leisure hours?"

"Why, as to that," he said, "I reckon a woman ain't none the worse for talk because she's stout and able to work. I calculate she'll mind her own business pretty much, and if she does she won't talk a great deal to me; that ain't what I got her for."

"But suppose when you get home she should be unhappy, and want to see her parents and other friends?"

"Why I don't allow she will; I didn't get her for that."

"But if she does," I replied, really anxious to touch some chord that might afterwards vibrate in the poor girl's behalf; "if she does feel unhappy? you know one's feelings are not always under their own control."

"Wall, if she does I expect I shan't mind it much, if she keeps it to herself."

The selfish brute!

"If she kept it to herself, as you say, would you not attempt to alleviate her sorrows? would you not take her on some pleasant ride or walk, and speak very kindly to her, and endeavor to make your new home and company agreeable to her?"

"Oh!" said he, laughing feebly, "I shall give her enough to eat and wear, and I don't calculate she'll be very *daunsey* if she gets that; if she is she'll git *shet* of it after a while."

My indignation increased at every word.

"But you brought her away from her home to be treated as a human being, not as an animal or machine. Marriage is a moral contract, not a mere bargain of business. The parties promise to study each other's happiness, and endeavor to promote it. You could not marry a woman as you could buy a washing machine, though you might want her for the same purpose. If you take the

machine there is no moral obligation incurred, except to pay for
it. If you take the woman, there is. Before you entered into this
contract I could have shown you a machine that would have answered your purpose admirably. It would have washed and ironed
all your clothes, and when done, stood in some out-of-the-way
corner till it was wanted again. You would have been under no
obligation, not even to feed and clothe it, as you now are. It would
have been the better bargain, would it not?"

"Why that would be according to what it cost in the fust place;
but it wouldn't be justly the same thing as havin a wife, I reckon,
even if it was give to you."

"No, certainly not; it would free you from many obligations that
you are under to a wife" (it was the first time, by the way, he had
used the word), "and leave you to pursue your own pleasure without
seeing any sorrowful or sour faces about you."

"Oh, I calculate sour faces won't be of much account to me. If
a woman 'll mind her business, she may look as thunderin as a live
airthquake, I shan't mind it."

"No, sir, I see you possess a very happy insensibility to the woes
or happiness of others. Your wife has occasion to congratulate
herself on the prospects of life with a person elevated so far above
the emotions which move the human herd."

I will not deny that the fellow's coolness somewhat enraged me.
There was a fair prospect that I should have read him a lecture
as long as he would find patience to hear, but at this moment his
wife came round the stern of the cabin. I thought she had heard
the conversation, for the usual insipid smile was replaced by a
slightly contracted expression on her dark brow, and her voice
sounded more as if it were the utterance of a soul conscious of its
own identity and requirements, as she said, "John, will you come
help me git to the big chist, the captain has had some truck put
on it."

"Wall, you ain't a baby, I reckon, that you can't tote it somewhar
else," was the amiable reply.

"But that's such a heap of it," answered the poor girl, unwilling
to be wholly refused—so early too!

"What if thar is a heap. Tote away ten or fifteen minutes, and
thar won't be so much."

She turned away without another word, but as she passed the
open window, I saw her wiping her eyes with the corners of her
calico apron. It was the most human manifestation I had seen in
her. Notwithstanding the intense disgust I felt for the base-hearted

tyrant who stood before me, I was constrained to make one more effort on behalf of his victim. I said, therefore, as gently as I could speak, that it was not customary to treat females so in our country; that a man would be pronounced a brute who would refuse to render or procure assistance for a woman under like circumstances, even if she were his servant, and such conduct was still more abhorrent toward a wife.

"Wall, I reckon the Yankees may do as they like about them things, and I shall do jist the same. I don't think a woman's of much account anyhow, if she can't help herself a little and me too. If the Yankee woman was *raised up like the women* here *aar*, they'd cost a heap less and be worth more."

This was the old key again. He was hopelessly benighted and brutified. His red flannel bosom and dark face inspired stronger aversion than ever, and I turned away, saying that I trusted his wife would agree with him in these opinions, or they might lead to some unpleasant differences.

"Oh, as to that," said he, "I reckon her pinions won't go fur anyhow; she'll think pretty much as I do, or not at all."

Thou beast! I exclaimed mentally; and sat down in the cabin pondering on the incredible brutality of such opinions in a civilized man, when the wife came in. She had just returned from her visit to the "big chist." There was no longer a doubt, from the expression on her face, that she had heard the conversation, and understood some part of it too. I left her to her own choice, whether to speak of it or not.

After a few mintues she said, "I reckon you'll think John talks hard about women."

I replied, that it was quite unusual to find persons who thought as he did.

"Well," said the faithful creature, "I reckon he don't think as bad as he says;" but her suffused eyes more than half contradicted her tongue.

There's too much of the true woman in her for this brute, notwithstanding her ignorance and silliness, thought I. It's an absolute waste of some of the fairest materials that compose human nature to throw her away with this selfish animal.

"How long have you been married?" I asked.

"Two weeks yesterday," she replied, the blood mantling through her dark cheek and brow.

"Had you been long acquainted?"

This question unsealed her tongue, and without waiting further inquiry, she ran on with her story.

"No, I never see'd him but three or four times. We was new-comers in the settlement whar his folks lived, and nobody knowed when he come back that he wanted to git a woman to take with him. He come to our house once after night, and him and the old man had a long talk out doors, and finally he come in and stopt a little, and went off. The next day, dad *ast* me how I'd like to come to *Illinice*! I didn't take his meanin rightly, but John come again afore long, and then he ast me. I told him I'd heern 'twas a good country, but I liked it well enough thar. Then he said the old man had told him he might have me to go back with him if I was willin to it, and he allowed I would be. So after two or three weeks, we got married and put right off for his place."

"And you expect to be happier in the new home than you were with your father and mother?"

"I hain't calculated much about that; but I reckon I'll want to see them and the young ones a little, till I get broke in."

I could scarce forbear a laugh at the significancy of this rude expression. It was a common one with her, but described the process before her more forcibly than the most elegant language. There was no hope for her but to settle into her slavery, and wear the shackles, if possible, without chafing under them. She had not character enough to redeem herself, and the brutal treatment to which she was doomed would tend every day to diminish the little that she had, and reduce her to the condition of a mere machine. Both parties were beyond hope; so that in gratifying my curiosity I had raised a crowd of painful emotions in my own breast, and turned a dark page for the poor over-grown child before me. They left us next day, the bride wrapping her light slippers in her pocket-handkerchief, and walking barefoot from the landing.

CHAPTER V

Our boat conducted herself much better in the latter part of her tour than the first. Her improved conduct gave the captain leisure, when he was awake, to spend some time with his female passengers. As I was the only one left after the departure of the Hooshier bride, these honors were concentrated on me. It would have been a troublesome distinction had the engine been less noisy or his voice louder, but as the one was "soft and low," and the other hissed, whistled, groaned, and sputtered continually, I was but little embarrassed by them. If his face expressed astonishment at what he uttered, I proceeded to look astonished myself. If he looked a negative, I shook my head; an affirmative, I nodded: sentiment, nothing was easier than to respond; profound, it cost little effort to look wise and inquiring. Every day he donned a fresh ruffle and white pantaloons; but the hose, I think, were the same—so that after two or three days, there were several transverse stripes of a dark brown color crossing the foot, which at a distance, with a little aid from the imagination, might be construed into ribbons, and so made to impart the appearance of a more elaborate finish to the fine pumps. He had a Leghorn hat, with a wide rim lined with lemon-colored silk, in which he aired his brainless cranium on very warm days, though he never pardoned himself for appearing in the cabin with it.

We worried on through the flood of water that was pouring down the bed of the Illinois and submerging its banks, till the night of the fifth day brought us to the landing place of our friends in the town of Pokerton. It was at that time the county seat of one of the largest and wealthiest counties in the state. Its name is faintly descriptive of its inhabitants in a double sense: one of their favorite recreations being a game at cards, which is indicated by the first two syllables of this name. A still more conclusive right to it was demonstrated before we left the town. We had a promise of a conveyance to reach our friends early in the morning, but our utmost efforts of coaxing, hiring, and remonstrating failed to bring it till one o'clock. My vexation may easily be conceived. After a journey of nearly four weeks, to be delayed so long within nine miles of the dearest friends I had on earth; to be doomed to sit in the wooden room of a wooden tavern, every beam and board of which was saturated with the juice and fumes of tobacco; to look out, hour after hour, into the sleepy street of a river town, thronged with rough boatmen, horse-jockeys, plaintiffs and defendants (for the court was in session) with their learned counsel, every man and boy of them armed with a cigar, or old pipe, brown with the absorbed fumes of the weed; to see among them all not a face that one had ever seen, and, tired as I then felt, not one that I could fancy I should ever wish to see again,—was insufferable. Reading, in such a state of suspense, was out of the question; and it was impossible to set foot out of doors, for the mud mounted half-way to the tops of the men's boots. I had not a few misgivings about the "new country," and they increased in arithmetical progression, till a nondescript vehicle drove to the door, and Hal came in to announce that deliverance had at last come. Cloak and hat were never donned quicker than mine on that occasion. I stood waiting long before the baggage was in.

The driver was a native. "Is this *hyur* the young woman that's goin out?" said he.

"The very same, sir."

"Wall, just wait till I get this truck aboard, and I'll help you in."

"Thank you, I can help myself. How long will it take you to drive to my sister's?"

"I can't rightly judge now; the roads is heavy and the slues deep, but I allow we'll fetch it about five o'clock, anyhow. I should a been here two hours ago, but my beast was out on the prairie, and I couldn't git him afore."

"Well, our patience has been amply proved, meantime; but now, if you can, accomplish it by five o'clock. Its just half-past one, and I confess I do not see clearly how one horse is to travel nine miles, with three persons and the baggage, over the heavy roads and those other phenomena that you named, whatever they may be, even in that long time."

"Thar, we're all ready now, that big piece of plunder can't go; seat yourself with the lady, Mr., and we'll put out;—jist hold on the lines a minute, till I go in."

When he returned he had replenished the inner man with a liberal potation of whiskey, and his resolutions for our benefit were multiplied indefinitely. He mounted a large trunk in front, flourished his whip, and we soon left the suburbs of Pokerton behind us.

It was a glorious April day. The very air was exhilarating enough to have routed a legion of azure tormentors, not to mention the circumstances under which we were breathing it.

Those who have ever experienced the emotions that fill the heart when one approaches the home of friends—a dear sister or brother, after a separation of years, can appreciate something of ours as the wheels rolled on and brought us nearer to this interesting termination of our wanderings. The deep joy which will not permit one to be silent and yet finds no relief in words, the questions which will continually force their way to utterance, though no answer is expected, the imaginary portrait of the home, its internal arrangements and external appearance, the changes which time has wrought in the persons of its old inmates, the appearance of the new ones he has introduced, the volume of the past which is to be opened by each party, its mingled contents of painful and pleasurable records, the new things that are to be told, and the old ones that are to be reviewed, the freshness of each to each, and the days that must elapse before this single charm can be diminished, the speculations upon the probable position and employment of each member of the family when you enter, and their surprise contrasted with your coolness which says, "Why, you didn't know we were so near, but we did and are not at all surprised"; all these thoughts and feelings, and a thousand others which human language can define, crowded our minds and kept every faculty upon its fullest tension.

The country itself had indescribable charms for the eye to which it was new. We had left the foliage of spring farther south, but I rejoiced more to see the prairies in their naked majesty, having in my mind the rich promise which the coming months were to fulfil. Where they had not been burned, the grass was still brown, and the trees and copses naked.

One of the great desires of my life that yet remained ungratified, was to see a prairie. Several smooth openings among the groves looked large enough to our uneducated vision, but the driver declared they were nothing — mere "little meadows which would make smart truck patches by and by. Jest nothin at all in the way of a prairie." But this did not restrain our exclamations of delight at the beauty around us. To all which came the reply "Nothin at all, ma'am."

I at last asked if we should pass nothing entitled to the name of prairie?

"None of much account," he replied; "thar's two or three smart little openings among the *baarens*, but the timber's scattered all over hyur."

We crossed a little stream at some distance from the town, and our road thence onward, for more than a mile, wound among beautiful heights, thinly wooded and covered with the clean brown grass. As we mounted one of these the country opened before us, and swept away to the eastern horizon, a distance of many miles — a smooth, open plain, undotted by a tree or other familiar object. I can never forget the thrill which this first unbounded view on a prairie gave me. I afterwards saw many more magnificent — many richer in all elements of beauty, many so extensive that this appeared a mere meadow beside them, but no other had the charm of this. I have looked upon it a thousand times since, and wished in my selfishness that it might remain unchanged; that neither buildings, fences, trees, nor living things should change its features while I live, that I might carry this first portrait of it unchanged to my grave. I see it now, its soft outline swelling against the clear eastern sky, its heaving surface pencilled with black and brown lines, its borders fringed with the naked trees!

No better proof of the reality of this prairie could have been given than the silence which it inspired in myself and my companion. We had burst into exclamations of delight a dozen times before, when the little glades opened around us, but now there was not a word uttered. Both were lost in contemplation of the sublime spectacle which lay before us. We had no inquiries to make. Nature spoke to us in her own unequivocal language.

But the view was short; the road soon wound again among trees, and afterward ran across a tract of low open ground from which the prospect beyond was cut off. It began now also to be worse than we had found it. The turf was wet and very soft, and the soil where it was cut, so adhesive that it was extremely difficult for the horse to make any progress. We had not yet learned what the *slues* were, and I was about asking our Jehu to enlighten us on this point, when a practical demonstration, much more impressive than the most eloquent description, superseded the necessity, and indeed, the opportunity of speech.

We approached a long narrow line of stagnant water, filled with bogs of tall grass and apparently very much broken up in the middle. There was no bridge in sight, and the road terminated abruptly on one side of this miniature swamp and emerged as abruptly on the other. It was evident that people crossed, or at least drove in from both sides.

The man on the trunk betrayed no hesitation, he only looked first to the right, then to the left, as if he contemplated turning out of the beated track if any better one offered; but apparently the examination was fruitless, for he advanced and plunged his horse at once into the thickest of the black pool. I was certain we should never get through. The animal sprung, floundered, and pulled his best, and drew the waggon (the driver, by the way, called it a *dearborn*) about twice its length, when he went down, and I thought was going to disappear altogether, but a sudden jerk showed that he still found footing. The fore wheels sank in the place he had just occupied, the driver lay in the pool between, the horse stood high and dry on the opposite side, the shafts dragging at his heels, and Hal and I sat looking all sorts of consternation, first at the driver, then at the horse, then at each other. It was but a

moment, and both broke into a shout of laughter that brought
Jehu in astonishment to his feet, and drew the attention of two
elderly ladies who were looking up some early sprouts of beans in
a garden near by. There we sat, dismally helpless, in a bemired
and decrepid waggon, the horse and driver a few feet in advance,
and both of us wondering how we were to get out. The man of
the whip soon recovered his self-possession, and merely remarking
that the bottom of the *slue* must have fallen out since he crossed
it, suggested that I should walk ashore as best I could and go into
the tavern, while he went to the blacksmith's shop for help, and
to get his fractures repaired. "It was right good luck," said he as
he drove off, "that we didn't get *slued* afore we got to town."

"To town!" said Hal, opening his eyes in astonishment; "where
is a town?"

"Why hyur, don't you see there's a tavern, and yonder is a
blacksmith's shop, and two *housen* beside. This is woodland."

"Yes, so I should think, in its natural state."

On due inspection, however, a sign-post was visible before the
smartest-looking of the three cabins. It belonged to the garden
where we had seen the elderly ladies, and now both their caps were
visible in front. People with traveling baggage could not pass through
the town without inspection, still less be *"slued"* in its very suburbs,
and not receive any proffer of hospitality from its principal inhabitants. On charitable thoughts intent, therefore, the good matrons
issued from the door to invite the strangers in till repairs were
made. While they approached I had time for a brief survey of their
persons. As we were within two or three miles of our sister's house,
these people must be neighbors, so I had some interest in the
examination.

Both were somewhat past the middle period of life. One was a
straight, tall, precise figure, trimmed at all corners into more than
puritan stiffness. Her face was expressive of much kindness, I
thought. I was not so well skilled in physiognomy then as now. Her
carriage was lady-like, and both her dress and manner indicated
that she was an emigrant from the east. The former, however, was
peculiar, and betrayed the presence of some strong prejudices in
the wearer. The waist was short, and the long skirt fell in narrow,
perpendicular folds to the feet. The sleeves (it will be remembered
that this was the period of maturity among large sleeves) were
confined to the long, slender arm half-way above the elbow, and
thence enlarged a trifle to the shoulder. A neat, square collar of
spotted muslin surrounded the neck. The cap was equally plain;

still all was in keeping with the person, whose whole mien was characterized by a stiffness that reminded one of a new made Quaker in a ball-room. Her companion was quite a contrast to this in person and dress. She was shorter and thicker. Her movements were quick and free, and indicated a woman who had moved much, and always with an object. Her dress was more conformable, as Mr. Weller, sen., would say. Her sleeves were larger, her waist longer, her skirt not so perpendicular, and her cap had a fuller border. All these observations were made in a much shorter space than it will take to read them, for we met in less than a minute from the time when they commenced. A courteous salutation from the non-conformist and a cordial one from her companion, were followed by a scrutinizing gaze through the glasses of the latter, and an exclamation, "La! it's Miss ———, Mary's sister, isn't it?" There was no denying the charge.

"I thought so, you look so much like her; come in, do. Why, you broke down in the slue, eh? Well, who'd a thought it?—but Mary's been expectin on you this good while. She'll be glad enough, I guess. Take a chair; you must be tired. And that's your brother Henry with you, eh? I thought I knowed you as soon as I looked at you. It beats all how much you and Mary looks alike. Why, when'd you come up the river? What, last night, and never got out here till this time? Take off your things; you'll have to wait some time for 'em to mend the waggon: the whippletree is broke; I see the fellow carryin it along in his hand."

"No, thank you," said I, embracing the first pause in the good old lady's interrogatories and salutations, to inquire the distance that yet remained.

"La! 'tain't but three mild; we're nigh neighbors. Well, how glad they will be to see you! Do take off your bunnut; they won't get the waggon mended right away."

I replied that I would walk rather than wait long, now we were so near.

"I massy, you can't do it,—the road is so wet and the *slues* so full of water. There's a *slue* right out here that you couldn't get across at all, so you'll have to wait."

I now turned my attention to a group of young girls who were gathered at the other side of the room. One of them, a pale, timid-looking child of fourteen, with large black eyes and a face singularly like that of the taller woman, came forward, and was introduced by the latter as her daughter Josephine. The others bore the like relation to the hospitable landlady. When the latter abated the tempest of her speech a little, the more dignified non-conformist entered into conversation with me. She told me who she was, a piece of information which had more interest for me than the reader may suppose; how long she had been there, and where she came from. It was all done in a very proper and precise manner. Not a single rule of etiquet was transgressed, either in question or answer.

At the end of half an hour the waggon was at the door, and we were once more ready to start. We inquired of the landlady for the house.

"It's the next but one," she replied. "You go by Squire O'Brien's jist out here in the edge of the grove, and it's the next one you come to. It's a story and a half frame-house, with a kitchen back."

Silence seize your tongue, good woman, for the next half hour, for that hint! I wouldn't have looked at the best painting that represented it, and here, within an hour of seeing it, I have the whole thing set before me.

We drove on, got over the *slue* without breaking down, rode through one or two little copses of hazel and sassafras, emerged on the open prairie with the same sky-bound savannah in front that has so charmed us a little way back, and continued thus till we struck the outskirts of a thin tract of barrens, entered a lane with fair fields on either hand, and saw two houses before us. But now we were all seized with a sudden mistiness of recollection. Nobody could tell whether it was the first or the second; something had been said about two close together, and it was finally settled between Hal and his Jehu that it must be the farther one. We looked hard at the first, to see if we could detect no familiar face peering from its windows, but they seemed deserted and lonely. The yard and garden adjoining were inclosed with picket-fence, some rose bushes and a few other flowering shrubs dotted the turf of clean cultivated grass, which was just springing from its winter bed, and there was an aspect about the whole that made me almost exclaim "This must be Mary's home." But we had passed, and were looking back, when a face appeared at one of the kitchen windows that settled our doubts, and turned the horse's head in the direction of our own rather quicker than was consistent with the safety of the *dearborn*. No accident befel us, however, and in another moment we were ushered through the unfinished hall into the room which served as kitchen, parlor, and dining-room. One was there whom our hearts bounded to see, but not Mary.

"Where is she?"

"She has stepped into her father-in-law's, the next house; but she'll be here in a moment, for she must have seen you."

The words were scarcely uttered when the outer door opened, and a thin, slight figure bounded in, and the next moment we were alternately clasped in her arms. My dear sister! My dear brother! were the only words we had need to exchange. Deep emotion is always silent.

CHAPTER VI

Mary was followed by a sturdy little boy, with cheeks like the rich side of a fall pear. He looked at us a moment, and then drew to the opposite side of the room.

"This is my Junius," said the proud mother.

"So this is the famous letter-writer, about whose wonderful doings and sayings we have been favored with such long passages in certain epistles from Prairie Lodge. He is not exactly as spiritual as old *Nominus Umbra* was at the last date, but he will be all the more interesting to us as mortals by and by, when his highness condescends to make our acquaintance. Now let us see the externals of Prairie Lodge."

"Oh, there is little to see now. Nature does most of our ornamental work here, and she has barely commenced the business of the season yet. I can show you what she has to work on, and you will soon see for yourselves that she is an elegant and unsparing artist here. Now, are you ready?"

"Yes."

"What, no gloves?"

"Never a one. I want my hands at liberty, having a special use for them: and, moreover, I hate gloves."

"But you'll wear a sun-bonnet?"

"Why, yes, I must concede as much as that, I suppose, though next to the articles just mentioned, your close, straight-forward sun-bonnet is my abhorrence."

"Yes, so I should think, and all other forms included, to judge from the color of your face and neck."

"Why, I have worn, as you see, a little open hat, that would let me look wherever I chose. I have not lost sight of a leaf, or rock, or anything either curious or beautiful, for the sake of saving a shade of brown on my complexion."

"But you havn't traveled from New York in that little ribboned nut-shell without a veil?"

"Exactly so, sister mine. I packed my veil in the bottom of my trunk when I started, to save all scruples, and relieve myself from two or three troublesome debates each day, on the propriety of dropping it over my face for five minutes. I put veils in the same category with gloves."

"And sun-bonnets too? Why you'll run wild on the prairie before the first flowers are out; if the Indians were crossing the country as often as they used to be, three or four years since, they'd take you along for a stray princess."

"Thank you; the rank would be flattering: but if it were due to our family on the score of color, I have an elder sister who should take precedence."

"Here we are. This little brook that is fringed by these willows, runs from a piece of springy ground above the garden, and falls into the little stream that crosses the road at the foot of that large tree. It is here all the year, except, occasionally, a few weeks in very dry seasons. One could scoop out a delicious little pool under those drooping willows, if one had time and felt no scruples about glove-less hands."

"Yes, I'll think of it. Now where does this clean path lead through that unparalleled gate and those bushes beyond?"

"To the spring."

"Ah, what a distance!"

"Oh yes, but we only bring water thence for drinking and cook-ing; we have, usually, an abundance of rain-water near the door."

"That's a blessing; but when the clouds fail?"

"That is a failure we very seldom hear of here. You'll see before you have been with us a week it is the last dispensation one would provide against."

"You have showers, then, sometimes?"

"The clouds will answer that question some day, in a manner that will astonish you."

"Is there anything worth seeing in this grove beyond your spring?"

"Nothing of much interest in the natural world; there is a little spot there—" and my sister's face lost its playful expression while she spoke. "But I must tell you the story some day, when we have leisure, and take you to see it."

"Very well, if it be melancholy, as I guess, let us dismiss it till some future time, when sorrow will be a pleasure. Whose house is that down the road?"

"That is Mr. R——'s, John's father. We call it 'the other house.'"

"It would be more convenient, would it not, to eliminate the last two letters of the article, and cut the phrase down to two words?"

"Undoubtedly. But I trust you will not claim the idea as original. It is one we have often availed ourselves of, since the erection of this, made a t'other of that."

"Very ingenious truly. But what are all these shrubs about the yard?"

"Here you see a row of forest trees: this tall one that bends so gracefully is an elm. John and —— placed them here two years ago. These are roses along here; yonder are two lilacs on each side the front door; farther on is another kind of rose between the gate and the large tree, and this is a seringa, but it has never flowered yet. Those scattered promiscuously yonder, are roses. I have been unable to procure a greater variety; indeed, if roses would bloom at all seasons I should scarcely crave it. As the roots increase I intend to divide and multiply them till the yard, all except my bleaching plat, is a wilderness of them. There is nothing in the flower world that I so much love. They grow very fast on our rich soil. If different kinds of shrubbery were to be had here, one could have a magnificent display in a very few years. I have the promise of some from Cincinnati this spring, by a gentleman with whom you are partially acquainted, I believe. Oh, I declare it's a phe-nomenon that red can be seen through so dark a brown! But this gentleman is to have a variety of plants sent on, and he offers to divide with me. By the way I had like to have forgotten one hor-ticultural curiosity. It is here on the west side of the house, under the bed-room window. These windows are not so bare in summer. I have a flowering scarlet-runner that clusters very thickly over them, and makes a more beautiful drapery than your damask and gossamer."

"I have no doubt; but show me your curiosity."

"Here it is, do you recognize it? But there's little need of asking; for a lady who abhors bonnets and veils, you blush easily, methinks."

"I scarcely know who would not blush to see themselves stared at by their own initials, done in green of that size, and in salad, too! common salad! By and by it will be plucked and eaten in vinegar. Who would not blush at the prospect of such an ignominious blot-ting from the face of nature? But who is that approaching us?"

"My husband. You'll hardly recollect him:—but come in. I must set about tea. Hal is whispering me that you havn't eaten since you left St. Louis."

"If he doesn't call such service as he did at the supper table last evening eating, it must be confessed we have not."

"Be seated; you will now learn the convenience of having your parlor and dining-room in the kitchen, that is, when you are your own servant. I take care of my family alone, but it will interfere little with our conversation; you sit there, I work here; so it all goes on harmoniously."

"But suppose I work with you, let me lay the table."

"Certainly, I shall refuse you no privilege of that kind."

In a few minutes the shining plates were laid upon the snowy cloth; a reflecter filled with tender biscuits glittered on the hearth; the tea-kettle bubbled into the fire; the cellar yielded its stores of golden butter, cheese, and honey, and a repast was before us that would have tempted appetites more pampered than ours had been. In the evening all the family were gathered, not excepting the gentleman whose plants were on their way from Cincinnati. There was also present a gentleman who had long been domiciliated with my sister's family—a man with a dark face, which seemed the home of the very genius of melancholy. A single word explained his connexion with the story which Mary had promised me at some future day. The evening was spent in the enjoyment of some of the richest emotions that belong to humanity; all retired at a late hour; we new ones, with a world of novelty yet to explore—the others with many wonders of the eastern world yet to learn.

CHAPTER VII

The next day calls were received from the other house, invitations accepted, and prairie life fairly begun.

There was everything yet to see and learn, but we were under progress very soon. Hal, I believe, advanced much more rapidly than myself—a natural consequence of his being abroad so much more. But we were no stayers indoor. When the household cares were disposed of for an hour or two, away we went into the groves and thickets, or out upon the prairies. There were some visits to be made at two or three miles' distance; these called for horses. Sometimes the call was responded to by one only, and I remember one afternoon enjoying a hearty laugh when Hal, who was to accompany us, came in and announced very gravely, that the horse was ready, and that he would mount and wait till we came out. He had built a small addition to him, he said, and quite regretted there was not a fourth person to accompany us. Mounted thus, one on the saddle, the other behind on a blanket, with Hal for our bridle knight—and never had two ladies a more waggish or humorous one—we scoured the prairies. Hal was generally in at the mounting and dismounting; but unless there were danger to be encountered, we saw little of him between the goals; what we gained over him by our speed being lost by the various explorations which curiosity or fancy led us to make.

The equestrian of the prairies enjoys the largest liberty which falls to the lot of mortals. Time and distance are the only checks he knows. He draws his rein for whatever point he lists, and gallops in straight or curved lines on till he tires or reaches the spot. Physical freedom is nowhere more perfect, and seldom is it enjoyed with a higher zest than we brought to these excursions, great as was the disproportion between steeds and riders.

Our visits were usually made in the afternoon. The hour for starting was the earliest practicable after dinner, which was always taken at twelve. When the morning had been auspicious within, and only the ordinary affairs of the house were on hand, the preparations could all be made by one o'clock. But the force of habit was too strong to suffer me to submit to this without an earnest protest, and I remember feeling very much annoyed one day at being dragged out to spend a long afternoon less agreeably than we should have spent it at home.

"What possible pleasure can it afford our hostess?" I inquired.

"I cannot vouch for the pleasure," said Mary; "but the convenience, I can assure you, will be very great."

"How, pray?"

"If we go at one she will have time to prepare tea; if we wait till two, she will be compelled to dismiss us without."

"Send a messenger then to assure her that we are coming; that will give her time."

"Yes, but it would be very awkward to take her in mid preparation."

"Not at all for us, and the lady, on your own showing, can be endowed with no very high degree of sensibility; so I think your argument fails."

"My argument may, but my experience does not. I have visited this lady, you never have, and I speak from positive knowledge when I say that it will not do to go later than one."

This was one of those obstinate cases—such as arise in many other affairs in life—in which one feels the reasons to be indisputable, but finds it difficult to set them forth in words. We repaired to our post at one o'clock; the hostess was already on the *qui vive*. She however sat about five minutes after our entrance, to give dignity to the reception, and then went about consummating the great event of the day—the tea table. The whole affair went on in the room where we sat, so that I shall be able to give its different stages and progress with an accuracy which, I trust, may be appreciated.

First stage—half-past one—a kettle of pumpkin is suspended over the fire for stewing, and a tea-kettle placed on the hearth, a few inches from the forestick; half past two, a patent oven is placed before the fire, filled with gingerbread, of which I will give the recipe to the next edition of the Frugal Housewife. Next, the pumpkin is taken up and prepared for baking, by sifting and mixing with eggs, milk, ginger, and molasses. I ought to have remarked that as all of this took place in the month of May, the pumpkin was dried. At four o'clock, the gingerbread was replaced by a pan of wheaten biscuit, and the tea-kettle was suspended from the hook whence the pumpkin had been taken. At half-past four, the table was placed in the centre of the room, and covered with a cloth. Dishes now began to drop around upon it. They appeared at random, of all ages, colors, and sizes, just as the congregation gathers at a country meeting-house. This continued till dark, broken at intervals by the attention necessary to affairs elsewhere. At five o'clock, the biscuits were removed, wrapped in a table-cloth or towel, and a pie placed in the oven. The fire was stimulated with a fresh basket of chips. Time was shortening now, and affairs began to wear a hurried look. I could not forbear taking advantage of a short absence of the hostess, to ask Mary whether her experience would enable her to guarantee us any supper, with all our punctuality. At six o'clock, a plate of dried beef and pickles appeared on the table, flanked by a saucer of honey and a preserve dish of plums. The tea-pot was scalded at half-past six, the biscuit and cake had taken their places at a quarter to seven, and just fifteen minutes afterward, we were seated at the table. The attention of the hostess was several times interrupted by the pie, which would not bake; at last she declared herself under the necessity of apologizing for its conduct, and asking us to excuse its appearance. We left a little before eight o'clock, and the naughty pie was taken from its hot berth a few minutes previous. When I was invited to repeat the

visit, it was impossible to forbear expressing myself so highly entertained that I should take great pleasure in doing so.

This is not an exaggerated report; but it is due to the females
of the country to say that such extreme slowness is not characteristic
of them. The person who figured here was an importation from
the Buckeye state, and would have been a snail even in Yankee
land.

This, though a literal description, is a fair representation of social
visiting in that country.

CHAPTER VIII

At Prairie Lodge our acquaintance with *Sucker** life commenced.
But it was not carried to any great intimacy here. My sister's home
had been little visited, even in earlier days, by the primitive settlers.
Their principal intercourse had consisted of business affairs between the men, and visits of mercy between the females in the
times of sickness or death, so that we saw little of them excepting
an occasional out-of-door call from some neighbor, or in passing
their residences or waggons in our various excursions.

One family of this kind occupied the next house west from the
Lodge. We often passed it, and the external appearance excited
the most intense curiosity to have a peep at the internal. But I
grieve to say that it could never be accomplished under any decent
pretext whatever. All the showers were either too early or too late.
No waggon ever broke down in the neighborhood, though the road
was at times bad enough to encourage hope for a long way on
either side. It was too near home ever to stop for water. It is true
there was an occasional illness, but this could not serve my purpose,
for the wife had a mother, to whom the lively doctor of our village
gave the name of Meg Merrilies (I fancy there was a little spite in
it, for she was his rival in this branch of the medical profession),
who would travel fifteen or twenty miles on foot in the morning,
attend to her patient, and return in the evening. Meg then offi-
ciated, to the exclusion of all the curious gossips of the neighborhood, and had things all her own way. The patient was generally
out the next day, and all went on as before.

The house was one of the meanest description of cabins. It turned

*The cognomen of the Illinoians, answering to the Buckeye of Ohio, the Wolverine
of Michigan, the Corn-cracker of Kentucky, &c.

its back upon the road, and showed only a four-light window, or rather sash; for soon after I first saw it, the third was broken out, and the fourth so fractured that its continuance seemed extremely doubtful. A patchwork quilt of blue jeans and red flannel was hung across the aperture a few days after, and never removed while I remained in the country. Directly beneath this, against the wall, which was on a line with the fence, was a green pool of about the dimensions of the house. It was of artificial construction, and re-dounded not a little to the taste of some eight or ten large swine, who delighted their senses in its aromatic depths, at the same time that they regaled those of by-passers.

The entrance to the house was in the rear. A low kind of shantee projected from the door several feet back, which served for pantry, milk-house, pig-pen, poultry-house, and possibly stable in winter. In the right angle between these was the well, just far enough from the corner to be visible in passing. The ground around this was the great theatre of action for mother and children. I never knew the exact number of the latter, but if called to testify in any matter concerning them, I should say the minimum was eight, the max-imum double that number. I rarely saw less than the former, sport-ing away the morning of life, in their rags and filth, on the banks of the verdant pool, or the hard-trodden ground around the well. Their dress and complexions were so uniform that I could never distinguish but one of them, a girl of some twelve years, whose face was always a little dirtier, her hair a little stiffer, and her clothes a shade nearer the color of the earth in which she burrowed. When any one approached the house, they all scampered like a herd of wild animals into the angle between the cabins, and peeped around the corners as long as the traveler was in sight. A general yell and shout announced his disappearance and their return to the several amusements from which they had fled.

The father of this family was a man of sense and much general information; his morals were unimpeachable, and his character commanded so much respect, that he was proposed for one of the highest offices in the county. His election was lost in consequence of some local division, not at all connected with the degraded condition of his family. He had a fine farm, valuable horses, and other property, and, away from home, appeared as well as any of his neighbors who lived more comfortably. His means would have enabled him to build a good house, surround it with cultivated grounds, and furnish it with every requisite for neatness and com-fort. Had such physical degradation been the result of extreme

poverty, the case would have excited compassion, instead of curiosity or disgust. But it was not so.

It may be asked, then, what was the cause? It was not that the
parties were misers, and hoarded their gains; for their means were
spent freely to procure whatever they deemed necessary to comfort.
What, then, was it? Merely the incapacity of the mistress of this
family to appreciate a better condition, or help to create one. I
afterwards saw many cases of a like mode of living, and am bound,
in fairness, to say, that the credit was due in nearly every one to
the females.

I once entered a cabin of this description, on a cold November
day. It had no window; all the light came down the wide chimney,
or through the open door. There was a long shelf in one corner,
on which two plates, two cups, and three saucers were arranged,
in conjunction with an iron skillet, a small bake kettle, and a tin
tea-pot. A broken table stood against the wall, on which the breakfast things yet remained, though it was eleven o'clock. In a back
corner of the room was a bed, and the only thing that indicated
the exercise of powers superior to the ingenuity of the beaver, was
a wide shelf over it, on which some husks were deposited, and
covered with a bit of filthy cotton cloth. This was constructed for
the nocturnal quarters of the blowsy little heir, who was then tumbling over and over on the ground. There was one dilapidated
chair in the room, besides a single bench and a double one. The
chair was standing back on the platform which had been laid for
the bed, and, as I entered, escorted by the husband, the wife rose
from her seat near the table, took her pipe from her mouth, and
placing it near the edge of the hearth, invited me to sit. A second
child was playing in the ashes. The door was wide open, and the
raw wind swept in gusts through the miserable place, filling it with
ashes and smoke. I have never seen more utter poverty or filth.

When I had gathered my skirts and seated myself as safely as
the circumstances would permit, the woman returned in her pipe,
and the employment which my entrance had interrupted. She had
a large paper of coffee in her lap, from some of which she was
selecting the foul kernels, et cet., preparatory to roasting. Never
was there a more perfect picture of self-satisfaction. She had a fat
figure, which seemed, when she seated herself, to settle away into
a circular mass of matter, in which life and motion were barely
manifest. Her children received but little attention; indeed, it was
not easy to see how one could bestow more upon them. The elder
was enjoying himself intensely; and the happiness of the younger

was abated only by the caution which the mother occasionally gave it, "not to swaller the rocks," which she threw from among the coffee.

It was impossible for me to contemplate this revolting scene, without endeavoring to ascertain the state of mind that could lead a human being to live willingly in the midst of it. I remarked, that it must be a serious inconvenience to live through the winter with the door open.

"Why, yes," she replied, "'tain't as warm *hyur* as it used to be in Kaintucky: 'twasn't of much account there."

"But we obviate the difficulty of a colder climate by windows; they admit the light without the cold."

"Yes, I reckon they're mighty convenient, but we hain't had one yet."

"How long have you lived here?"

"Four year."

"Have you never had a floor?"

"No, we hain't yit; but I reckon we shall git one afore long. It's might bad to have the old man to work around the house, so I don't say nothing about it: he wants to put it down, but I don't allow 'twould make much difference; I reckon that out thar," pointing to the little platform, "will do us yet."

It would weary the reader to give further details of a conversation that evinced only the most disgusting indifference to the common comforts of a more civilized condition. I rode several miles on the same day, with the husband of this woman, and had an opportunity to learn that he would prefer a better manner of life, but that her aversion to change or action rendered so great an effort necessary on his part, that he had never undertaken it. He had ample means for surrounding himself and his family with every comfort. Beside a fine farm, which he cultivated near a good market, he owned a valuable stock of cattle and other property, and had between a thousand and fifteen hundred dollars, in specie, lying in a black chest by the head of his bed. He had no disposition to hoard it; he would spend it the next day, for anything that they could agree on as conducive to happiness. He was likewise possessed of superior natural powers, which he had used in acquiring knowledge of various kinds, and was then capable of making himself a very pleasant companion, by the use of his varied information. His mode of living was never the subject of remark among people of his own class. No one thought it strange, or wondered whether it would ever improve. The women, who, with more household industry, lived better than "*Miss Andrews,*" probably thought she lost a "heap of comfort" in her windowless, floorless, dirty house, but so a smart Yankee woman would have thought of them.

These extreme cases, however, are fortunately rare. In the homes of most of the first settlers there is much more regard paid to cleanliness and comfort. In many of them the neatness and order are perfect. Of necessity they have fewer artificial luxuries than the inhabitants of older regions, but these are not evidences of talent or worth. The inherent virtues of cleanliness, order, and self-respect are often more manifest in a simple than a complicated style of living, and are not less productive of happiness in one than the other.

CHAPTER IX

The beautiful progeny of spring began now to gather around Prairie Lodge. Animate and inanimate nature teemed with the loveliest creations. The showers that had been so emphatically foretold on our arrival did not disappoint us. They fell almost daily for several weeks, and were generally accompanied by lightning and thunder, such as the dwellers in the east have no conception of. Nothing of the kind can be more magnificent, unless it be the marshalling of the same storms on the vast plains farther west, where they are said to be even more terrific. They come more generally toward evening, and not unfrequently continue till near morning. Nothing can exceed the rapidity with which they gather after the first signal is given. A little cloud not larger than a man's hand rises on the horizon, and in fifteen minutes the earth is deluged, and the pealing heavens seem on fire. There are few showers here unaccompanied by the most striking electric phenomena: sometimes the whole arch is lighted by a continuous flickering glare, rent occasionally by a more intense vein. The thunder roll is ceaseless, with such lightning! The deep peals that accompany the brighter flashes only strike with a more appalling tone. At other times the whole vault is filled with a darkness that seems ponderable, till a mighty flash rends the pall and searches the very soul. It is gone, and the solid earth trembles under the mighty concussion. Again darkness, as if eternal night had come, wraps the scene till the flame leaps forth with a more blinding glare than before, and a crash follows that seems to shatter the foundation of the world. The third or fourth signal is followed by the storm, which breaks through the sable rack as if half the ocean had been lifted from its bed and were wandering in the upper air. In an inconceivably short space of time the plains around you are deluged, so that every succeeding flash is reflected from innumerable little pools as if you were in the midst of a shallow lake broken by islands of sedge and grass. I never appreciated the sublime power of the elements till I witnessed these storms. They are one of the most glorious features of the country.

Their effect was heightened too by contrast with the scenes which followed them. The vast expanse of country over which they ranged was in a few hours after as quiet and smiling as if the upper elements had dispensed only peace and sunshine from the first hour of creation. And beauty born of these awful warrings stole over every rolling height and into every green glade in our landscape. The swelling bud, the unfolding leaf and flower followed in the path of their majestic progress, making rich and beautiful what had before been desolate and wintry. The spirit that had all the night perhaps raved with such fearful and angry power, seemed, when the bright and peaceful morning came, to have borne a magician's wand after his wrath, and kindled life, beauty, and joy on the plains it had threatened to devastate. The trees around our lodge, now began to put on their summer garb; the hazel copses unfolded their young leaves. The prairies spread their green carpets and even went so far as to variegate the pattern with the violet and the scarlet-painted cup. The strawberry came out in her bridal flowers, and blushed herself into luscious maturity beneath the ardent sun. It was not confined to beds and patches such as delight the eyes of the urchin roving through forbidden meadows in the east, but reddened whole acres around the lodge. The pleasure of gathering it was surpassed only by its delicious flavor. When we came in heated, and just enough fatigued to make rest delightful, our blushing treasures were cleansed of the leaves and grass, sprinkled with sugar, and deluged with delicious cream fresh from the brimming pan. Oh what a feast! and while we were enjoying it the soft breeze floated in laden with the odors of the young world, and the music of its varied populace. The grove in the rear of the house was tenanted by many little songsters, busily employed in these days of universal industry in announcing their return and preparing for the duties of the season. My favorite was the Quail, the merriest, the happiest, and most business-like bird of them all. He rejoices in the showers, and so do I. The harder the rain, the livelier his cheering when it is over. He makes the dripping wood ring with his shrill note. If you walk out while the drops hang upon the leaves, and the grass bends with the weight of its gems, you hear his merry greetings floating by as gaily as if a bevy of children had escaped to the woods and were playing hide and seek with an omnipresent "Bob White," who would only answer when called with a whistle. You hear it in every tone, the imperative, the plaintive, the querulous, the dignified, the entreating, the congratulatory. "Bob White!" soliloquizes one philosophic-looking fellow from the second story of a hazel clump. He looks about a moment, and repeats in a higher and more intense key, "Bob White!" Two or three more turns of the smooth little head and the sagacious little eye seem to raise his temper, and he adds the epithet "Old!" as if Bob White were rather sensitive on the score of his years and would be drawn out to repel the injurious insinuation. "Old Bob White!" he exclaims, and it is responded to from below. Presently out trips a neat, industrious, thrifty-looking bird, who appears to be keeping house in some of the snug little apartments to which these clean paths lead, and exclaims "Old Bob White!" He starts and looks smartly about for the individual who has perpetrated so unjust a slander. "Old Bob White!" And, as if the enormity grew with the repetition, he hops upon another branch, adjusts his plumage, and boldly as an eye can defy, he defies any libeller to prove his charge.

The altercation is becoming sharp, when presently a softer and entreating voice from below, cries out "Bob White!" His anger is dissipated in a moment. With a look of universal charity toward all Quail slanderers, he alights from his post of defiance, and trips away up the leafy aisle. He runs along in haste, looking expectant but determined. He evidently anticipates some appeal to his feelings as a husband and father; but is resolved to yield to no indiscreet solicitation. He reaches a little nook near the edge of the thicket, where low herbage has crept in and woven a thick bed, soft and odorous. The branches are closely knotted above it, and two or three stems of the *Geranium Maculatum* droop gracefully over, looking with their meek pale eyes at the nestling little group which Mrs. Bob White is vainly endeavoring to keep in order during her husband's sally in defiance of his youth. When he arrives, he finds a dozen callow Bob Whites tumbling about with the manifest intention of rebelling against parental authority. The mother entreats, the father remonstrates, but to no purpose. He finally changes his tone to that of instruction, and warns his inexperienced children against the many dangers which wait on the life of a Quail, but more especially against traps. In due time order is again restored, and the exercise of the parental authority has so elevated Bob White's estimation of himself, that he can now forgive all that previously excited his indignation. He feels that respectability established on such a basis is not easily overthrown; and thus reconciled with himself and the world at large, he walks forth beneath the dripping boughs with a complacency which mere epithets cannot disturb.

The Grouse is another member of the feathered tribe, peculiar to these beautiful regions. He is a large, mottled grey bird, with a heavy ruff of feathers running over his head, which adds much to the watchfulness and timidity of his appearance. Their nests are built on the open prairie in some thick knot of grass. This bird has no proper song, and is in general a very silent inhabitant of these vast plains. When hunted or overtaken by the traveler, they rise suddenly with a whirr, somewhat similar to, but not so distinct as that of the pheasant, and fly very rapidly. If not disturbed they describe the half of an ellipse between the points of rising and alighting. The strokes of the wing are short and rapid, and the flight is very swift and direct. These fowls are rarely heard to utter any noise except at one chosen hour of the day. On a spring morning before sunrise, if you are in the vicinity where grove and prairie meet, the air resounds with a peculiar noise, between the whistle of the quail and the hoarse blowing of the night-hawk, but louder than either. You inquire what it is, and are told it is the prairie cocks greeting the opening day.

Spring morning on the prairies! I wish I could find language that would convey to the mind of the reader an adequate idea of the deep joy which the soul drinks in from every feature of this wonderful scene! If he could stand where I have often stood, when the rosy clouds were piled against the eastern sky, and the soft tremulous light was streaming aslant the dewy grass, while not a sound of life broke on the ear, save the wild note just mentioned, so much in harmony with the whole of visible nature, he would feel one of the charms which bind the hearts of the sons and daughters of this land.

We are within the borders of a little grove. Before us stretches a prairie; boundless on the south and east, and fringed on the north by a line of forest, the green top of which is just visible in a dark waving line between the tender hue of the growing grass and the golden sky. South and east as far as the eye can stretch, the plain is unbroken save by one "lone tree," which, from time immemorial, has been the compass of the red man and his white brother. The light creeps slowly up the sky; for twilight is long on these savannahs. The heavy dews which the cool night has deposited glisten on the leaves and spikes of grass, and the particles, occasionally mingling, are borne by their own weight to the earth. The slight blade on which they hung recovers then its erect position, or falls into its natural curve, with a quick but gentle motion, that imparts an appearance of life to that nearest you, even before the wind has laid his hand on the pulseless sea beyond. A vast ocean, teeming with life; redolent of sweet odors! It yields no sound save the one which first arrested our attention, and this is uttered without ceasing. It is not the prolonged note of one, but the steady succession of innumerable voices. It comes up near you and travels on, ringing more and more faintly on the ear, till it is returned by another line of respondents, and comes swelling in full chorus, stronger and nearer, till the last seems to be uttered directly at your feet.

But the light is gaining upon the grey dawn. Birds awaken in the wood behind us, and salute each other from the swinging branches. Insects begin their busy hum. And now, the sun has just crowded his rim above a bank of gorgeous clouds, and pours a flood of dazzling light across the grassy main. Each blade becomes a chain of gems, and, as the light increases, and the breath of morning shakes them, they bend, and flash, and change their hues, till the whole space seems sprinkled with diamonds, rubies, emeralds, amethysts, and all precious stones. Nothing can be conceived more beautiful or joyous than such a scene at this hour. The contiguous wood conveys an idea of home, such as you have borne from the forest-clad states of the east. It is a refuge from the vastness which oppresses the mind, because it can never wholly compass it. You rejoice, you exult in the friendly presence of the trees; not because they afford you a grateful retreat from the ardent sun; not because they adorn your rude dwelling; not because they promote the growth of fruit and flowers; not even because they congregate the dear little birds about your home; but because they afford the natural and familiar alternative to which the mind recurs when it is weary of the majesty which lies beyond them. You have sat under them in childhood; you have swept the fragments from the little spaces among their roots and carpeted them with moss, and festooned them with the wild flowers which nodded near. You have peopled these magic palaces with fairies, and felt a joy which words can never tell, in dreaming how happy the little beings might be where nothing is visible to their tiny eyes but exquisite beauty, and no sound falls on their small ears but the melodies of growing life. You have listened to the winds, sighing plaintively through the boughs, and felt your soul grow fit for companionship with all things whatsoever that are beautiful and lovely. And now your heart turns fondly to these tall tenants of the plain as to elder brothers, and for a moment you look coldly on the naked expanse beyond. But stop! the sun is fairly up. The flashing gems have faded from the grass tops; the grouse has ceased his matin song; the birds have hailed the opening day, and are gaily launching from the trees: the curtain which has hung against the eastern sky is swept away, and the broad light pours in resistless. The wind comes coursing gently up from the far distance, bending the young herbage, and bearing to your senses sweet sounds and odors, nursed on the unsullied breast of Nature.

The tenants of the farm-yard are now astir; the cows are milked, and all the animals whose services the farmer does not call to aid his labors, are dismissed to ramble in the boundless pasture. The generous oxen are summoned to the yoke, and the labor of the day commences. If I have lingered long over this revel of nature, a spring morning on the prairies, with the grouse be all the blame!

Among the more accomplished feathered artists here are the Bob o'Link, a species of mockingbird, sometimes called the Brown Thrasher, the Robin, and the melancholy Whip-poor-Will. These inhabit the barrens and the prairies in their vicinity. They are seldom found at any great distance from the woods. There are some small birds who love the free plain, but they cannot boast of much genius as singers. It is beautiful to think, however, that as man creeps outward from the groves and builds his cabin, opens his garden, and nurses a few shrubs and small trees around him, the little wood songsters construe it into an invitation to accompany him. Trees are of very rapid growth on the exhaustless soil of the prairies. A few years' care will bring about your house a dense grove of the locust, the cotton wood, aspen, and several other species, so that one need not be long deprived of bird-music. There are several varieties of the Woodpecker; but they will not visit a new home so soon. They look upon young and thrifty trees as humbugs, so far as they pretend to any present utility, and regard them rather as estates to be held in trust for future generations, than as available funds for the present. They decidedly prefer the aged and established to the young and ambitious. In the heavily wooded bottoms of large rivers, and their tributaries, is found the Parroquet; not so finished a speaker as the Parrot, but quite as ready. He is a lively chatterer among the stately trees in the summer months, and when winter comes he betakes himself to the dark deep forests of the south. Like the most voluble consolers of our own species, he shrinks before the approach of stern trial. There are also several coarser tribes, which I never loved, and shall therefore only name for the gratification of the curious. The Crow caws here as everywhere else, but he has been rescued from the general detestation in which he was formerly held by the magic pen of Bryant. No other could have done it. And yet, who can read the "Death of the Flowers," and not entertain a higher respect for him, and feel more melody in his croakings than before? The Hawk screams above the wood top, and over the poultry yard, all through the bright summer day. But nothing could make him other than an object of abhorrence to me since he bore my favorite chicken away before my very eyes, many, many years ago. I could not love him even with such an introduction as made his croaking cousin acceptable.

Next in kind, but more loathsome, is the Buzzard, an indolent, gluttonous bird, who wheels lazily over the great plains, till the decaying carcass of a wolf, deer, or other animal attracts him to the earth. He then descends, gorges himself with the foul carrion, and often rests beside it after eating, from sheer inability to rise. The Turkey, whom this infamous fellow so much resembles, that he has succeeded in stealing his name as a prefix to his own, is a much pleasanter member of the feathered tribe. Great numbers of them abound in the woodlands, where the stately march of the old cock gallanting his hen and her lively brood through the forest is one of its most delightful features.

The landscape grows more beautiful every day. The prairie puts on its richest garb about the first of June. The painted cup, mocassin flower, and geranium, come out; and there is more repose in the vegetable world than there has been. Nature, like a notable dame, has cleaned house in proper season, got her furniture and ornaments arranged, and now seated complacently in her easy chair, challenges the admiration of beholders. In the vicinity of farms, the landscape is enriched by herds of cattle feeding on the prairies. If you walk or drive among them in the afternoon, they are panting like gourmands after a turtle dinner. Their very ribs are distended with the luxurious fare in which they have reveled all day, and their breath perfumes the air. As the sun declines they wander homeward, the cows bearing a treasure that almost flows without the pressure of the housewife's hand. When the milk is strained and set away, the cares of the day are over, and then we wander out among the hazel copses or through the grove, to enjoy the gorgeous sunset, and the long dreamy twilight that lingers over these peerless lands.

The hazel copse is one of the most picturesque features of our landscape. It grows very abundantly, and in autumn yields an inexhaustible harvest of the most delicious nuts. It is found several miles from the woodland, and grows in clumps from three to six feet in height. At a little distance these shrubs have the appearance of green mounds thrown up on the smooth surface of the plain. Its shelter is much sought by the rabbit, the most tender and timid inhabitant of the prairie. Where the hazel has a strong compact growth it uproots the grass and leaves the soil unoccupied, except by an occasional flower or creeping vine, whose long tendrils make a beautiful festoonery for such little aisles. Along these the timid hare skips and feeds during the day, and when twilight favors his faint heart, he may be seen leaping out into the more dangerous paths trodden by man and other beings whom his instinct teaches him to dread as foes. Let him hear your footsteps and he flees the sound as if it foretold his death. We stroll through these miniature groves, treading carefully, and speaking in low whispers not to alarm the quick ear of their little tenants. By and by, we emerge from the winding road into the more open barrens. We wander onward, talking of olden time and the time to come, when presently a sharp, shrill sound breaks upon the ear, followed by the bounding of light feet. Away flies the deer, startled by our white dresses moving among the green foliage, and fearful every moment of the cracking rifle. Poor innocent, we shall not harm you! You might have cropped the twigs unmolested, and been spared that pang of fear, had you known that we love mercy, and find no pleasure in depriving any created thing of the joys which are its natural inheritance.

But while we have mused and talked, the magnificent drapery of the west has been folded away. The gorgeous piles of gold and crimson have melted and left the sky, faintly tinted with their departing glories. The curtain of night is creeping slowly over the earth; the breeze steals gently through the foliage, and shakes the large leaf of the sassafras with a soft hollow sound, which, with the quick, liquid rustling of the aspen, and the fuller notes of the forest tree, pours a delicious harmony into the ear of night. Half an hour later the light is gone out in the west. The night-hawk has ceased his airy, sounding swoops, and the whip-poor-will has come from his retreat, to tell again the melancholy tale he urged so mournfully last night. There he sits, in the top of the tall oak before the door, and will not cease his plaint. What is it troubles thee, poor Will? Hast thou been engaged in some naughty affair, wronging thy neighbor, or looking sweetly at the daughter of some sour old worshiper of Mammon, who scorns thy poverty, and threatens thee, unless thou desist? Or has some gay gallant misled thy dame, and is thy song a cry for vengeance? Methinks it is too melancholy in its tone. Some sorrow surely is its burthen. But our ears are grown familiar with it, Will; and thine, perhaps, is lighter than that we turn away from every day, though uttered more intelligibly. They say thou art a merry little fellow all day; that joy dances in thine eye, and that thou hoppest from branch to branch, laughing under thy wing at the anticipation of the melancholy pranks thou wilt play at night, with sentimental maidens and moonstruck lovers. If so, Will, thou art a sad rogue, and deservest some real sorrow, little masker that thou art!

But, good night! I turn my ear to a tale of more unequivocal sorrow than thine. Sister has promised me the story of the dark man's griefs.

CHAPTER X

"Sit with me here," said Mary, "in this dark, unfinished room. It has been the theatre of some of the scenes which I shall endeavor to delineate, and do not prepare yourself for any high-wrought romance. My story is one of reality too palpable to be recurred to, even now, without the most painful emotions. It is one of the many I could relate illustrative of the trials which sometimes wait on the settler in new countries. But you were down at the graves to-day, and have already guessed the import of what is to follow, so I will begin in my own way.

"I must premise that, from our first settling here, we have been under the necessity (often a pleasant one) of entertaining many strangers, for the most part gentlemen, who come to view the country. Persons landing at any of the river towns in our vicinity, and wishing to spend a few days or weeks for that purpose, were generally referred to us; and when they came, it was impossible to deny them such a home as we had to share with them. It has been a severe burthen to us females, overtasked as we have been, with the cares of our own families, and the arduous labors which the imperfection of the mechanic arts imposes on the good houskeeper of new countries; but we could not, and often did not wish to escape from it. When we moved into this house, most of these persons came to us, probably because my family was smaller than Mrs. R.'s, and my house larger. Sometimes such guests have been attacked with fevers, and lain on the threshold of death for weeks, requiring such care and attention as only an accomplished nurse, otherwise unemployed, could give. I have, in such cases, had to divide my time and ability between them and my family, watching by night and working by day, till they have recovered, and gone from our roof bearing the recollection, that humanity is not always confined to the homes in which physical refinement contributes so much to the comfort of the afflicted. Happily, no one of these wayfarers ever expired among us, though I have many times lived in the daily expectation of such an event. We watched one young stranger on that bed for ten weeks, during three of which we expected each day would terminate his sufferings and our hope. But he recovered to thank us, and bless his Maker for the energies which had borne him safely through the fierce conflict.

"But this is not my story. I relate these events merely to convey some idea of the claim which strangers have to our hospitality, and of the feeling which links us as brethren to those who are homeless and friendless in our land. This feeling breaks down all the barriers of ceremony wherewith we are restrained in more populous regions. It brings strangers together without the frigid medium that makes them mere objects of sight to each other; it seats them at your table and invites them to partake of whatever your home affords, with a freedom and genuineness that make the recollection of the cold and heartless ceremonies of more artificial society sickening.

"Such was the feeling that opened our doors to the solitary man whom you see still among us. But he came not thus alone. When he landed, three years ago this spring, at the place you left a few days since, he was accompanied by a young wife. They had set out together from one of the eastern cities, to seek happiness and fortune at the west. Having no definite place in view, they landed at P——, and there the young bride remained, while her husband visited the interior in search of a spot where they might make their home. He came to our neighborhood, and finding a piece of land which he liked, about a mile beyond us on the prairie, returned and brought his wife to see it. They stopped at our house, and I was more than willing they should find a home here till their own was ready to receive them.

"Mrs. K. was a dark-haired woman, with an eye that made her whole face glow when it was lighted up with pleasure or expectation.

She was rather above the middle stature, with a well-formed person, and a clear, happy voice. It was easy to see that her husband, silent and grave as he was, loved her with a strength that is rarely surpassed in man. They seemed to me a happy couple. They boarded a few days in our family, and then commenced housekeeping in this room. She was a pleasant companion, and being nearly of my own age, and possessing a cultivated mind, there soon grew up a warm friendship between us. Each could enliven the solitary hours of the other, and during the long days when our husbands were at work, we were much together.

"Their farm progressed quite rapidly; one or two fields were broken by the plough, a house built, and an enclosure made around it the first season. The next spring they removed. Their place, as I said, is about a mile east of this; it is farther out on the prairie, and commands a beautiful view to the south and south-east. It was delightful, after they removed there, to see near us another tenanted home. You cannot appreciate this feeling till you have passed a deserted one on some wide prairie. A sign of life, about one of the thinly-scattered houses here, stirs the heart with joy, though you have never seen its inmates; but a deserted prairie home, with smokeless chimney and curtainless windows, is one of the loneliest objects on which the eye can rest.

"A new source of joy cheered the young wife in her labors. She was soon to become a mother; and what task sweeter than to prepare her dwelling for the expected guest. She toiled faithfully and patiently, as if her hands had been trained to it from childhood; and her labor was directed by a capacity that made it effective. Her rough house grew into a pleasant habitable abode, and the young harvest springing around, gave cheering promise for the coming season. I saw her often after their removal, and always found her happy and rejoicing in the prospect before her.

"On the 24th of April of that year, there commenced the most remarkable series of storms ever known in the country. They occurred daily and sometimes twice a day, till the last of June, accompanied by the most terrific thunder and lightning ever witnessed. You may judge of the terror they inspired, when I tell you, that much as I loved the conflict of the elements before, the roll of thunder even now always produces a temporary faintness and nausea; then it completely overcame me. Language can convey no idea of those terrible days. The storms gathered with such fearful rapidity. A small cloud would be seen somewhere,

"When all the rest of heaven was clear,"

and in a moment the deluge was upon us. It seemed as if another flood were coming to purify the earth. The falling of the rain was frightful, to say nothing of the lightning that cleft the atmosphere, and the crashing thunder that followed so close upon it, that the tread of the latter seemed to extinguish the light of the former.

"These terrible scenes, following each other without the intermission of a day for more than two months, seemed to blight the country. The prairies were saturated, and in many places submerged, and yet the rain came. Sometimes when it had stormed thus all night, the sky would be clear till noon, and the sun pour his rays upon the steaming earth, till vegetation seemed scalded. Perhaps, just as dinner was set, a little cloud would gather in the west, or a faint roll of thunder strike the ear. My appetite would vanish in an instant; and with blanched face and trembling limbs, we would set away the meal untasted. The men always came in, though they were generally drenched before they reached the house. But such was our terror that we could not have remained alone. When a shower commenced, we knew not that its termination would see us alive. One flash and thunder-peal, I remember, were so awful that they brought us all to our feet with pale faces, and eyes that looked as if they were gazing on death. When the shock had passed, and we found that we could still move, the people of each house rushed to the doors, expecting to see the other on fire. But the lightning had rifted that large oak, the stump of which still stands about midway between them. After a while we ceased all employment when these awful periods came, and sat like people awaiting their doom. I have never seen anything of the sublime or terrible that approached the storms of those seventy days.

"But the consequences were still more dreadful. The earth was filled with water, and every little hollow upon the prairies became a stagnant pool to engender disease; so that after the fierce storm-demon had scourged us and departed, the silent pestilence rose from the green plains that smiled beneath his reign, and stalked resistless among their inhabitants.

"It was a critical period for my friend. The new cellar beneath their house had been half-filled with water, and I dreaded extremely its effect on her health. But there was no way to escape it, except to leave the house, which was scarcely thought necessary, while the danger seemed so remote. She preserved her spirits and energy through all, till her husband was prostrated by the fever. Then came her time of trial. Except the laborer who had assisted her husband on his farm, they were alone, and ours was the nearest family with which they had any acquaintance. I rode over nearly every day after my work was done, and frequently spent the night with her. There was a long period of dreadful suspense. The same disease was raging elsewhere with a fearful malignity, and it was impossible, for many days, to say whether hope or fear predominated. I knew that the effect on herself must be great, whichever way the scale turned. When the excitement was removed, she must sink. It was even as I dreaded. She was attacked long before the recovery of her husband, and both lay helpless; dependent on the skill of their hired man and the kindness of neighbors. I watched with them every alternate night for several weeks, and spent a part of almost every day there, after she was brought to her bed. Her attack commenced with a fever and terminated in a premature confinement. The babe that had been so long and joyfully expected, was thrown heedlessly aside, and all attention concentrated on the sinking mother—but vainly. She survived only till the third day; and the first time her husband left his house, was to follow his wife and child to the little spot you visited to-day, beneath those trees. His grief was appalling. Sickness had blanched his dark face into a ghastly hue, and drawn deep furrows in his cheek, which were immovable as if chiseled in granite. He had seen little of her lately, for his mental faculties had been partially suspended while she was watching by his couch; he knew she had been with him, but in terrible affliction which he had not soothed. Her last days were days of intense mental suffering, which he had not alleviated; and, finally, her life had closed in fierce agonies, which he had been compelled to witness, but could neither share nor relieve. He seemed to be a stranger to himself in these new circumstances, that has so suddenly changed the aspect of his whole life.

"Her grave was the first that had been made among us. We selected the spot for its quiet beauty, and the repose which its situation promised the dead, even when all who are interested in them pass away. When we arrived at the tomb, it seemed impossible for him to resign her without one more look. The lid of the coffin was removed; he gazed a brief moment, bent over it, imprinted one long kiss on the cold brow, and turned away. The mother and child were lowered, the grave filled—and thus departed the stranger who had come among us so recently, filled with hope and joy. His home was now too desolate to be endured. All that had made it home was gone for ever. He returned to us sick, dejected, melancholy; all the brightness which had gathered round his life turned to darkness—all his hope to despair. The house now stands untenanted, a cheerless sight to us who have known its better time. He spends his days at work on his farm, and his evenings as you see. But, notwithstanding his misfortunes, he still loves our country, and will, I think, remain in it."

"That, I believe," said I, "is the choice of most who ever spend any time here, and it was to me a mystery very difficult of solution, till I saw what enchains them. I do not now wonder that a person who has senses to be gratified, with all the various objects of each, that surround him here, and higher faculties to be elevated by communion with nature in her loveliest forms, can never willingly leave the land in which they are so daintily fed."

"Yes," replied Mary; "there is a charm in this country which cannot be resisted. But what is it? I have lived here five years, and am yet unable to say. It may be in our majestic streams; in our glorious prairies; in our delicious springs and summers; our profuse and glowing autumn; in the variety of free and joyous birds and animals that revel here; in the unrestrained freedom which we enjoy, or in all these combined."

"Undoubtedly, if my short acquaintance entitles me to an opinion, it is the latter."

"Social and physical freedom exist here," said Mary, "in their most enlarged forms. In less favored portions of the earth, man is more or less enslaved. Want, custom, artificial desires, or some of the thousand phantoms which tread upon the heels of human enjoyment, restrain his freedom. They limit his action, give complexion to his feeling, oppress his thought, cut off his communion with the primal sources of truth. His necessities have each an individual voice, and call loudly for effort. He may not rest till this is made. Here, it is to a great extent otherwise. Our genial climate and exhaustless soil afford an abundant and ready return for his labors. He is soon released from want, and his faculties, rebounding from their depressed condition, go leisurely forth in quest of happiness. There is just enough of ease in his outward circumstances to excite, instead of enervating the tone of his energies; and with enlarged capacities for enjoyment, he finds himself surrounded by the most propitious array of facts and objects for promoting it. Nature in her loveliest and benignest aspect is spread before him. She invites him to her acquaintance; and while he courts it, the jarring selfishness in which his life has been spent softens into greater harmony with the good, the true, and the beautiful in creation. He becomes a better, wiser, happier man. His fetters crumble, and he begins to reach forth to ascertain the boundaries and qualities of the new sphere in which he finds himself. These are such as to afford him a greater degree of pleasure than he has probably ever before experienced. Freedom from want, purchased with a moderate use of his physical powers; freedom from social trammels; freedom from the struggles of an emulation founded in vanity, or other vitiated desires; from the myriad forms of ruinous and slavish excess which feeling takes in more populous regions, where man's intercourse is more with his fellows, and less with Nature and his God."

"These elements," I replied, "create a happiness which all can enjoy and appreciate, the cultivated as well as the rude. Hence it is no longer a problem with me, that one possessing tolerable powers of mind may leave the most refined society of the older world, where material as well as mental elegance have previously surrounded him, and, coming here, find that charm in his life, though stripped of everything that had before constituted happiness, which will not let him sever himself from your fair land without many a pang and heartfelt longing to lay himself once more upon its broad and beautiful bosom."

"There is another thought," said Mary, "which has always constituted a strong bond between my heart and the land of my adoption. It is that of the mighty Future which lies before a country possessing resources like ours. To bear a part in developing this, seems to me equally calculated to stimulate and gratify our noblest powers."

"Unquestionably; but are such thoughts enjoyed by any but the nobler class of minds? Have they existance among the unthinking and uncultivated?"

"A better defined one, I suspect," replied my sister, "than you are disposed to concede to them. Indeed, I think them born of the country, and nursed by every day's acquaintance with it. One could as well gaze upon the rising sun and not foresee the splendors of midday, as live in these magnificent plains, and have no vision of their future greatness."

"You are probably right. At least, I have as yet no authority to dispute opinions growing out of five years' experience."

"I think your longer dwelling here would lead you to the same conclusions. It is impossible for the commonest mind to resist the united influences of which we have spoken. It must be elevated and made happier by them. Hence, if I were asked to name the

charm that binds the prairie settler to his home, I would say, it is
not merely the fine climate, the beautiful lands, the diversity of
the natural world, nor the majesty of stream or plain, nor even
the bountiful seasons. It is the combined effect of all these, giving the widest freedom of thought and action, and inspiring each
individual with the consciousness that his acts, be they few or many,
tell upon the development of energies that have slumbered for
ages, but are now fast growing into gigantic stature before the
world. Nor is it necessary, in order to constitute a part of that
which prompts us to action, that these ideas should have a distinct
existence in the mind. Men often act from motives that are buried
beneath an ocean of lighter feeling, and are but partially recognized
by themselves, till, like the electric shock, which compels the sea
to reveal its most startling secrets, some mighty event, searching
the depths of their being, brings them to the surface, to astonish
their possessors. Many a man has mouldered into dust, whose life
has been shaped by motives which, clothed in words, would at first
have appeared strangers to him, but which he would soon come
to recognize as a part of himself."

"But it is bedtime for people who rise with the day, and tomorrow
you have another half-day's penance to perform at ————"

"Which I shall rejoice to have accomplished, I assure you. Good
night; I am certain I shall see that dark face in my dreams."

CHAPTER XI

Our life at Prairie Lodge soon became more quiet. Visits having
been received and for the most part returned, we were left to the
enjoyment of our own circle. But I had still seen so little of the
Suckers that every opportunity of coming in contact with them was
gladly embraced, and just as we were beginning to cast about for
some excursion that should furnish one, the kindest of all chances
sent along a traveling menagerie and circus. A most rare conjunction of attractions for the "*natyves.*"

The "Zoological Institute and Grand Corps of Equestrians" was
to exhibit on Friday the ———— day of June, at the town of Wash-
ington, about ten miles north of us. It contained an elephant, two
camels, a Numidian lion, a royal Bengal tiger, and several other
less important personages, all whose claims were duly set forth; in
addition to which, the "Grand Equestrian Corps" would exhibit

the "most remarkable acts of horsemanship," and "Messrs. Sands and Turner would perform some of the most striking feats of physical agility ever witnessed." In short, the enterprising proprietors had determined to spare no pains to make these wandering entertainments as attractive as possible. But the certainty that the native population from far and near would be gathered was sufficient for me, without reference to the wonderful attractions set forth in the bills. Master Junius was anxious to see the elephant, lion, tigers, et cet., and his father and mother to see him enjoy the novelty; so it was determined without debate to go to the menagerie. It rained nearly all the night preceding, but the eventful day opened bright and clear as became a day in June. The horses were harnessed to the large farm-wagon, from eight to twelve chairs placed in it, some sidewise for better stowage and some facing each other. All the umbrellas, from our smart newcomers, to the old mutilated ones whose heads had grown grey, and whose limbs were fractured and luxated by five years' service in a new country, were put in requisition. Everything being ready, and the party seated, we set forth.

While we are making way over the wet prairie and through the *"Slues,"* I shall, with the reader's leave, introduce to him the steeds by the aid of whose good limbs we journey. They are emigrants, and have always held themselves very much aloof from the natives of their species, so that, notwithstanding a residence of five years, they are not on visiting terms with one of their neighbors. The one whose character and career are most interesting bears a name which has suffered much since the time when he gloried in it. This cognomen is *Tyler.* At the time of which I write, and for several years before, the adjective "old" had been prefixed, but it was purely in honor of his years, not as an epithet of insult. Tyler had some peculiarities which made him rather a pleasant object of contemplation wherewithal to diversify a long ride. His physical eccentricities deserve precedence. There was about the forward extremity of his neck a sort of decayed or constricted appearance, as if he once suffered the extreme penalty of the law and the impression of its instrument was never effaced. This gave his head the air of not being at home with his body. It looked as if he had drawn it in a lottery, and not being pleased with his bargain, had refused all pains to make the best of it, and put it on in the rudest style,—a lifelong warning to all horses who would speculate in like manner. But the other defensive member so indispensable to all quadrupeds, was characterized by the reverse of all these appearances. It had been robbed of its natural fair proportions, so that only a fraction of it was left, but what there was, was perfectly at home and very useful in the small sphere in which it moved. Its principal office when the body was not at work was to refresh the memory of flies, and add bitterness to the natural prejudices of these insects against the owners of all such appendages. It was not as efficient in defence as in offence, but was tireless in both capacities, to the extent of its abilities. No one ever saw it still. Its most brilliant achievements, however, were displayed when the owner was employed; and of all the kinds of labor which he performed, traveling before a waggon seemed most to favor its powers and pretensions. Tyler had a gait which I think was an anomaly among his species, though his friends called it a "trot." It was considerably slower than a walk, but was characterized by such a harmony of the whole animal, mental and physical, that it was really a pleasure to see him perform it. He settled into it naturally, after one or two applications of the lash, and instantly there was such an air of repose and contentment in his face, and such a harmonious moving of the whole body and its appendages, that it was delightful to see him. On these occasions the organ of which we speak played its most brilliant part. It seemed to govern his entire machinery, to be as it were the music-master of the choir, and by its beats regulate the whole. So perfect was its supremacy, that even the engrafted head yielded and swung from side to side in exact time with it. Flies could now light with impunity, for the harmony was not to be broken for a trifle.

Tyler had a habit which it seemed absolutely marvelous how he could preserve, of appearing very much astonished when any means were taken to quicken his gait. He, however, used his ears and tail principally to manifest this feeling. The former would prick up and the latter flash out of all time, as if some wonderful phenomenon had burst upon his senses. But he recovered from it in an incredibly short space; the tail resumed its swing and the ears their unwondering position, before he had described a distance equal to the length of himself and the waggon. Then if the request were repeated at the end of that time, he experienced the same surprise, and manifested it in the same manner, with the addition of a shake of the head if it were pretty sharply conveyed. There was but one argument for increased speed which wrought any conviction in Tyler's mind. To this he always yielded on its first presentation. If you exhibited the corner of a buffalo robe to him over the side of a waggon, he construed it into a necessity that could not be resisted, and away his heterogeneous body flew over the prairie, helter-skelter, one eye ever and anon cast back to see whether the reason were still good. Such an event always gave a shock to his feelings from which he did not soon recover; unless the remaining distance were long, it was certain to be accomplished in much less time than if his tranquillity had not been thus disturbed.

Tyler was sustained in his labors by a companion of the feminine gender to whom he had been long and faithfully attached. But she was Xantippe to his Socrates. If his conduct was at any time offensive to her taste, which it must be confessed was more refined than his, she informed him promptly by snapping his ears and otherwise showing the most unequivocal symptoms of wrath. I fancied that her affections waned as the graces of youth departed from her companion.

But Tyler has swung his head, tail, and feet to some purpose, for here we are in the suburbs of the town whose name will, if its proprietors are to be believed, redound not a little to the honor of the Father of his Country. It is prettily situated in a grove, through the borders of which runs a stream of considerable size. As we come upon the high swell south of the village, we have a full view of its principal street. At this moment it is lined with a crowd of all ages and sexes, dressed in a great variety of styles. We descend the slope, cross the bridge, and are at once in the midst of them. Let us alight here. This is my menagerie. I wish to fall in with that tide of females, and hear what they say. There are three walking along together. One of them has on a pair of paper shoes, and is obliged, as she wishes to keep her feet in them, to tread rather daintily; the others, more prudent, have walked in their substantial leather shoes, and carry the finer ones wrapped in their pocket handkerchiefs. They are talking busily while they pick their steps in the black mud. One of them addresses her friend on the right.

"I expect there'll be a power of folks *hyur* to-day."

"I reckon," is the brief reply.

"Was you ever in one of these hyur shows?"

"No, I never was; but Irene has been."

"Whar was it at?"

"In Indiany, 'fore dad moved hyur. She said there was a heap of droll beasts in that, and dad says they're pretty much alike. They tote the same critters about every summer in different parts of the country."

"Well, it's just as good, I reckon, for them that never seed 'em afore," said the third party, who had hitherto been silent.

"Yes, I reckon so, and two bits ain't much anyhow, if they should bring the same back."

"Where be they?" exclaimed the one in advance of her companions, looking up as she approached the public square; "I don't see nothing *hyur.*"

"No, I allow you won't," said her friend, laughing, "they don't keep 'em runnin about the roads. They ain't many would pay two bits to see 'em if they run out."

By this time we had reached the centre of the village. The two prudent ladies turned into the house of an acquaintance to change their shoes, and we went on toward the immense canvass pavilion, which was erected just beyond. The usual noises which proceed from a collection of the kind were issuing from it as we entered on the flood-tide of Suckerism that was setting into the narrow, winding door. A large number of grated boxes were placed around the sides, and one stately elephant was vibrating at the upper end, between a large and small camel. An immense number of seats rose to the very roof from the spaces between the waggons, a part of which were already taken, though it was early in the day. While the young letter-writer went one way, to delight his father and mother with his original remarks and profound questions on the animals, I turned another, to study what was by far the more interesting to me—the human part of the show.

It would be vain to attempt any description of the external of this crowd. The philosophy of Sartor Resartus himself would have failed in the endless variety before me. Here were garments whose age must have exceeded that of their wearers;—bonnets of a fashion which must have prevailed in the last century, for nothing like them had ever been known within the memory of the oldest of our party; vandykes in imitation of the Elizabethan period, and caps, whose fantastic proportions and trimming would have irritated the risibles of Hogarth's sleeping congregation. There was one young girl barefoot, her head covered with an antique Leghorn, trimmed with black, and projecting enormously over her face. Her dress was silk, of a hue which no language will describe. It was compounded of the color of apple-tree bark, old soap, and sole leather. The waist was too short to let her arms fall into their natural position; when they did, the blood-vessels ceased to perform their office, as the crimsoned broad hands and protruding wrists gave too palpable evidence. The brevity of this part, the length of the skirt, the total absence of all *tournure* in that part of the figure where it has been fashionable of late years to admire it, and the naked feet, made one of the most extraordinary *tout ensembles* of the day.

Another miss, of more mature years, sported a pair of light cream-colored shoes with the hose which nature had given her, and these in quite an unsophisticated condition; a coarse red and black calico dress, a silk apron of mazarine blue, and a black cape of the same material, over which one of the capacious tamboured collars of the olden time was spread, its lateral extremities drooping from the elbow. On her head was a pink sun-bonnet with a square frill which covered her shoulders, and a pair of green cotton gloves, the wrists ornamented with wide lace, were displayed upon her hands.

There was little conversation while they were examining the tenants of the cages. Sometimes an expression of wonder or admiration was elicited, but the hum which tires one's ears in an eastern assemblage on like occasions was not heard. I took an advantageous position on one of the seats, and gave myself up to the examination of the crowd. Presently Mary came up, to point out a character. He was a middle-aged man with dark hair, and eyes which seemed to look out at the sides of the head, so continually were they rolling from side to side. He was clad in a blue jeans coat, and pantaloons of the same, and held a large riding-whip in his hand, wherewith he employed himself in whipping the dust from one leg of the latter. He was looking about with the air of a man to whom the emotion of surprise was no longer possible. If he had just returned from the African deserts with a full collection of every species of animal which they contain, he could not have regarded these with more coolness. But for his garb and one other circumstance, one would have affirmed he could be no other than Van Amburgh or Monsieur Martin himself. That other circumstance was a certain constrained expression of the face, and, when it rested upon a new object, a gleaming of the eye, which, closely observed, showed that the man in the jeans coat and pantaloons was not quite so familiar with elephants, lions, tigers, &c, as he wished the Yankees to think him. He was evidently playing a part for their edification. I watched him sometime, not a little amused at the assumed indifference with which he suffered his eyes to wander about him.

The crowd increased every moment, and began to form about the entrance a dense, heaving mass of heads which, for aught one could see, might have been floating on some buoyant medium, so perfectly were the bodies which belonged to them concealed from view. It was a very pleasant amusement to guess, when a new head appeared, what sort of body belonged to it, and follow it to the skirt of the crowd, to test your own acuteness. The contrast between the fact and your expectations was often highly ludicrous. Presently there appeared in the midst of the scene an upper extremity which left one in no doubt as to the character of the pedestal on which it was supported, for the shoulders and part of the chest towered clear of the crowd, and bore aloft one of the most extraordinary heads—its furniture included—I have ever had the good fortune to see. The face indicated that it might have seen some fifty-five years. It was a long face, sharp at the lower extremity, and rather rounded at the upper. The eyes were between a grey and a black. They had a quick and penetrating, but not a restless glance; they were eyes which had been compelled to serve their owner in scenes of danger, and had contracted the habit of looking too strongly to be able to abandon it when the necessity was removed. The mouth seemed to have been originally drawn up at the corners, as if nature had made it to laugh, but the events of life had thwarted this purpose, and hung so heavily upon them as to draw them a little below the straight line. Yet there was ever and anon an effort made to repair this wrong, which lent an indescribable mixture of the sorrowful and comical to the face. The eyes shared in giving utterance to these blended emotions, but when anything decidedly comical presented itself, they supported the melancholy expression, and put on a look—partly of resistance, partly of defiance—which was very curious. Thus the face was continually hovering between a smile and a cloud; but the former seemed to be laboring under some disgrace, so that before it could fairly show itself, it was hissed down, and shrunk away in shame. The forehead was surrounded with short hair, which had in former times been black, but was now an iron grey. A very wide but scant cap border hung over it, and the whole was surmounted by a capacious sugar-loaf Navarino scoop, which had once vied with the raven hair, but was now faded, and mottled with bluish grey spots, that corresponded well with the lead-colored ribbon that fastened it. The crown mounted from the back of the neck, in a cone, to the height of half a yard, and the ribbon climbed over this, holding loosely in its place a circular piece of pasteboard, which supplied the absence of the original top. Let no one suppose, however, that the old lady had repaired her black hat with white pasteboard. It had either been inked, or dipped in a black dye; probably the latter, for ink must have been a rare article in her domicile. So much for the head. Her shoulders were covered with a small black shawl, and a blue and white cotton handkerchief supplied the place of a cravat, though neither could possibly conduce to comfort, in the heated crowd.

At the first look, it was impossible to avoid the ludicrous idea that the old lady had provided herself with stilts, the better to enjoy the spectacle before her; but this thought was instantly put to flight by the character of her face. Besides, her gigantic stature was too well proportioned, and each part too much at home in its elevation, to admit the idea of temporary or artificial foundation; for she advanced when others stood still and gazed with wonder at her amazing stature and progress. She fairly divided her honors of the day with the elephant, and stalked up to the camel in a menacing attitude, as if she thought he did not see a woman of her presence every day, and might as well confess it at once. Sometimes her scoop bonnet covered half my field of vision, at others it was turned so that the paper-capped crown towered above everything else. As the people began to take seats, preparatory to clearing the ring for the monkey ride, I was very desirous that the old lady should get a post in my neighborhood. I rose on my feet, therefore, and as her eye was wandering in search of an eligible spot, beckoned her to approach. She looked hard at me a moment, as if a little bewildered, and then, suddenly changing the expression of her face, came down at her most rapid pace. As she approached, I made room for her beside me.

"I reckon," said she, while adjusting herself in it, "you're Miss Roberts' sister that's come lately from York. You look a heap alike."

"Indeed," said I, "has my sister the good fortune to know you?"

"O yes, I've know'd Miss Roberts ever since she come to the country, and a right smart woman she is, if she is your sister."

"Really, do you consider her 'smartness' any the more reasonable on that account?"

"No, I didn't jist mean that, but I've all'us thought a heap of Miss Roberts, and like to say it."

The old lady's panegyric was interrupted by the voice of the manager ordering the more curious to "fall back," and clear the ground. My neighbor's head was instantly turned and elevated several inches to command the theatre of action. A beautiful little brown pony trotted out into the ring, and was very soon followed by a sagacious and most respectable-looking monkey in regimentals. He was introduced to the gaping multitude as Gen. Jackson, but his servility made it a poor compliment to his Roman prototype.

The master of ceremonies on this occasion, as on all similar ones which I have ever witnessed, was a very tall man in a long-skirted frock-coat and rather short trowsers. The fact is one which I would recommend to the attention of naturalists—not a little ingenuity may be exhibited in its solution. Whether it is one person who, gifted with ubiquity to a certain extent, presides over all the monkey rides of the country, or whether there is a peculiar affinity between these animals and tall men, are questions beyond my depth. Any one who inclines to the latter suppositon will please bear in mind that the principle, whatever it be, must cover the long frock-coat, the short pantaloons, and a tall seedy hat. I have never known these adjuncts to fail. On the present occasion the performance was not very brilliant. The pony threw up his heels and whirled exactly with the crack of the whip, the monkey was quite as in-elegant as usual in his postures, and not a whit more excited with the novelty of his Sucker audience than if he had been performing for a common New York assemblage. I did think he winked a little quicker when he faced the Navarino, but it might have been imag-ination. The most edifying part of the whole spectacle was the comments of my neighbor.

"Mighty!" she exclaimed, as the pony took his place, "what be they goin to set on that little horse's back? That great feller ain't agoin to mount him, I'll knock him off myself if he does. He's too long for such a powerful little beast. The great lazy *ramaffin.*"

The good old lady, in her friendly zeal for the pony, forgot that the *feller* whom she was denouncing was several inches below her own stature. But while she was in the high tide of her anathema, the monkey appeared. She looked for a moment quite bewildered, and at last broke out.

"Well if these Yankees don't go ahead of heaven and airth! I reckon now they made that little fixin a-purpose for that horse, but he ain't very handsome no how; he looks like a baby with his grandfather's head on. They mought a made the tail of his coat longer, and he'd looked better than he does now—but the Yankees don't care what's decent, for the young women goes with their necks bare a heap more than I ever seed anybody else."

Dropping the tone of soliloquy, and addressing herself to me in the most earnest manner, "Look at them two critters," said she, "I s'pose they are, for they say that one that's ridin ain't a boy, for all he looks so powerful like one. That horse'll throw him off yet, and stomp his brains into the ground if he's got any."

Two or three whirls of the pony wrought the old lady's sympathy and indignation to the highest pitch.

"If everybody felt like I do they wouldn't set such a fool as that a horseback, whether he's a monkey or not. He's alive, I reckon, and that's enough to make a christian take him off o' that critter's back, anyhow."

The tall man came in for his share of denunciation at every new feat which he commanded the monkey to execute, and before the three performers retired, the good old lady had denounced all Yankees and "Yankee doins" for the fortieth time. The man in the jeans clothes and riding-whip had watched the whole affair with such evident admiration, that the look of contempt which he remembered to assume after they retired was extremely ludicrous, and served better than a volume to reveal his whole character. But he was too remote for his comments, if he made any, to be audible to us.

Next came Mr. Turner with his dog, and their wonderful feats drew whole volleys of exclamation from my transparent neighbor. But when the young man climbed the centre pole and suspended himself from its top by a cord around his wrists, the poor woman could restrain herself no longer.

"Mighty Heaven!" she exclaimed, or rather shrieked, for her voice was sharpened by her excited sensibilities. "Does the 'farnal Yankee think we come to a hangin? I've saw one in my life, and that'll do me. But if he's a mind to hang thar he may, I won't look at him," and the giant hat swung quickly round, facing the audience above.

"It don't make you feel like it does me," she remarked, touching my elbow, "or you wouldn't look that way. I reckon you never seed a real hang, did you?"

"No."

"Wall, you'd never want to see another if you had, nor any such shammin as that. 'Tain't fit for folks to look at that knows what christians is."

I expressed so hearty an assent to this opinion both in relation to the real and the sham hanging, that the old lady looked earnesty at me for a moment, and then said, "Well now, I allow you've got some christian feelins in you. I like to hear anybody talk like that. Come and see me. Mr. R—— will tote you and Miss Roberts up some day, and I should be mighty glad to see you, and so would my old man."

While this little complimentary by-play was going on, the man whom we left suspended had come down, the crowd had relieved its excited feelings by two or three hearty rounds of applause and several interchanges of opinion among themselves. I lost sight of the man with the whip, but, to my great joy, he presently appeared in our immediate vicinity. I pointed him out to my neighbor, and asked who he was.

"O, that's old man C——; everybody knows him for the biggest liar ever lived in these parts. It's no account what you tell him, he'll *all'urs* break up ahead on you. And one thing is strange, he all'urs tells his lies as if he b'leeved them himself. He was in the *milichary* under Gineral Harrison a good many year ago, an if they should set down together anybody that heerd him would reckon he was the first man of the two. There ain't nothin on airth that anybody has ever seed or know'd, but what he's seed somethin a powerful sight bigger. You'll see afore long, now he's come so nigh."

While my friend was thus enlightening me, the ring had been again cleared, and a springing board elevated upon two blocks placed within it. In a few minutes, one of the most athletic-looking riders appeared in knit garments fitting closely to his fine, muscular form, and was introduced to the audience as Mr. Sands, who was about to perform some surprising gymnastic feats.

"I hope he won't hang himself," said the old lady, looking earnestly at his splendid figure, "he's too handsome, and there's been enuf of that *jimnasty* now."

But Mr. Sands, after a few preliminary performances, to assure himself that he was all right, relieved the good woman's apprehensions by setting himself into a sort of rotary motion in the air, like a human windmill. I counted twenty-nine of these surprising aerial evolutions, and then turned away, for the spectacle grew painful.

"He'll kill himself," said my excitable neighbor, "why don't they take him away? Stop him!" she screamed; "he can't stop himself! Why don't you catch hold of his legs and arms, some of you? I could hold him myself if I was thar," and the sympathizing creature rose on her feet and stood expostulating with the heartless audience some seconds before the performance ceased; when it did, there was a great deal of confusion for a few moments, and then a shrewd neighbor, who understood the constitutional infirmities of "Old man C——," remarked to him,

"Well, Mr. C——, for a Yankee boy, that was pretty fairly done, eh?"

"Oh, I reckon it'll pass among Yankees, but it's no account among us. When we was in the army, we used to do that every day, and we had some fellers who would turn them somersets sixty-feet right up a tree!"

"What, branches and all?"

"No; we cut away the branches of some of the trees round the camp, a purpose to have 'em ready. It's no account to do that. A right smart man would turn eighty or ninety without stoppin to breathe; that fellow, now, is a puffin like a beat horse."

"Yes, he does breathe a little quicker, it's true, but we think he has done well."

"Oh, it's right for you that never see anything better to think so, but I've got smarter blood than that myself."

"Ah! how?"

"My grandfather fit the British under *Begyne*, thar in old Virginny; and when orders was give for every man to take care of himself, he took a knapsack from a feller that was dead close by him, and put it on hisn, and started. Jest as he got to the fence, a powerful, big, old nigger that he know'd a long time, hollered to him for help, for both his legs was broke by a cannon-ball, and he allowed the Indians 'd scalp him if they got hold on him. So the old feller just throws him over the two knapsacks, and jumps the fence. But the British was most on his heels when he cleared it. He retreated *fifteen miles in sixteen minutes*, and then he come to the race-way of a mill eighteen feet wide; that he jumped, and the British halted on the other side for a raft, and so he got away."

"With the two knapsacks and the black man?" said the listener.

"Yes, and the next day they weighed 'em all, and what do you reckon they all made?"

"Two hundred pounds?"

"Two hundred? The knapsacks weighed eighty a piece, and the old man weighed two hundred and fifty without his legs, for they cut 'em off before they weighed him."

"Indeed! your grandfather must have been a very powerful man, to retreat so rapidly under such an immense burthen."

"Yes, he was a right smart old feller; but I've seen younger men that could do more than that."

"Ah, and who were they?"

"Why, 'tain't of much account for a man to brag of himself, but I've done better than that ar in my own time" (whipping his boot more vehemently than ever). "When I was with Gin. Harrison, we wanted to make a forced march once, when the roads was mighty bad, and the streams all in a fresh. So the gineral he come to me in the mornin, and said he calculated I'd be the best man to go ahead, for if anybody could do it—I could; and the men would follow me better than any other man. So jest to oblege him I started on, and told the boys to come, for I'd clar the road for 'em. We went on till after night, and it growed so cold, we thought everything would freeze up anyhow. At last we come to a stream that had ris a right smart sence morning, and left the ice under water: I halted here, and waited for the gineral to come and insult with him afore I tried it. We waited an hour, and at last the rare-guard come. I told the gineral that I reckoned we better not try it that night, but he said he wanted to git over; and he allowed I could git the boys to follow. So I never waited for him to say it agin, but I put right in, and swum my horse through, and broke the ice all the way. When I got on t'other side, I toted four or five old trees to the water, and laid 'em across myself, 'cause you see the stream was narrow, though it was right deep.

"At last they all got across, and then we marched five miles afore the gineral would let us camp. When we come to the place, I started to git off o' my horse, and couldn't stir. I was froze fast to the saddle. It was growing colder and colder, and I didn't know what I should do. Some of the boys allowed they could warm some water, if I'd set still, and thaw me up. So they went to building fires, but I didn't want to set there and wait; and, at last, I give a mighty spring that lifted the horse right off his feet, and when he come down, the ice cracked all around, and I got loose."

"You must have been sick after it," said his listener, "and so lost the battle the next day."

"Not a bit of it. I never was better than I was the next day; and I'll tell you what I did. I had a boy to load my rifle, and while he was doing it, I fit the Indians with a hatchet. I shot twenty-one, and—" but here a surge of the retiring multitude took the speaker and listener beyond my hearing.

"There," said the old lady, who had caught the last few words; "didn't I tell you right? He'll lie like that as long as anybody will stop to hear him, and that's a wicked man that's keepin him agoin."

"I have heard," I replied, "of story-tellers who would never suffer themselves to be out-done by others, but this man seems determined not to be surpassed by himself."

"That's jest it," replied my friend. "If he should ever tell so big a lie that he couldn't tell a bigger one, I reckon 'twould kill him. But I see my old man yonder waitin. Good bye! come and see me, and tell Miss Roberts to come with you." And with these words the old lady departed.

I began now to experience some trepidation, lest it should not prove so easy to rejoin my friends. I looked long and anxiously over the moving mass, but nowhere were their faces visible, till a sudden jog of the elbow brought me to the right, and showed Mary standing with Master Junius in her hand.

"Come, 'light down,' " said she. "John has gone for the horses, and you will not find another Mrs. S. here to-day."

"Nor anywhere else, I apprehend," said I. "Women like her must be rare."

"Yes, they are, more's the pity, for, with all her eccentricities, and they are interwoven with mind and body, she possesses some of the finest elements of character. Kind, just, generous, and hospitable, with clear perceptions and a ready humor, blended with the best feelings which belong to humanity, yet almost wholly devoid either of the arts of cultivated life, or the prejudices of her class, she is a model of a frontier housewife. Poor woman! she has endured much physical hardship and suffering, as well as other afflictions. They seem to have bent her naturally buoyant spirits almost to the ground, so that one is constantly reminded, while conversing with her, of the purple frost flower we used to admire so much at the east, which, always bent under the strong November blasts, seems ever vainly seeking to regain its former position. You may laugh at my comparison, and think that a woman over six feet, with such a Navarino and other appurtenances, should remind one of flowers only by contrast; but when you have lived as long as I have, away from the world where clothes make the man or woman, you will learn to see and appreciate beauty of spirit, irrespective of garb."

"I scarcely needed such a lesson as I have had to-day, sister, to teach me that. You know I never placed undue value upon dress, nor other material refinement; and if I had, I could not have failed to discover some of the spiritual beauties you have enumerated, under the coarse exterior of your friend. She seems an excellent-hearted woman! With some cultivation, and a little training in the hands of a posture-master, she might have carried even her enormous stature into any circle, and awakened only respect and affection. As it is, I have no doubt these are the predominant sentiments with which she is regarded by her acquaintance. Still it cannot be denied that the Navarino is an extraordinary adjunct of such a figure; see, now, if it is not," said I, pointing to the huge Pennsylvania waggon, in which the good woman was seated, beside her little husband. "It is an admirable keeping, all but the man, is it not? The very horses seem to copy their mistress: but the husband must be a cipher!"

"No; you are mistaken. He is almost the equal of his wife in excellence, and enjoys as undisputed supremacy in his family as if the size were all on his side."

"That is the best thing you have said of her yet. But I am going to visit her some time, and then I shall see for myself. Here are our steeds, and, I think, by the time Tyler has accomplished ten miles, we shall be willing to discuss something more substantial than external or spiritual beauty."

Just as we were crossing the stream I looked back. The great tent was struck, the cages were all converted into closed waggons, the circus horses and riders had off their holiday garb, and were each ready for the journey before them; the camels had shouldered their bundles, and the elephant, acting as his own porter, though under a cloak, was advancing towards us. But we soon left them out of sight, for Tyler plied his six organs of locomotion with such praiseworthy celerity, that we reached home just as the sun was sinking before us into a range of gold and purple mountains.

The adventures of the day led to some lively discussion of men and things in the west. I found the descendant of the "*Begyne*" hero was quite as notorious as he had been represented by that eccentric show. The stories which he told that day were declared to have formed a part of his honest belief for the last ten years.

"It cannot be otherwise," said my brother, "for he has, within that time, repeated them so often, and so earnestly, that he would have convinced you yourself of their truth, unless you had argued their probability in your own mind after each telling; and certainly, he has a right to indulge in the luxury of such hard-earned belief.* His stories no longer amuse me; but his absurd misapplication of words has not lost that power. It is only a few days since he called on us in the field to inquire for 'strays.' We told him there was one among our cattle, and were about specifying its age, et cet., when he stopped us, and said we ought always to make a man who was looking for strays '*subscribe*' them himself. 'Now I'll *subscribe* the beast I am looking for, and you can tell whether it's this one or

---

* These passages may serve to show the almost incredible influence of habitual falsehood in warping the judgment as well as the moral sense. The anecdotes related in the text were narrated with as much gravity, and, ultimately, I have no doubt, with almost as earnest a belief in their truth, as the demonstration of any proposition could be recited by a grave professor.

not.' When he had finished the 'subscription,' as he called it, we informed him that it did not belong to our 'stray,' and he plumed himself not a little on the shrewd lesson he had taught us."

I afterward saw a deed, conveying a considerable amount of real estate, of which this experienced gentleman had taken the acknowledgment. He had never held the office of magistrate, nor was he in any way qualified to perform an act of the kind. It was, therefore, "of no account," either in a legal or a common sense. But it had the merit of originality, both in structure and orthography. It was briefer, too, than those forms wherewith more learned gentlemen certify the legality of like documents. Here it is, verbatim et literatim: —

"hear i dothe surtify that the said ——— his wife and the said ——— is the said peepul that has maid this said dead and they allow they did it without compunctions or fears of themselves or enny body the said wummen aint 'feared of her said man nor him of her— Thereunto i set my hand an seal

                                        ———   ——— (seal.)"

But everything has an end, and I know of no class who should be more grateful for this truth, than people who are continually making themselves absurd. Even "Old man C's" ridiculous blunders ceased to excite our laughter, and after the cows had been milked and the chickens fed, we retired to rest, with a hearty welcome to the kind "Restorer," after the lengthened amusements and labors of the day. Our repose was not broken till deep in the night, when the growling of lions, tigers, etc., and the heavy rumbling of waggons, with the tramp of horses, roused us. The menagerie was passing on its way to the next town to exhibit. The following morning the elephant was found to have left the print of his foot in the soft turf beyond the house. It was about fifteen inches deep, and large enough to allow a child of six or seven years to sit down in it. It was not obliterated for many weeks.

CHAPTER XII

The time had now arrived when I was to leave Prairie Lodge and try my fortunes among strangers. This was in truth the commencement of "Western life" to me; for in my sister's home the ruder and less pleasant conditions of life in a new country had been

softened down by innumerable little arts and resources. The peculiarities of the people had been only so many sources of amusement or themes for speculation. They had never come so near as
to embarrass or annoy. Now the chances were that they might
assume a very different aspect. Instead of provoking mirth or awakening only cool curiosity, they might and probably would conflict
painfully with my previous habits and long indulged preferences.
Nevertheless the trial must be made, and the first difficulties to be
solved were, where and how? that is, in what particular house should
the new home be found? Every habitation in the little town, on
which our choice had fallen, was already crowded to excess. Several
were in progress which offered prospective homes, and in one of
these quarters were finally promised when it should be completed.
Meantime some six weeks or two months must elapse, and a temporary "place" must be found, in which to wear these away. Far
and near was the country searched therefore to find it. Suitableness
was a consideration quite out of the question, for be it known to
the fastidious that seeking board in the west is very different from
the same thing in New York. Here the host is favored, there the
guest. After several days of fruitless inquiry the anxious seeker was
commended to a Quaker family about a mile and a half from town,
where many of the citizens had boarded while building their own
dwellings. I had lived so much and happily in the neat quiet houses
of these people at the east, that the bare suggestion filled me with
delight. My imagination immediately conjured up the most delightful pictures of order and neatness. This house was visited on Saturday afternoon, and found to offer a very tolerable prospect of
comfort. The mistress was absent, but her husband gave assurance
that we could be accommodated. We could come the next week.

Behold us then landed at the door, the next Saturday a little past
one P.M. The house stands on a hill which is bordered on the west
and south by a grove, and commands a fine view of the prairie
north and east. The spot is really quite beautiful. I shall find many
charms "in the wood and by the stream" to lighten the long and
lonely hours, if such come, as come they must to one among
strangers. The exterior of the house looks very respectable. It has
the western stamp; the tall chimney is turned out at the end, and
there are four outside doors, two in front, and two in the rear,
opening opposite each other. The windows also are uniform, two
between the doors and one beyond each. A slat-fence of some
pretension incloses a part of the yard, but, most wonderful of all
our claims to gentility, the house is painted. It is a dark red, bor-

dered at the angles with a stripe of dull white. The window frames have a dubious hue which I cannot name. We alight and enter the southernmost of the front doors. It is a warm day in July, and the opposite entrance is thrown wide to allure the current. But oh, what an elysium it breathes upon! We gain the floor by one step, though it is of rather inconvenient height, and here the full view bursts upon us. The room is unequivocally filthy; near the opposite door sits the patriarch, his chair standing at an angle of forty-five degrees with the floor. He has on neither coat nor waistcoat, the whole of his simple garb being made up of a pair of blue cotton pantaloons, and a muslin shirt of very doubtful hue. On the right as we enter is a large open fireplace, the hearth of which is covered with ashes that in some places even encroach on the floor. Among them stand several baking-kettles and spiders, in which were apparently going on some very moderate cooking operation. Opposite the fireplace, partly under the stairway, stands a table, spread with a dark-figured india-rubber cloth. Beside this stands our lady hostess manipulating various parcels of dough; a process rendered particularly interesting from the fact, that a current of air enters the fireplace every few moments from the south side, and departs at the northern to make the circuit of the room; having during its brief stay taken a heavy freight of ashes and smoke. As it travels around to the opposite side, a very considerable portion of these cargos is deposited upon the table; and the principal object of the woman's labor seems to be to distribute this brown coating fairly through the mass. Each time that the parcels are taken up, the space they have covered is left comparatively clean, and though I will with an earnestness that starts the perspiration, that the operator shall lay them on the same spot again, yet she fails to do it in every instance. She must be proof against all magnetic influence! The old adage of a rolling stone is utterly refuted in those loaves. Locomotion was never more successfully proved to be favorable to gathering. My eyes grow to those balls of dough, and will not be persuaded from them, till they rest quietly in the filth of a single spot. The transition is then very natural to the person who has been operating with them. She is a woman of ordinary size, with two black eyes settled very near each other on a lymphatic face. Her hair is drawn tightly back from the forehead, leaving the grey temples entirely uncovered, and fastened behind in a most slatternly twist with a small white comb. She is clad in a dark blue calico, made very short in the waist and very narrow in the skirt. A small cape of another color, finished at the neck with a rectangular collar, is, I suppose, designed to cover the space left bare by the dress. But the various duties to which she is called, have so reduced it from its fair proportions, that two-thirds at least of its office is left undischarged, and that in the most important point. A part of these duties is very soon explained, for a cry is heard in the next room, to which she responds by rubbing the dough hastily from her hands, and presenting herself in person. In a moment she returns with a child of some twelve or fifteen months in her arms, and seating herself directly in front of the gentleman, proceeds to offer, without a spoon, the universal cordial for such woes. Shocking as is this proceeding, it does not prevent my noticing for the first time her feet. It is no tiny slippered member that peeps from beneath the flowing folds of her dress; but a broad flat foot, partially clad in a homeknit stocking of brown linen. The heels of both have long since got leave of absence, and the toes are earnestly soliciting the like indulgence, but with less success. The most melancholy state of the epidermis is manifest where these rents appear, and the sight of them reminds me so strongly of the anecdote of Dr. Abernethy, and the old woman who won a guinea from him by the exhibition of her lame foot, that, notwithstanding the horrors of my situation, I can scarcely resist the involuntary smile that rises to my lips.

There are two children in the room; girls of seven and nine, who from the moment I entered have politely turned their attention from ornamenting the loaves on the table with finger marks, to the inspection of my dress and person. Let the reader figure to himself, then, the dirty house, the dirtier man, the dirtiest woman, and the most dirtiest children, for nothing but a double superlative will convey any idea of their condition, and the writer sitting in the midst clad all in white of the most unsullied purity, and he will have some faint conception of my début in "Sucker life." Perfectly astounded by the scene before me, I had dropped upon the first chair, and sat gazing at the objects I have attempted to describe with a consternation that, had it been observed, would, I fear, have lead our host and hostess to doubt my sanity. The two girls dodged around me in all directions. The whiteness of my dress seemed to amaze them. They took hold of it in various places, and lifted it from the floor to get a look at my feet. I drew them back instinctively. What if the hose had by some mysterious process become such as I saw before me! I could scarcely persuade myself that they had not, and felt agreeably relieved when the elder, who had assumed this part of the inspection, exclaimed in a half whisper to the other, "*She's got on new stockins!*" But their most profound wonder was called forth by an embroidered sewing-silk shawl. I could not keep their hands off it. The pure white of the fabric, and the bright and delicate tracery of flowers, could never be sufficiently admired. At last my gloves drew their attention. They seized the one which I had unfortunately laid off, and bore it away for a more minute examination. I looked imploringly at the father, and was understood; for after he had several times repeated an order for its restoration, they returned, and a few minutes more, very much to my relief, brought the examination to a close. When it was over, the juvenile committee retired precipitately to the yard in front, and throwing themselves down "*on all fours*," scampered at full speed through the grass for several minutes, uttering all the time a noise so nearly like that of the wild turkey, that I started with surprise.

"That's the girls thee hears," said the hostess, half adjusting her dress, when the uncleanly baby signified his willingness to get down. She slid him to the floor, and, without washing her hands, walked directly to the table and recommenced her baking operations. The loaves had been very freely sprinkled several times during her absence, and the dark table-cover was quite whitened by the repeated deposits of ashes, so that the present working over was to some purpose! How could one ever eat that bread? I made a random estimate of the number of days one might subsist without food; and calculated the chances of getting boiled eggs twice or thrice a week, but the prospect was very dismal.

"Let us walk out," said Mr. F.

I gladly accepted the proposal, and stepped hastily forth, relieved, like one oppressed with nightmare, by the blessed name of the outer world. When we were fairly out of ear distance my husband spoke.

"You cannot live even for a few weeks in that place, can you?"

It was a difficult question to answer. Three minutes before, with that horrid spectacle around me, I should have said, without hesitation, No! But now it had faded away. Nature was pure and beautiful here as elsewhere. The deep wood, with its clear leafy aisles, was doubly inviting, by contrast, with the filth from which I had just escaped. The winds that sighed around us were fresh, and birds were chirping and singing pleasantly in the trees, as if the house had been the home of all the domestic virtues. I should have a little place of my own somewhere, that could not be proof against hot water and soap, and there I could sit alone and enjoy its neatness. Beside all this, I knew that a better, or, indeed, any other place was out of the question; and it seemed quite inconsistent with duty or comfort, therefore, to show any adequate appreciation of the disgusting realities of this. Moreover, retreat was now impossible. The conqueror of Mexico, when he had landed his forces on the shores of the new country, destroyed his ships to prevent the possibility of return. We had followed this illustrious example, not with so imposing a motive, perhaps, but to scarcely less purpose in regard to the alternative of escape. Weighing all these things in my mind, in much less time than they can be written, I answered decidedly, "Yes." I will not deny that the answer was rendered more energetic by a discover made at the moment, that the grove abounded in wild fruit, as the plum, blackberry, cherry, &c., which would soon be ripe, and afford a most luxurious fare without that loathesome bread. So much was I encouraged by these unexpected accessories, that it really cost but little effort to dress the prospect in colors which comforted both very much. After a deliberate survey of the external, we turned our feet reluctantly houseward, for homeward, as yet, it was not. On reäpproaching, I noted, for the first time, a little cabin almost adjoining the large house on the northern end, which gave every indication of being inhabited. The entrance looked neat, and there was a cleanliness about the pails, kettles, and other household implements standing without, that quite revived me. "Here must be something," I exclaimed, "that can be seen, at least, if not participated in. It looks familiar and cheering."

I set my foot reluctantly upon our dirty threshold, and, as I entered, saw a young woman sitting within sewing. She looked so cleanly and wholesome, that I set her down at once for the tenant of the cabin. She was introduced as the married daughter of our host, and the housekeeper aforesaid, a ceremony, by the way, which would never have been performed but for another announcement that followed it, and made me almost embrace her in the joy it produced. We were to eat at her table! Judge of my relief, any one who can, to be transferred from this dreadful place, to be no more haunted by those loaves, to get leave of absence from those stockings, and the children, and the vile india-rubber cloth! My happiness seemed perfect! I wanted to take my young hostess by the hand and say, Let us leave this place, and go to your own neat home. But this would not do. I was obliged to restrain my transports, and reconcile myself a little longer to the apartment of her lady-mother. But, alas! true happiness is always brief, and mine was a little briefer on this occasion than usual. It suddenly occurred to me, that some place must be provided to spend the night in, and the hints I had heard of congregated sleepers among these people, combined with the fact that there was but one other room in the house, threw me into a greater trepidation than I had yet experienced. To settle the question at once, I asked the young woman where my room was.

"Room!" she replied, regarding me with evident surprise, "thee can't have a whole room, but thy bed stands in *thar.*"

"Show it to me," I said, while a cold shudder passed over my frame.

She led the way, and I followed to a room corresponding exactly, save the staircase and fireplace, with the one we had left. There were three beds in it, two occupying the front corners, and one at the back. The latter was pointed out as the one assigned to my use, and I thought, from the tone in which it was done, that I might consider myself fortunate if the whole of this were left to me. Beside the beds, the apartment contained four flour barrels standing in the corner fronting mine, a cast-off tin oven near them, two chairs, a large bundle of old calicos and muslins lying under my window, and a few bits of board covered with fragments of broken plates, cups, et cet., with which the young ladies before referred to, doubtless amused their elegant leisure. The floor was not so hopelessly bemired as that we had just left, but it was strown with all descriptions of loose litter — flour, meal, potato rinds, plum pits, apple cores, chips, rags, feathers, et cet. The young woman apologized for the disordered condition of the room. But this was the least dreadful of the realities it presented to me. The other was enough to make the greatest heroine that ever lived in romance, stand aghast. I inquired who occupied the other beds.

"The boys sleeps in this hyur," was the reply, "and ————— —————, the country surveyor, in this, when he's hyur; but that ain't more than oncet or twicet a week."

The tone in which these facts were communicated was such as utterly to defy remonstrance or appeal. The proprietor of a first-class hotel could not have shown his best suite of rooms with less expectation that they would be complained of. I must demur to these arrangements, but where to begin was the question. At last I observed that it was so at war with our eastern usages to sleep in a room with other people, that I scarcely saw how I should become reconciled to it.

"Thee'll soon git shet of that," said my hostess, " 'tain't of much account anyhow, and a body gits so they don't mind it after a little."

"But the initiation," I said, "is terrible. I would rather have a couch on the floor of your garret, or sit up in a chair all night, than sleep in a room where there are two other beds occupied by strangers."

"Oh, thee needn't mind the boys, they'll be asleep long afore you go to bed, and up afore you're awake, and I — won't be here to-night. He allowed he'd be gone till the middle of next week. So thee needn't make thyself any more trouble. I reckon thee hain't been in the country long, has thee?"

"Not long enough," I replied, "to be accustomed to this, and I never shall be. I don't intend to be," I added, waxing somewhat warm at the nature of the supposition. "I shall never sleep in that bed till some partition is thrown across the room. I have some ideas of exclusiveness, which shall not be outraged by any degree of necessity."

The good-natured creature laughed in my face.

"If I see thee next year at this time," said she, "thee won't feel so."

"That may be," I replied, "though I doubt it exceedingly. But how I may feel a year hence is a matter of no consequence. The present is what I care for. If I degenerate with the lapse of time, I will lament it then, not exult in it now. Be assured I can never attempt to sleep in that bed as it now is. I only regret that there is not another day between this and the sabbath. If there were, I would show you what the ingenuity of a Yankee girl could do. As it is, I shall live outdoors most of the time till Monday morning, and then you shall see."

"Very well," replied my hostess, "but I reckon thee won't care much about it after a little."

I had forgotten to say that before we left Prairie Lodge, Mr. F. had purchased a little roan pony for my progresses over the country, and that she was the only living thing here, beside ourselves, in which we felt any personal interest. We were not, therefore, altogether so helpless as the great conqueror after his ships were destroyed; for pony was still left, when our carriage returned; but for all practical purposes of escape we were equally so, since the flight of two persons could scarcely have been effected in any manner, with such small means of locomotion, not to mention trunks, valises, et cet. If any lady wonders how pony finds a place in this arrangement for the night, I will tell her. I contemplated dispatching a boy to town on her to procure the wherewithal for my temporary carpentering, and, as I stepped quickly to the door for this purpose, the faithful creature, who was feeding in the yard, came up and laid her head in my hand, as if she would offer me any service in her power. But night was too near at hand; I was obliged to abandon the enterprise till Monday morning came. I, however, requested (for ordering was no part of my prerogative there) that the flour barrels might be removed, the tin oven set away, and the playhouse and bundles of rags carried to the other side of the room. When this was done, I borrowed a broom, and made clean work with the flour, chips, et cet., that covered my part of the floor. The trunks were then placed, and so much done toward domiciliating in this unparalleled place. Never did anybody rest more unwillingly than I from these labors. But tea came, and the white cloth and shining dishes quite reconciled me to the delay I was obliged to endure. Besides, there was a glory in originating and prosecuting such a scheme, to reward one for submitting to a little restraint. I determined to keep my own secret; and the complacency with which I sat up in the great naked room till a late hour, and, finally, lay down in a wrapper to rest a little before morning, excited no little wonder in the sharer of my vigils.

CHAPTER XIII

The Sabbath, spent in quiet wanderings through the woods and fruit thickets, and reading on the clean turf, and another night like that described, brought us to the morning which I had so ardently desired. No scrupulous housewife ever longed more earnestly for the absence of the male part of her household while her slaked lime was waiting, and her tubs of water ready for the onset, than I, till Mr. F., with many adieus and ceremonies, and much condolence for my condition, at last took his departure for the day. At the end of the next three minutes my working toilet was finished, and my labors commenced. I had bespoken a supply of the necessary articles from the cabin, and having cleared so much of the floor as I intended to occupy, proceeded to put these cleansing agents to their duty. Their efficiency exceeded my most sanguine expectations. The floor came up from the superincumbent mass, with a distinctness which no one would have anticipated. Blistered hands and lacerated fingers were matters of no moment to one intent upon a great purpose like mine. I toiled away, therefore, in spite of a variety of these little incidents, till the dinner summons came and found me still in the high tide of successful effort. But the room, for it had now become one, had undergone a great change. A heavy partition of quilts doubled on each other twice or thrice, had been run across above the head of the bed, and the whole space inclosed by them was exclusively mine! The little floor was covered with a piece of carpeting. The two chairs were scoured, the window washed, and the wooden work of the walls thoroughly cleansed. Between the window and door was a space for a mirror, and here I had set a toilet made of dry-good boxes, and covered with brown linen damask. The trunks were snugly stowed under the bed, and I fancied, as I looked about, that I might safely challenge any home of six hours' growth, for an equal air of comfort and neatness. My door and window looked out upon a green lawn, dotted with the wild cherry and other trees, and still farther, upon a rich and distant stretch of prairie and grove. Now that I had brought affairs within to so improved a condition, I could regard those without with more complacency. Even the beauty of the distant landscape was much enhanced by the environments from which I now beheld it; and still more, I suspect, by the better state of feeling induced in myself by the latter. I piled my books—the best companions of such a quiet retreat—upon the toilet, which, by a curious, and I flatter myself ingenious, arrangement of the boxes, was made to answer the purpose of toilet-table and bureau, and dressing myself hastily, answered the call to dinner. My hands smarted and ached with the wounds they had received, and I felt a degree of fatigue which made rest welcome, but a more delightful feeling of satisfaction is rarely experienced, than was mine when contemplating the result of my morning's work. And then the anticipation of Mr. F.'s surprise when he should come in, and find such a snug, neat little home grown up since morning! My only sorrow on returning was that there remained nothing else to be done. But I borrowed a broken pitcher, and gathering such wild flowers as could be found at that season, placed it between two piles of books, and then sat down to compose my mind for reading.

I had seen nothing of my neighbor in the next room since the day previous, but how could I forbear inviting her to witness the superiority of industry and order over her own miserable house-wifery? She seemed to have an idea of being quite exclusive, so that I thought there could be no risk in inviting her to look in upon my new quarters. I confidently expected a burst of admiration, or at least some hearty commendation of my industry. Judge then of my surprise, when the good lady seated herself, and, after looking coolly about her, exclaimed, "Wall, I reckon thee thinks it looks

better than it did before! but I shouldn't like so small a room!"
Comment was unnecessary. I did not even name the window which
would stand open all night, nor the door which might remain ajar
likewise, nor, bad as is the foul air of a small bed-room, the things
which were even worse than that to me, but dismissed the old lady,
more than ever confirmed in the opinion that she was destitute of
everything which could awaken in me the least interest.

My young hostess was not equally stupid: she appreciated the
advantages I had gained, and particularly the satisfaction arising
from a sense of cleanliness in everything about me—a sensation
unknown to the other. She could likewise understand something
of the feelings which had prompted my labors, and participate, to
a certain extent, in the joy of success. She loved to have her own
little cabin neat and orderly; and so far there was a bond of sympathy between us. Beside, she could estimate the joy of the surprise
which I was continually hovering over and studying to heighten;
and this made her seem far more human than if she had looked
with indifference upon it.

At last the time came. Just as the sun was setting behind the
woods, pony came dashing gaily up the hill, and in a moment more
the "gude mon" stood in the door, looking very much as if he had
entered the wrong house. I pass over the repetition of the details
which I was obliged to give, and the lamentations that were taken
up over my hands, and simply say, that we found ourselves so happy
under the new arrangement, that the more commodious apartments
of Prairie Lodge were pined for less than we feared. My principal
regret was, that pony could not walk in and share our comfort;
but she frequently came up to the door, and, putting in her head,
looked as if she were convinced that it was all right, although the
means of making it so were not quite so apparent. I had more
difficulty in making arrangements for my morning ablutions than
anything else. Towels I could furnish myself; but the best ever I
could get was an old pail, and the best basin, a tin one, holding
about two quarters. These would have answered the purpose very
well, if I could have been left in undisturbed possession of them.
But they were sure to disappear at least half a dozen times during
the day; and then it was exceedingly difficult to track them. When
found, too, they must always be cleansed; for no one could tell to
what uses they had been put during their absence. I had several
times, while thus engaged, met the patriarch of the establishment,
and thought he cast an evil eye on my proceedings. But as I knew
no reason for his doing so, I had gone on in all the consciousness

of innocence, to assert, practically and theoretically, when occasion required, my right to these articles. Judge, then, of our astonishment, when, after bearing with his disturbed spirit several days, the old gentleman took my husband aside, and, after expressing himself perfectly satisfied with our deportment, et cet., added, "But I can't allow thee, nor thy wife, to wash in my house. I reckon outdoors is good enough for anybody; thar's a basin by the well, and plenty of water in it; and anybody that can't wash thar, I expect mought as well go without."

Ridiculous as this may appear to the reader, and does now to me, I scarcely knew at the time whether to be most amused or indignant.

"I will wash in his house," I said, "so long as I sleep in it, whether he is accustomed to it or not. If the other ladies who have boarded here were weak enough to yield to this barbarian prejudice, I will not. Of that I can assure the venerable gentleman, in one moment, if he wants my decision. Does he think I shall sally forth every morning, and stand at the well, waiting my turn for that vessel, which lies on the ground all day, and answers every conceivable purpose, from a pig-trough to a washtub—for the baby's linen. It is so completely encrusted with filth, that you might safely defy a legion of chemists to name the material of the original form. Out upon the old savage. I'll maintain my separate establishment in spite of him."

But as there were some four weeks yet remaining, it was thought prudent to indulge his prejudices so far as to appear willing to comply with them. Accordingly, after bathing and completing my morning toilet, I usually transferred my basin from the wooden chair seat to the sill of the door, and made a very circumstantial display of a sham washing outside. If the patriarch passed anywhere in the vicinity during this time, I esteemed it particularly fortunate, and, if possible, advanced the basin a little further into the outer world. This *honest* compliance brought its reward; for although it did not quite meet his views, he was pleased to express the pleasure it afforded him "to see so much goodwill in the young woman." Poor Mr. F. was obliged to recompense my rebellion, by taking the basin to the well, and performing ablutions equally superfluous there among the young gentlemen.

But it is time to introduce the reader more particularly to the senior personage. He was a dark complexioned man, of some fifty-five years, with an eye that had nothing peculiar about it when his face was in repose, but which had a keen piercing look when anything excited him. He bore the name of an illustrious preacher of the sect to which he claimed alliance, and had originated in the same neighborhood; but the branch of the family to which he belonged had left Long Island many years before, "Virginny;" and as their fortunes declined, had gone farther west, till he now occupied the outpost in Illinois. He had speculated himself into several fortunes which he had lost by the same means; was a shrewd calculator of his gains; (but would risk them all when a "right smart *spec*" offered;) and had that peculiar kind of industry, which led to continual scheming, but to little manual labor. He loved the country and his mode of life. But this feeling was subsidiary to those already named. If he could have schemed as well in an eastern city, he would have relished life there; and only found occasional cause of complaint in the absence of game, which he loved to shoot. He would never have hesitated to place his family anywhere. An introduction to the Court of St. James would have flurried him less than a private dinner party does many people. Himself arrayed in his jeans suit, and long furred hat, and Catharine in her ancient pongee and quaker bonnet, he would have "reckoned" they were "fixed enough for anybody." He was tyrannical in his family, and "allowed that boys was made to work," an opinion in which his sons did not so heartily concur, as to evince thereby the highest degree of filial respect.

The daughter with whom we boarded, and the eldest boy, a youth of sixteen, were the children of a former wife, and, if rumor were to be trusted, did not find the paternal fireside so agreeable as the darlings of the second mother. The only dowry which this daughter had received, was the name of Sidney; though as she said "she never know'd that was a man's name till the Yankees come to board thar." She was a good-natured girl, with no great depth of feeling or thought, but all that she had of both was expended on her coarse, long-haired husband, a Hooshier of the broadest stamp. She appeared to have had her *native* buoyancy suppressed by some unnatural process in early life, for her face was always grave, even in her happiest moments. If she laughed it was a fleeting laugh, gone as soon as it came, and succeeded by a reproving expression, as if it were a thing to be repented of. She had grown up in the most abject ignorance. Reading could scarcely be included in the catalogue of her accomplishments, and writing was to her as mysterious as Egyptian hieroglyphics. The simplest arts of cultivated life were unknown to her, and she was at the same time ignorant of those other branches of knowledge which may be almost universally found among females of her class. Poor Sidney had, therefore, few resources within herself, and fewer still in the indulgence of the filial and fraternal affections. No wonder then that what capacity she had for love was concentrated on her husband. Beside, he deserved it; for though somewhat rough in the exterior, his kindness was inexhaustible, and his faith in her perfection impregnable. They were really pleasant models of domestic happiness. He had more physical industry than his father-in-law; the forests of Indiana had perhaps cultivated it; but when the labors of the week were closed, and Sidney had prepared an extra meal after breakfast on Sunday morning, he would "gear up," and, seated side by side in the immense Pennsylvania waggon, they drove off to "meeting," or to some friend's to spend the day, and returned at night pleased with themselves, with each other, and with the prospect of returning next morning to their labors. They were far happier with these rude enjoyments, than thousands who live in luxury and ride in spendid carriages, with liveried servants.

CHAPTER XIV

For many comforts in the household affairs of the little cabin, we were indebted to those who had preceded us. Sidney had taken the title of Mrs. the preceding year, and the festivities of the occasion had been superintended by a family of "York girls," as she designated them. During their progress she had been initiated into the mysteries of pound-cake, jumbles, and apple-tarts. And these now constituted the principal delicacies with which she tempted our appetites. It is needless to say that having only an imperfect knowledge of the rule by which they were compounded, she was not always successful in her attempts; and as we were little addicted to the consumption of the articles when she was, her ingenuity was not greatly taxed in these matters. Her style of serving the cake was quite original. She shaved and laid it on the plate as one would old cheese; and her notions of the quantity which should be indulged in at once, were extremely moderate, not covering more than one of these thin small slices. This should be the rule at many other tables than that of Sidney.

We fared very well for four weeks. My residence grew more and more pleasant as the summer advanced. The blackberry and plum ripened all around us, and afforded delicious desserts at breakfast, dinner, and tea. I could gather any quantity myself, in the grove and thicket below the house, and used to spend many hours thus when Mr. F. was in town. The only drawback to these pleasant rambles was the fear of snakes, and the danger from these was more imaginary than real; for I never saw.but one or two (and those were harmless) in all my wanderings about the place. And I may as well take this occasion to say that dangers of this kind are very much exaggerated both in books and the minds of settlers on the prairies. I resided nearly five years in the country, and spent a large portion of my time abroad on foot, on horseback, and in waggons, and was never once menaced or frightened by a venomous or dangerous serpent. That there are many there, cannot be disputed; and so there are in all country regions which I have ever visited. But if unmolested they are mostly harmless; and when a bite is received, nature has an antidote immediately at hand. You scarcely walk ten yards on the prairies without passing several tufts of an herb, the leaf of which is said by old settlers to be an infallible remedy if applied within a short time. The bite of the rattlesnake is, therefore, little dreaded among those who understand this. In the rich bottom lands are two or three larger species whose speed is equal to that of a horse. They sometimes give the incautious traveler chase, and are dangerous, from the heartiness of their embrace, when they overtake him; but there is little danger in the prairies from these tenants. It takes time, however, to become convinced of this, and I, to make assurance doubly sure, made my sallies under the protection of a pair of boots, which, though they impeded my progress and threatened to forsake me at every step, quieted the little fear I had, and left me free to wander and look for something beside snakes—a hateful search anywhere! On one of these excursions I was overtaken by a citizen who was riding along the same road. Skirts were not so long then as now, and I felt a painful consciousness of my feet, that drove me to the tall grass to await his disappearance. In my haste I nearly lost one of the boots, and had to stop and replace it just as he was opposite me; but a beautiful flower that was springing up where I stood, afforded a graceful pretext for stooping, and so relieved the awkwardness of my position. When he was out of sight, I promised never again to wear the boots, snakes or no snakes, a vow which I kept religiously ever after.

I saw no company in my temporary home, except the inmates of Prairie Lodge, who sometimes rode down and paid us brief visits. The reception of strangers was out of the question in my narrow apartment. Every night brought a report of the progress of the house whose completion we were awaiting, and every morning sent forth most fervent aspirations for the day when its walls would be tenantable. Six weeks spent in this retreat, seeing scarcely a face, save those of our neighbors in the next room and cabin, made me begin to feel that society would be welcome. Beside books and my wanderings, the only amusement I had, was to make observations on the character and domestic arrangements of the elder lady. The former was soon exhausted: the latter afforded a more protracted employment. There was one little mystery that I felt some curiosity to solve, and that was how the house should have had so cleanly an aspect on the Saturday when Mr. F. first visited it, and been so incredibly the reverse when we arrived. In due time the solution came. The thrifty housewife had a regular rule for cleaning, which she conscientiously observed. No accident, as of storm outdoors or an upsetting within, ever induced her to swerve from it. She washed her floor every other Saturday, and Mr. F. had hit the happy day. We were half-way between, and hence the different complexion. But even these cleanings were not such as to satisfy more scrupulous housewives. Many an eastern dame would not have hesitated to denounce them as mere pretence; and they always seemed to me to be made more from the force of habit than from any sense of duty or increased comfort. They served, however, to make sitting down in her room less dangerous for a day or two, and so were very acceptable.

I had been for several days dreading an invitation to her table, and could only pray that, if it must come, it might be on the afternoon of the clean Saturday. But no such fortune awaited me. It came in the middle of the last week, when the disagreeableness had nearly reached its climax. What could be done? Excuse or evasion was impossible there, under such convenient observation. If one could have become suddenly indisposed; but that was an alternative to which I had neither the patience nor artifice to resort. I had no confidential friend to send for me, saying that my presence was indispensable; and after examining every loophole of escape, I gave up in despair. Here was another act of semi-martyrdom four or five hours in duration, and indefinitely worse than any I had suffered at Prairie Lodge. Determined, however, to endure as little as possible, I stepped into the cabin and petitioned S—— to share it. She readily consented, and seemed disposed to make quite a formal thing of it, by putting on her Sunday gown. At half-past one, the latest moment she declared that we could wait, we presented ourselves in the good woman's room. The resignation of a lamb going to the slaughter was nothing compared to that into which I compelled myself, as we took our seats. If the dirty casket before us had been riched with a single gem of thought or feeling above what its exterior appearance indicated, one might have forgotten its uncomeliness in their light. But the disagreeableness had no such qualification. To sit a half day with her, was to sit with the mere physical material of a woman, put together in a somewhat exceptionable style, and sadly soiled. The afternoon wore away in discussions of the fruit harvest; in some uninteresting reminiscences of life in Ohio; and a detailed account of the babyhood of her promising daughters. Meantime the young ladies were demonstrating their emancipation from this period, by tumbling about in the grass before the door, and imitating the cry of turkeys, grouse, owls, et cet. They had the most incorrigible love of locomotion *"upon all fours."* Wherever business or pleasure summoned them, unless great haste were requisite, they journeyed in this unique style. One could not avoid being reminded of a species of animal to which they seemed allied by other similarities as striking as this.

When tea-time approached, the *dodger* was mixed and placed at the fire, the "salt risin" loaf that had stood in the corner all the afternoon was examined (with hands that had not been cleaned since we entered), and put to baking; and in due time the india-rubber table-cover was garnished with a variety of dishes, empty and filled, and we were invited to take our places. Then came the time that tried my stomach. There was nothing on the table that was not of home manufacture; not even that last refuge of the distressed, a "store cracker." The milk had passed through sundry pails, strainers, and pans, so that it stood little chance of being purer than the bread; the butter was not to be thought of by one who had seen the churn, and the hands with which its contents were removed; the preserves were, if possible, more impracticable than anything else; the fried bacon was too loathsome in itself; and the chicken radiated pin feathers from every part of its surface; beside having gone through with all the stages of preparation in our presence. Graham himself never took a more temperate meal in point of quantity than I on that memorable afternoon. I had made up my mind to devote myself exclusively to a piece of bread. I attempted the crust, but there was the table-cover on which it had been kneaded staring me in the face: then the inside; but this was soft, and it was impossible to swallow it without remembering the hands that had been thrust through and through it. The hostess pressed me in the kindest manner to eat. Dish after dish was offered and rejected, till, at last, when my stomach was on the eve of uttering a protest that could not be mistaken, I withdrew, and retreated as hastily as decency would permit to my own room. Scarcely was my equanimity restored, when a considerable bustle arose in the apartment I had just left; and presently one of the girls came in to say that the baby had a fit. I stepped in, and found the child lying in a stupor upon its mother's lap. She was chafing his feet, hands, and temples alternately, and appeared more like an animate being than I had ever seen her. In a short time the boy revived, and his mother then informed me that he was "often took that way, but he soon got shet of it." The table was still standing, and she ordered the elder girl, who was in her favorite attitude before the door, to stop "cutting up," and come in and clear it away. "And git the basin," added the fastidious woman, "and wash the dishes off: thee can do it as well as I, if thee's a mind to."

I sat a few moments, till the poor baby seemed quite recovered, and then rose to return to my own room. One might suppose, after what I had seen, that no evidences of uncleanliness could surprise me, yet when I cast my eye at the table in passing it, and saw the cups from which we had just drank piled into the basin that had been commended to my husband for our morning ablutions, I was obliged to confess a new cause of wonder. The sight drove my digestive apparatus to open rebellion. I fled as from an embodied pestilence; and the whole affair was soon settled, by my resigning all claim to the few morsels of bread I had swallowed, and promising never to abuse myself thus again. But I little knew what fate had in reserve for us. The week before we left, some near relative of our young landlord was taken ill, and his wife was obliged to leave us to the tender mercies of *ma chère mère*. It would have been seven days of a fast unbroken, at least at her table, if we could not have been supplied with boiled eggs, plums, and blackberries. The former could not be contaminated, and the latter we could gather for ourselves. So that affairs were still sufferable, and the more so that relief was in speedy prospect. Indeed, those days might have been quite agreeable, but for the necessity of appearing at table. One could not take a meal in a private room without giving offence, and thus producing a state of things that would by no means enhance our comfort.

I had nearly forgotten to mention one very novel feature of our entertainment in this place. Our "old man," as he was familiarly designated by his sons, had been, and in truth still was, so great a lover of sport, that he had at one time kept a large band of dogs for the indulgence of this taste. They were now dwindled to four sturdy fellows, who seemed, like the few retainers of some decayed knight, to mourn the days that were gone. Their leader was a noble old brown dog, who bore the name of Lion; I prefixed Cœur, and made him a hero. He was a famous fellow, of lordly presence and magnanimous spirit. His supremacy over his brethren was never disputed. In all quarrels he was the final umpire. In all expeditions he was the commander. In all difficulties with foreign powers, he was the diplomatist, and his terms were never dissented from by the democracy. But notwithstanding this confessed greatness, Cœur de Lion wore a sorrowful expression, and, except in periods of excitement, walked humbly about as if conscious that the sun of his glory had set. He looked an Othello, his "occupation gone." He was patriarch of a race whose power was diminishing, whose greatness was decaying before his eyes, and how could he be other than melancholy? There were seasons however when he seemed to enjoy partial relief from this oppression. Moonlight nights were the chosen of these. The silence, the cessation of man from those plebeian labors which no well-bred dog can share, the partial light, friendly to illusions elsewhere, as well as in the mind of Cœur de Lion, all favored the revival of olden memories and the imaginary participation in scenes of bygone power and usefulness. On these occasions he was wont to stalk about in a contemplative mood, not suffering his followers to be heard, and scarcely to be seen, till night had fairly set in and the moon rode high, the undisputed source of light.

His friends were then summoned; and after consultation, one or two, as the case might demand, were dispatched to the woods, and the noble leader with the remaining force took up his station near the house. In a few minutes the scouts commenced their reports, and the replies and instructions began to be sent forth from head-quarters. This always continued, each waxing warmer as their duties seemed to grow more real, till the din brought the "old man" suddenly to his feet, and the ignominious "git out!" repeated two or three times with increasing emphasis, and a most irreligious expletive at the end, silenced the home department. On such occasions, Cœur de Lion's ears and tail dropped suddenly; and looking at his company with a mournful resignation, he led them away, the picture of abject and hopeless shame. It was doubtless mortifying to him beyond measure; but obedience was one of his many exalted virtues. He could not have been guilty of its opposite to save the whole canine race. Cœur de Lion was no noisy radical. He preferred disgrace and suffering under the existing order, to reform in defiance of it. But there was a difficulty in enforcing this rigid discipline, of which he was not the master when his forces were divided. He could compel the party under his immediate command, to silence; but the scouts were not so easily reduced Distance was favorable to the maintenance of the authority which had been delegated to them; beside which it was impossible, without a personal interview, to inform them that no more reports could be responded to that night. This could not be had without leaving the post which he had pledged himself to maintain, and thus poor Cœur de Lion, placed between an imperative order on one hand, and the calls for his opinion to be audibly expressed growing every moment louder and more pressing on the other, was in a most pitiable state of perplexity. He ran from one side of the house to the other; he snuffed the wind, and scented the grass, and at every renewed call from the woods seemed on the point of bursting forth again into oral communication with the distant party. At last he grew desperate; and, hopeless of restoring order while he was dumb, sent forth a sharp and brief command to "come in." This astonished the other division, and always led to some inquiry into the cause of the order. Disciplinarian as he was, it was impossible for him to produce perfect obedience without a word of explanation; and while he was giving this, footsteps were again heard, the door opened, and another shameful "git out!" issued, followed by the irreparable ignominy of a broomstick, an old hat, or a billet of wood, to enforce it. And then poor Cœur de Lion, broken in spirit, sorrowful, disgraced in his own eyes and those of his followers, slunk away by long, slow steps around the corner of the house, and was no more seen or heard till the following morning. His friends, left to the discouragement of reporting to a silent camp, usually came in about half an hour after; and having learned the true cause of the apparent neglect with which they had been treated, received apologies, and all retired to rest.

Such scenes diversified the early hours of nearly every moonlight night. When they were conducted with spirit, and one was not too far pledged to Morpheus, they became a source of much merriment.

CHAPTER XV

Our house progressed more moderately than we expected; but at last, to my great joy, it was within three days of completion. I was anticipating the pleasure of having a whole room, and the inumerable little appurtenances of comfort "thereunto belonging," when one day Mr. F. returned from his office much earlier than usual, and informed me that our apartment was already occupied by others, and that he had taken a tenement, and determined, with my concurrence, to commence housekeeping. Here was a most unexpected state of things! I was as ignorant of the great art of housekeeping as if I had been a child instead of a woman. But that which so disqualified me for undertaking it, made me all the more ready to begin; so that fifteen minutes' pondering over the proposition made it seem even pleasanter than our original plan. I was ready to go the next day, or even that, if it were practicable. "But the house—what kind of one was it, how large, how many rooms? which way did it front? was it painted, finished, had it a garden, et cet.?" All these questions were answered in a breath. It was a small house with two rooms, fronted south, stood back from the street, leaving a fine yard, which, however, was not yet fenced, and there was any extent of land back, for a garden. The front room was not finished, but would be in two days, and the house cleaned, ready for moving. Two days were left for preparation, and though I had nothing to prepare, I was exceedingly busy. Meantime, on Mr. F.'s return each day, I could not but fancy that he had very much the air of a man who had been engaged in some severe labor, but I questioned him in vain to find out what it was. I was quite too inexperienced myself to come to the correct conclusion: the shrewdest guess I could make being that he was buying furniture, &c. to save me the trouble after my arrival. On the morning of the third day, the house was reported to be ready, and having packed my partition, taken up my carpet, and undressed my toilet, I stepped into the waggon, and in twenty minutes made my entrance into the town of ———, and my dèbut as housekeeper.

I must give my own description of this theatre of my future exploits; for the one given by Mr. F. is too meagre to do justice to the place. We alight at the back door of a building, so small that I fancy it is one of our outbuildings, till the sight of some chairs, turned helter-skelter over each other, and a Franklin stove standing within, convinces me that this is the veritable house. It was reported to be small, and I do not find the report exaggerated. The door by which we enter is so disproportioned to the house, that one thinks it was designed to allow the house itself to walk out. It is made of heavy rough oak boards, and parts in the middle, as if it opened into a carriage-house. It is altogether one of the most extraordinary of doors; but this is explained by reference to the fact, that the building has once been used for a grocery store. The adjacent lot, on the right as we enter, is occupied by a gaping cellar, all uncovered, and affording, therefore, readier ingress than egress to sundry small pigs, chickens, et cet., who perambulate the vicinity. Its walls, however, are so weather-washed, that one of them offers a practicable way of escape when the wits of the small prisoners are sufficiently collected to try it. Beyond, on the same side, the near view is diversified by the rears of several wooden stores of different lengths, the ground about each being picturesquely or-namented with broken crockery, soiled sheets of wrapping paper, rifled boxes, and crates. On the left, is a row of three buildings, which were afterwards called "Globe Row," from the fact that the "Globe Hotel" was opened in one of the farthest from us. They contain a room each and an attic. The middle one is occupied by our nearest neighbors, the family of a worthy mechanic recently from Philadelphia. The old lady's first call was made in about half an hour after our arrival, and accompanied by the tender of a barrel of rain-water, a kindness which those only can appreciate who have undertaken to clean such a house with lime-water, and that to be brought a distance of some dozen rods. Now that I am speaking of water, I may as well add, that there was no well be-longing to our house, and the nearest one was at the distance just named.

Thus much for the view from the back door. I should add, that all these buildings were uninclosed, and thus presented temptations which wrought lamentable corruption in the morals of the swine. Young pigs were thus tempted, nay, heartlessly allured into all manner of offences which grow out of too close an investigation of pails, kettles, boxes, mops, brooms, and other articles that usually consort at the back doors of dwellings which have neither closet, cellar, chamber, nor entry.

But I must leave moralizing, and finish my picture. We shall have to pass through the house to get a front view, and on our way may as well take a cursory glance at its finish, proportion, and contents. The entire tenement is sixteen feet by twenty. It has a door and window in each end, and a partition of very thin boards dividing it into two rooms. One of these is nine feet deep, the other eleven. The preponderance in size has been given to the rear apartment, which is finished inside the boards of the same description as those outside, and put on in the same manner; except that, instead of lapping, they do not quite meet, and therefore hold out the most unlimited invitations to winds and vermin, to enter and examine the premises. Nearly opposite the doorway, for as yet there is no door, which leads to the other room, stands a Franklin stove, making every possible effort to look social, as if it had been an old acquaintance in some of the pleasant sitting-rooms of the east. But it appears to great disadvantage, being besmeared with a mixture of paste and tar, with which Mr. F. has been trying to fasten strong brown paper over the cracks in the ceilings. Half a dozen green wooden chairs stand about, trying to give a home look to the room. But some appear to have become disgusted with the effort, and turned themselves on their heads, in the laps of their neighbors.

We pass through into the next room. This is got up in very creditable style. The proportions, to be sure, are not just what one may call elegant, being sixteen feet one way and nine the other. But the walls are plastered, and there is a very large front door, with a very small window beside it, and a narrow side door, which affords an advantageous view of the cellar aforesaid, and the dead wall of a brown framed store, about thirty feet in length, beyond it. But the grand prospect is from the front. Here is the little niche left between the grocery next door, and Globe Row, which will be a front yard when there is a fence thrown across it. At present it is a very interesting area of black soil, on which the vegetation has been so often disturbed by ploughing matches between gentlemen who combine in themselves all the advantages of team, plough, and driver, that there is not a blade on its surface. Beyond lies the pride of the town—the Public Square—an open space of ten acres, which has had trees enough lithographed for it to cover it three times with a dense forest, but which yet remains an obstinate and ungrateful piece of prairie turf. Still beyond this, is a hollow, or slough, which traverses the centre of the town from east to west; and divides it into "Trade end," and "Court end." The latter is on the opposite side, and, exclusive of a few straggling houses, contains a large two-story framed building, without a chimney, painted white, and denominated the Court House. Here the ministers of justice assemble twice a year, to terrify honest and peaceable citizens, and annoy rogues who are less adroit than their compeers. That other appendage of civilization—the jail—is in another part of the county. The last man who was in it, after staying some four weeks, begged the jailer to excuse him from keeping the key any longer for him, and assured him that he should take pleasure in transacting any little business he might have in the part of the state to which he was bound!

But this by the way. The few remaining evidences of public

enterprise will hardly bear notice here; so we will omit further description, and return to our house, which is at the opposite extremity of the town. Upon a more deliberate examination, I find it has neither cellar nor chamber. The entire establishment, including the privilege of bringing water from a distant neighbor and cultivating any degree of intimacy which fancy might dictate with the swine of the town, most of whom were distinguished for their pedestrian powers, consists of these sixteen feet by twenty, inclosed within the four walls already described. Mr. F. had, it is true, endeavored to avail himself of a trap-door in the back room by making an excavation beneath it sufficient to contain a firkin of butter or a small basket of vegetables. But this did not promise to be eminently serviceable, inasmuch as one foot of the Franklin stood upon the corner of the door, so that the latter could never be opened without first swinging the former round; a process not easy of accomplishment, and attended with imminent risk to the pipe. The floors were thoroughly wet, and exhibited every evidence of having been recently visited with other implements of cleaning than those usually employed by females. But they were still far from clean; and we addressed ourselves therefore, broom and cloth in hand, to bring affairs to a more wholesome state. If any delicate lady asks how I could have undertaken the scrubbing myself, I reply, that if I had not, no one would. No consideration could have procured the assistance of a stout Irish or colored woman, because none such were there. I might have sat myself down, folded my hands, and wept over the disorder; but that would never have brought order out of it. A much pleasanter and more efficient method was the one I adopted. It cleaned and curtained my windows, brought my stove out from the rubbish which covered it, made my chairs fit for use, and restored the floors to a comfortable degree of cleanliness before sunset. Our first meal under my auspices, consisted of crackers, cheese, and cold water, served on the lid of my bureau toilet. Our first night's rest, and welcome rest it was too, was taken on a straw bed laid in the six green chairs.

The next day advanced my housekeeping operations very much. My closet, consisting of four short pine shelves, was built in a corner of the back room and filled with dishes. My hollow ware was purchased and put in order. My floors were visited with another deluge of hot water and soap. Still the bedstead and table came not, and housekeeping was necessarily imperfect, to a certain extent, without them. Making purchases is not the same thing at the west as here. One does not go out to select sofas, chairs, bureaus, toilet stands, mirrors, carpets, tables, et cet., but to take such as can be found, and consider it lucky to find one article or set of the kind required. The question, too, is not how much you shall buy, but how little. Because, where shall you put it when it comes to you? This requires calmer judgment than any other part of the business. In my little box I could not have entertained twelve persons in any manner, unless they had been so good-natured that part of them would have remained without half the time. Yet I must purchase a dinner and tea set for twelve, to cumber the frail shelves of my small closet. Dining, breakfast, and tea plates, at least half of which had not the remotest prospect of coming into use, were therefore stored away, to the imminent risk of the whole.

These injudicious purchases gave me much trouble. My shelves were the favorite resort of whole troops of mice, to whose obtuse senses the volume of experience was a sealed book. For though they explored every aperture and crevice daily, and found not the slightest morsel to gratify the appetite withal, they returned each day as eager and expectant as before. Nothing but personal inspection satisfied them, and nearly as often as this was repeated, I had to follow it with the application of water and soap. Before a month was over, I wished my unlucky dishes fairly back in the shopkeeper's hands.

In due time the bedstead and table arrived. A carpet was found large enough for the front room, and a piece to make the back one look comfortable; some parlor chairs, a mirror, and bureau were obtained. My toilet was re-dressed, a door was made for the space between the rooms which had hitherto been curtained; and thus the whole affair became in time quite respectable. Our family consisted of Mr. F., myself, pony, and another member who ought to have been introduced to the reader before. This member bore the cognomen of Susannah, a name which was bestowed in consideration of her circumspect and exemplary character. Susannah belonged to the Swine family; but it seemed a melancholy perverseness in nature to have placed her there. She was a pattern of all the virtues that ever dwelt in her race. Comely in person, grave and dignified in manner, she carried in her whole deportment that air of humble merit that quite won the hearts of beholders. Susannah made but little acquaintance with the town swine. Their corrupt morals and lawless habits seemed to disgust her. She never joined their foraging expeditions, never put her nose into a pail, nor looked in at a door as if she thought she had a right to enter. She always advised against the scaling of garden fences and the stealthy visiting of neglected corn-fields. Susannah was therefore not so popular among pigs as many who were less worthy. She was voted an aristocrat, a Tory—a pig of no spirit—a pig whose example, if followed, would reduce the intelligent, enterprising, and highly-favored pig democracy of the town to a spiritless set of man-servers; a set who would eat when food was given them, and mind their own business at other times. What could be more disgraceful or dastardly? Whence then would come that large liberty which pigs of talent, courage, and enterprise had wrought for themselves, in spite of dogs, fences, broomsticks, and hot water—those infamous agents of wrong and oppression, against which their ancestors and themselves had so long and fearlessly protested? Such addresses, coming from the influential leaders among the pigocracy, frequently led to Susannah's expulsion by violence from their circles. Cries of "down with the advocate of order!" "put her out!" "long live the enterprising democracy!" were heard, and poor Susannah ran forth sorrowful and alone, a persecuted victim of principle. Being of the feminine gender, she had no opportunity to make head against these enemies. She knew they were demagogues, but what then? The very principles for which she suffered forbade her over-stepping the bounds of order and taking the field against them. So she grew up from early pighood to maturity, preserving her integrity in the heart of a corrupt community, a flower wasted, a model lost. But exemplary as she was, Susannah had some enemies among the biped citizens; some, I suspect, who bore in mind that very homely adage, in which it is alleged that silence facilitates the process of deglutition; and at last she met her death at the hand of one of these illiberals. She was found one morning to have been assassinated in the vicinity of the sheriff's office, the place having been chosen, doubtless, to give a legal coloring to the act. She was lamented as her worth deserved among those who knew her, and her descendants are to this day the most respectable pigs in the town. This passing tribute was due from one who knew her many virtues. The *morale* of the picture may often apply to a higher race.

Pony was quite a different personage from this. She was neat and compact in person, with a freckled complexion, that looked as if she had been thoroughly wetted and then covered with unbolted wheat meal. She was mirthful, affectionate, and withal not a little eccentric. Her favorite place of feeding was on the prairie, in the rear of the house. There she stalked very demurely about, cropping the rich grass till she was filled, and then, all on a sudden, she raised her head, snuffed the air, pricked up her ears, and stood an instant, as if listening to some mysterious communication, when she started at the top of her speed for the house. On she came, like the wind, looking as if she had something very wonderful to tell; but when I met her at the door and inquired what it was, she laughed in my face and said "salt!" When she had eaten a quantity from my hand, she would lay her head against my shoulder, and apologize in the playfulest manner for the article. Pony, as might have been expected, was a great favorite among ladies and gentlemen who were fond of equestrian exercises. Her docility of disposition and rocking-chair gait made her very popular. I could throw my rein over the horn of the saddle, take a book when I did not care to look about, and had no companion to entertain me, and gallop up to Prairie Lodge any morning and back at evening, never uttering a word, except in a pleasant solloquial way, the whole distance. If I dropped my book, discovered a flower or other natural object which I desired to inspect more closely than was practicable from her back, I informed her of it, sprung from the saddle, and left her to feed till I was ready to remount. This was not so difficult a process as one might suppose it would be on the open plain. The distance from the ground to her back was very trifling; and I think she would have looked with contempt on any lady who could not have accomplished it, without aid, at a single spring. If you failed, however, her contempt never overcame her patience; she merely looked around, as if she thought the failure ought to have excited your own indignation, and putting her head to the grass, left you to repeat it at your leisure. When all was ready, away she galloped again, looking about as if she enjoyed the prospect as much as yourself, and would like, if she had time, to point out some features of the scene which might escape your notice.

We loved pony, and so would any one who had known her as we did. She had but a single weakness, and that was one which she shared with many of our own species. It was a dread of showers, more particularly those which were accompanied by electrical phenomena. On these occasions she would run to the house at full speed, and standing close under its lee, if it happened to be on the windowed side, look in so entreatingly, that I was almost moved to open the door and invite her in, or go out and share her trouble. There she would stand, cowering and shaking before the wind and the thunder-peals till it was all over and then trot away to crop the moistened grass. The words of an old lady who had enjoyed some opportunity of becoming acquainted with her merits, are the briefest and most appropriate eulogy than can be uttered to her memory. *"She was an ornament to her speeshy."*

CHAPTER XVI

But it is time I left my domestic circle, and introduced to the reader some of our neighbors and fellow citizens, and their doings. Our town had been settled two years before, by a colony compounded of New-Yorkers, Bostonians, Providence people, and a few random Yankees and adventurers, that were said by an ancient *Sucker* lady in the neighborhood to have been "hove in to fill up." They had organized in the east and come to the west at random, knowing that there was plenty of territory there whereof to manufacture farms, cities, et cet. The honor of being the shire-town of this large and wealthy county was then vibrating between two villages, both of which were settled mostly by western people. The Yankee colony came, took this tract of unbroken prairie, laid out a square mile into lots (the wealthiest men holding the contiguous farms under promise not to refuse room in case the town should outgrow its original boundaries); and by the aid of a little capital, some notes of hand, more brains, and still more cunning, bore off the prize for which the open-mouthed Kentuckians, Tennesseeans, and Buckeyes were disputing. What equivalent was offered the Commissioners, who were appointed to select the most eligible spot, for their choice of this, was never known to the public; but it has since appeared that they were pretty *"shrewdly done"* to a considerable amount in promises, the payment of which was afterward refused on the plea of want of consideration! One may guess, therefore, that we have a pretty sharp population, and he will not very widely err. It is but rendering honor where it is due, however, to say that most of this kind of public spirit dwells in a few of the original company. The majority are thriving, industrious mechanics, farmers, and tradesmen, who, possibly, contributed their quota for such purposes when called upon, but otherwise pursued their occupation peaceably—content with their daily gains and the prospect of a rise in the price of property. The latter formed by far the largest item in their expectations of becoming capitalists. The most matter-of-fact citizen who had paid six hundred dollars for a choice lot at the sales, could not but see his money doubled, interest included, within the first two years. Nearly every citizen owned one, two, or three such lots, besides farms of immense value in the vicinity, so that we had also a wealthy population.

In politics the balance was pretty nearly equal in point of numbers between the two great parties. The four leading spirits, those on whom the responsibility of public efforts rested, were equally divided. But like true men and patriots, they suffered no party questions to divide or weaken their efforts in the common cause of personal aggrandizement. In truth, political considerations among them were rarely suffered to outrun community of interest. Not that men were less rank politicians there than elsewhere, but causes that affected the price of town lots were superior to all other considerations; and as this was the great point on which golden expectation turned, nothing was allowed to interfere with it. Our religious zeal was much more heated and less suppressed. Sectarian piety ran high among the professing heads of the community; and, as people who buy town property, et cet., for the most part care little whether a man has any religion, and still less what particular sect he adopts (his choice in these matters not affecting his vote), we were less restrained in the expression of these opinions than of those which bore on the more embarrassing question of politics. *Orthodox* and *heterodox*, therefore, were terms in frequent use among us. The precise meaning attached to each was known only to the initiated (if indeed to them); but this very indefiniteness was one of their greatest charms. Nothing more restrains vituperation and combat than an exact use of words. A term which has great latitude of meaning is much more easily hurled at an antagonist, than if it were precisely defined and did not touch his case. As in metaphysics, imagination is made to cover every phenomenon for which no other cause can be assigned; so in our discussions of character and morals, orthodoxy and heterodoxy were made the sources of all sin, or the parents of all virtue. Unlike political opinions, these extended to the feminine population, and were, I rejoice to say, the single cause of whatever dissension or difficulty existed among us. Let me not be understood to rejoice that this existed, but that it was the only one known among us.

The most important personage in all village affairs was one of our nearest neighbors, who, for certain good and sufficient reasons, I shall call Mrs. Esculapius. The reader will suppose now, that Mrs. Esculapius was the wife of the physician, but his sagacity is entirely at fault in the supposition. The occupation of her husband is a matter of no moment whatever to us. If it were, it would exceed his own importance in his family, for never man had less. The law that size is, *cœteris paribus*, a measure of power, has been much discussed of late years; I only wish those who doubt its truth could have seen the complete illustration of it afforded by these worthy citizens. In no fact that ever fell under my observation was it more fully demonstrated, than in the relative size and power of Mrs. Esculapius and her husband. Both these qualities were in the extreme of contrast in them. He was the smallest of men, she at the opposite end of the scale among women. He was less of a master in his household than any other man, she quite the reverse. He was good-natured; this did not spoil the contrast. He was submissive, she imperative. He was timid and retiring, she was always foremost in every domestic movement. But beside these points of difference, Mrs. Esculapius possessed some other peculiarities which will, if permitted, stand alone. She was endowed with a sense of hearing, the acuteness of which was perfectly astounding: neither walls nor distance offered any impediment to it. She knew as well the topics under discussion at her neighbor's houses, and the opinions expressed upon them, as if she had been present. She could report all these opinions the next day with as much certainty as if she had participated in the utterance of them herself. Her optical sense was equally keen; and, what was still more extraordinary, both these wondrous powers could be used at once; and hence she could report the expressed opinions, and the unuttered thoughts, of persons in any part of the town. We should have voted the phenomenon magnetic, but for two reasons; first, we were all unbelievers; and, secondly, a stronger faith in the possible than any of her friends exercised, would have been necessary to believe that she was ever in a magnetic state. For no one ever saw her asleep. But all conjecture and speculation of this sort were rendered superfluous by reference to the plain demonstrable fact, that, at the time when she was taking notes for these reports, she was always pursuing her ordinary household avocations; to all appearance as unabstracted by such employment, as any person to whom this power was denied.

The only circumstance which threw any light upon this wonderful faculty, was the necessity of waiting till the next day, and possibly till the second, before she proceeded to report. It was suggested, that a troop of fairies had chosen her for their general post-office, and were making her the victim of their harmless pranks. If any more ingenious solution can be offered, the case still waits for its light. Passing these peculiarities, this lady is a pattern housekeeper, a kind friend to those whom she likes, a sympathetic woman at a sick bed, a hospitable and generous hostess in her own house. She takes pleasure in sending specimens of her excellent cookery to neighbors who are less skilful in the art, or less favored with conveniences for plying it. I take pleasure in acknowledging myself still her debtor for many such little kindnesses.

In the front ranks of our religious community stands Deacon Cantwyne—a man celebrated in all the "country side" for his piety, his love of money, and his affectation of philosophy. Deacon Cantwyne's house is the resort of all the clergy of his own denomination; and the philosophy which he affects, leads him to extend his hospitalities to many others. So that he lives in a theological atmosphere, so to speak, an atmosphere musical with expressions of the religious feelings. This is his chosen condition. But if denied him in the presence of others, he is capable of creating it to a great extent for himself. He prays three times a day, and reads the Scriptures each time. He never neglects religious worship, takes an active part in the orthodox Sabbath-schools, frowns on open vice or dishonesty in any shape, is scrupulous in the observance of the Sabbath, even to leaving the room in which so profane a thing as the Pilgrim Fathers is sung on that day, and loses no opportunity of exhorting his non-professing neighbors to "come out from the world," and "fight the good fight of faith." Deacon Cantwyne is a business man, and he declares that a profession of religion, so far from interfering with success in business, as many worldly-minded but mistaken individuals think, is no little aid to it. He speaks from experience, for his religious pretensions have enabled him to pray his way to the bottoms of hundreds of pockets, which he could never otherwise have approached. All the while that he is doing it, he will lavish the most hearty expressions of esteem on you—esteem grounded on the virtues which he has discovered in you, for, as a Christian, he can admire no other qualifications. If you are in affliction, he will console you, pray with you and for you, commend you to the Bible, and to those sources of comfort which he has found so potent, and in the next moment, count the dollars which some proposed operation will enable him to make out of the confidence his speech was designed to create. When any special enterprise of this kind is in prospect, he prays longer and more fervently than usual; and if the victim is present, in the shape of a purchaser, or a debtor whose all lies under a mortgage which he holds, he is apt to be quite overpowered with his love of duty and his charity for his neighbor. Ten chances to one but he makes you the subject of a special petition, and closes with a request that you may be preserved from the devouring influences of the carnal appetites, from vanity, and from love of riches. He feels for you already, and wishes that your sufferings may be light when he shall have sounded your purse. His piety is never more apparent than on these occasions. If the operation is one of considerable magnitude, he solicits the brethren of the neighborhood to unite in a protracted meeting, for he feels that the gospel is losing its influence on the hearts of men. When he has consummated the affair, he will meet you with the blandest face, and enter into a conversation on electricity, the aurora borealis, or the last Arctic expedition. But he never fails to turn to the pole of his thoughts before he leaves you, and exhort you to remember that all these "phenomeny," wonderful as they are, are the handiwork of a power to whom your highest services are due, and that the best of us can but poorly glorify Him. Or perhaps he reads you a page from his own experience, telling you how, when he was a young man, he began life with the hope of achieving some worldly honors and possessions, but soon found that to do so, he *"should have to set his face like a flint,"* and close his ears to all the petitions of mercy; how this struggle between his better nature and the desire to do his duty had almost ended in the triumph of Satan; how thankful he is that it did not, and how much he hopes that every young man whom he sees entering life may be preserved as he was. And all this is said with a grave face as if he had not just defrauded you of your last penny, and were not ready to do you the like favor to-morrow.

Deacon Cantwyne's exhortations are uttered with a face and tone that would subdue a Philadelphia mob. These are natural gifts — at least I set them down as such. If they are not, they must have been cultivated in early life; for nothing of the kind can be more perfect. The face leads you to anticipate the voice, and vice versa. Deacon Cantwyne has been pretty intimately connected with the affairs of the colony, and some of his transactions would edify men whose kindred genius is restrained by stone walls and sheriff's processes.

He was originally from one of the principal cities of the east. While there he was employed in a highly useful trade, from which he seems to have realized a handsome equivalent for his labors. To this he has added whatever has fallen in his way, beside several things that have not been able to get out of it since he came west; and he is now one of our wealthiest men. He is not so ardently beloved in the neighborhood as many persons I could designate, but he never discovers this unless it is forced on his attention; and when it is, he sets it down to the account of his rigid piety. "How shall a devoted christian expect to command the love of the children of darkness? He ought to glory in their hatred, and would if it did not argue such deplorable wickedness in them"—and show that they would be on their guard against his long prayers. His piety is embellished by a liberality as striking as itself. This, however, partakes more of a public than a private character. Any public bequest which will enhance the value of property, he makes freely, provided it be expended in the vicinity of his own possessions. There are many little tales afloat in the village and country, illustrative of Deacon Cantwyne's peculiarities, which his biographer will doubtless gather for the purpose of doing justice to his memory. If I have drawn his picture correctly enough to have it recognized by himself and his friends, I have done all that I proposed to do on this page. If occasion to refer to him again should arise, a single stroke will bring him before the reader. That is a principal advantage in having his character well defined at the outset.

CHAPTER XVII

Our village abounded in professional men. Not to mention the youthful Cokes and the unassuming Blackstones, who asked no loftier place for their names than gilt or gamboge letters on a black shingle nailed beside their office-doors; we had magistrates, judges of law and probate, retired counsellors, waiting a favorable opportunity to embellish some of the more elegant walks of life. But most indispensable and popular of all was our doctor. He was the ornament not only of our professional classes, but of the village. His personal appearance is worthy a livelier pen than mine. He is actually of middle stature, but seems considerably below it, from the excessive deficiency of anything like hauteur in his character. His head projects well over the eyes, and towers above the forehead into an immense table-land, on which you might heap offences that would outnumber the hairs that cover it, and yet find forgiveness. This preponderance brings the head forward and upward in a right line, but it is the most graceful departure from a perpendicular that could be imagined. His strong perceptions leave about him no air of stumbling abstraction, but, combined with a boundless benevolence, lend the delightful expression one wears when looking for objects of sympathy or admiration. Leaving the doctor's head, the next most striking thing about him is his gait. Various were the attempts at description which this wonderful gait elicited from his fellow citizens. A walk it certainly was not, if by this term is meant a straightforward, or indeed almost any other use of the limbs given for that purpose. I do not mean to say that he performed locomotion without the use of these organs at all, because that would imply that he walked upon his hands or head—arts which I am not aware that he ever cultivated; and which it will be conceded must have been extremely inconvenient, unless his pockets had been made to correspond, for they were his medicine-chests. If he had been an importer of drugs, he would never have wanted any storehouse but these, and the privilege of depositing samples that were unsaleable, or robbed of their virtues by age, upon the shelves of his wife's closets.

But to go back to his gait. It certainly was a curious one. It was made up of incredibly short steps, that followed so fast upon one another as to give the idea of a man with two pairs of legs, each running on a wager against the other. If one could conceive a sheep with his two fore-legs lengthened so as to give him an erect attitude, yet still preserving his peculiar motion, with a perfect resemblance to the human figure in all other respects, he might have a tolerable idea of the doctor's gait. I am aware that this is a labored illustration, and that the idea at best is complicated; but no one knows how difficult the subject is, nor how long I might search the whole kingdom of animate nature in vain, for something whereunto to liken this motor phenomenon. It is true, that the terms "*nudge,*" "*shuffle,*" "*trot,*" and sundry others were used among the puzzled villagers to designate it; but they are all feeble, and so I believe will be anything I can add to them. There are things in nature which words hover around in vain: they never touch them.

The other eccentricities of our Galen were not so indescribable. He had a versatility of genius, which never failed to respond to any appeal. An Indian war-dance, or the amputation of a limb; the old woman in Robin Roughhead at a private theatrical entertainment, or a post at the couch of prostrating, withering disease, were matters of equal facility—I had almost said of pleasure; for the warm exercise of his sympathies on the painful occasions, and the relief which his skill and tenderness often enabled him to afford, were high sources of pleasure. As might be expected with such a constitution, our doctor had been a merry youth. He had spent a very considerable fortune in early life, for the purpose of reducing himself to terms of equality with necessity, whom he could not coax to his acquaintance in any other way. And he seemed even now to have a fear that she would forsake him again, for he never collected his dues, never informed any one that his services were to be paid for, unless by way of assent when the proposition originated with themselves. When he returned from a ball one winter morning with his splendid wife and brother, and found the house which they had jointly occupied burned to the ground, with everything it had contained, he stood a moment, and then said, "There are plenty of houses about here whose inmates will receive Mary for a few days, and there will be sick enough this season, heaven help them, to whom I can do some good, in return for which they shall enable me to build her a better home. I'll have it all right in a year or so, except the little mementos and trifles endeared by association and otherwise. Those cannot be replaced, so I suppose we must mourn over them a little." And the doctor kept his word; catching the means which fortune threw at him for his poorly-paid, arduous, and ceaseless labors, he purchased a beautiful building-spot in "Court-end;" build a cottage with a roof so sharp that it was described by a stage-driver, who had a passenger to set down there, as "the house with a ruff that split the rain-drops," made a sort of bird's nest of it, whose chief ornament was his peerless wife: and there he lives, or rather, the lady and her babes; for he is too much abroad during the warm season to have a proper residence anywhere. And there a hospitality and social charm are offered to guests, which is rarely surpassed in more elegant mansions.

At this time the doctor is accompanied in his professional visits by a faithful old horse, who is known throughout the country by the name of "Pomp." It would, perhaps, be as correct to say that the doctor accompanies Pomp; for the latter, if harnessed and left loose, under the false impression that his friend was in the seat, would doubtless have gone alone to visit their patients. I say *their* patients, because it always seemed to me that the doctor and Pomp were partners. What share the latter had in the profits was never know, though his share in the labors was, for he sometimes traveled sixty or seventy miles a day, beside stopping for calls. The estimation in which the doctor held Pomp was very high. To have struck him would have been treason; yet I ought to add, as an evidence of the inconsistency of man, that he would allow him to be driven till his bay coat was white with foam. But how could Pomp complain when his master treated himself in the same manner! Seated in his light waggon, reins in hand, the doctor announced his readiness to set off by speaking the name of his four-footed friend, in an tone which seemed to be agreed on between them as a signal for moving; and away they went; never a blow was struck, nor a harsher word spoken. I apprehend it would not have been safe for any person to have attemped either. I remember riding out with the doctor once, to see a sick friend. On our arrival, a coarse fellow came up, and seizing Pomp by the head, called out to know whether he should "*ondo him?*"

"Ondo him!" exclaimed the doctor. "Ondo Pomp!" and he cast a look at him which might have been translated into a volume; but, passing on, he merely said "No! you may give him some fresh grass, if you have any here. I should like to see the man," he added, in a muttered parenthesis, "who would dare ondo Pomp!"

The doctor's mode of communicating his opinions and wishes to Pomp is very convenient and pleasant, not only to themselves, but to the settlers whose habitations they visit. You may foretell their approach when two miles distant on the prairies, at any hour of the night, by listening to the mono-syllable Pomp! Pomp! And pleasant sounds they are to those who leave the bedside of languishing pain, and step forth an instant into the cool silent night, to breathe and catch the signal of the visit so ardently longed for.

In sickly seasons they travel all night. The doctor moves the seat of his waggon back, has an extra cloak or buffalo robe, of which he makes a bed, and, when he leaves a house, curls himself up in it, gives Pomp the signal, and starts on, leaving the latter pretty much to his own choice about the road. And they thus go on admirably; for the doctor has such a habit of speaking to Pomp, that, though fast asleep, he articulates his name in the usual tone, about once in twenty minutes, and the latter knows the roads so well that he always goes right, if not left to his own pleasure too long. In those latter cases the doctor is likely, on awaking, to find himself before the sharp-roofed cottage, for Pomp, among his other virtues, is eminent for his love of home. This goes on till poor Pomp is incapable of traveling longer at such rate, and then a stranger is hired for day-driving, and Pomp kept for night-driving.

For himself the doctor has no substitute. He goes night and day for weeks, snatching rest as I have described, and sometimes, when he goes into a house, after examining his patient, lying down upon the floor, or on three chairs, with a strict injunction to the watchers not to let him sleep over half an hour. This and a cup of tea twice a day, strong enough for the brother of the Sun or Moon himself, were all that the doctor required to keep him going till the pestilence abated. It is only in rare seasons, however, that their duties are so arduous. Ordinarily, the "sickly season," as it is termed, extends through some two or two months and a half at the close of the summer and opening of the autumn. During those weeks bilious fevers prevail more or less through the whole country; but especially in the vicinity of streams and low grounds. Here they are very general, and more malignant than in the prairies and higher regions. In many cases, where the medical adviser is unskilful, or proper care is not bestowed, the patient is left with the *"shakes,"* this term being merely a shorter name for the disease which others choose to call *"Fever Ragy."* Exclusive of the short period just specified, little sickness prevails. More than half the numerous forms of disease which poison society and baffle the physician here are there unknown. And, judging from my own experience, I should say that a large proportion of those which do prevail, might be avoided, by ordinary attention to the laws of health. Regularity in sleep, temperance in diet, personal cleanliness, and due share of exercise at proper seasons, would reduce materially the frightful amount of disease which now makes these western summers alarming. A residence of nearly five years, with only a tolerable attention to diet and regimen, brought me not a week's indisposition from the causes incident to the country.

But I have left our doctor to speak a word of caution to settlers. I know his good-nature so well however, that I am assured of pardon, even though my advice should shorten his bills. And why not, since the length of so few of them is ever estimated? In periods when his professional cares relax, the doctor is the most efficient of our village sociables. Always ready to converse well with those who wish to do so, or play the mountebank for those who prefer amusement; ready to flatter a lady into good-nature with herself, if it be necessary, or argue political tendencies with her husband, if this be more agreeable; he was indispensable in all social meetings, and nowhere a more delightful companion than at his own table or fireside. Though not an accomplished singer, he was sometimes prevailed upon to do his devoir even in this behalf. I never heard but one or two exhibitions of his vocal powers, and these were made at the pressing instance of friends who could not be refused. He had one favorite piece which served on both occasions, though doubtless he was master of others equally elegant in diction and charming in composition. I more than half suspected that he had played Mozart himself to the following lines—

> "At the battle of the Nile,
> I was there all the while."

These lines were burthen, chorus, and all: they comprised the entire piece. And the third or fourth repetition, in a tone incomparably more monotonous than the words, generally drew such peals of applause from the gentlemen and such a waving of handkerchiefs from the ladies, that the doctor was quite overcome, and took his seat in a very interesting state of confusion. As a mere artist the doctor was rarely excelled in what he undertook. A negro dance or a lofty flight of admiration for the works of nature, with which he was so continually conversant, were executed with nearly equal excellence, except that to the latter he brought the strength of a fine mind, as well as a high degree of artistic skill. In short our doctor was a rare character, and we prized him as such. His very faults and weaknesses, and he had plenty of them, only made us pity him and wish they were not — one could scarcely be indignant at them.

CHAPTER XVIII

Summer had worn away, with its wealth of golden grains and flowers. The luxuriant harvest had disappeared from the farms in the adjacent country, the tall corn was in its sere and yellow leaf, the late fruits began to ripen, the prairies faded from their rich green, save where here and there a *"late burn"* showed the tender grass, like an emerald island in the vast brown ocean. Autumn in the prairie land is scarcely excelled for the richness of its charms by any other season. Coupled with the perfection of the wide vegetable world is an idea of repose which fills the soul. An immense country, whose energies have been springing all the previous months with ceaseless toil, whose rank luxuriance evinces the employment of tremendous powers, now lies all around you in the deep quiet which ushers in a truly natural death. The sun pours forth a rich, mellow light; dim and soft, as if like a tender nurse he watched over this sleep of nature. The native birds, happy in the abundance which they cannot consume, fly cheerfully but quietly about, as if, their labor done, the season of rest had come to them also. The quail whistles and dances among the brown hazel thickets; the grouse flies from field to field, dividing his depredations through the neighborhood, and bearing off, when unmolested, a full crop to the plains, which he loves better than the abodes of man. The crow calls from the wood top, or wheels his long and lazy flights above the naked prairies, seeming really more amiable than at any other season. The air is filled with the smoke of distant fires; some day they creep up into your own neighborhood, and when night comes, light the heavens and the earth as far as the eye can reach. These are magnificent spectacles. I have stood upon the roof of our large hotel in the evening, and looked into a sea of fire which appeared to be unbroken for miles. These incidents occasionally interrupt the dreamy rest to which everything tends, but they pass away in a few hours, and the next day is as quiet as before. Sporting parties are made up among the gentlemen, and fruit parties, including ladies, to visit the nearest groves in search of haws, nuts, et cet.; or if any orchard has been cultivated in the vicinity by some ancient settler, this is resorted to, and small parcels of its rare fruit purchased and taken home. Our fruit parties usually resorted to a grove about a mile distant, on the west, and returned after an hour or two of delightful rambling, with baskets laden with the delicious haw-berry, a feast for many days. The paw-paw and persimmon did not flourish in our vicinity. They love the bottom lands of streams.

The groves at this season are indescribably charming. There is not in the large foliage that gorgeous variety which we find in the eastern forest. The trees wear a more sober and uniform complexion; but there are a thousand minuter beauties which touch the heart. A few flowers linger in the borders of the woodland and skirt the small streams. In the deeper recesses some sprightly ones are found, indicating by their vigor and freshness that they belong to the season of frost. Among these is one which I dearly love. It grows upon a tall stalk sparsely set with leaves, and forms near the top a beautiful shaft, studded with myriads of small flowers of the most exquisite hue and loveliness. They are like so many bright eyes looking gaily out into the pleasant world around. This flower does not belong to the deep groves, but is found in the little glades or openings in the woodside. And there, when October winds play among the leaves, and the bright sunshine pours through a sea of mist and smoke, into little nooks and corners, by decaying logs and upturned roots, where it has not gained admittance during all the leafy reign of summer, this bright flower is seen nodding and dancing merrily in the breeze as if it rejoiced in the approaching gloom. The squirrel searches timidly about among the fallen leaves, making provision for the winter; and the hare, whom he often meets, skips by him, half in sport, half in earnest, seeking the tender twigs whereof to make her dinner. The ripened nuts dropping among the leaves often startle her from her contemplations, and drive her to seek refuge in the nearest clump of grass or bushes.

These wood-parties are delightful recreations. Armed with thick shoes and provided with a basket each, for trophies of all descriptions—or if the distance be too great to be traversed on foot, mounted, as we could be best provided (the reader will remember pony), without our riding dresses, that we may not be cumbered with them when we reach the wood—away we go, free as the winds. North, south, east, or west, the way is equally open. The wild Indian, mounted on his hunting horse, has scarcely a larger liberty than we. We scour the plain, leap or plough the "slues," and gain the grove. Here our steeds are fastened to trees and boughs, and we scatter. Oh what a joyous afternoon is before us! And some at least know it, though all do not seem to do so. Toward evening, when the shadows begin to lengthen on the turf, and the winds to sweep more chillingly through the grove, we gather at the rendezvous; bring forth the shawls and other cautionary articles, spring into our saddles, give free rein, and after a swift and exhilarating ride, stop at our own doors filled with happy recollections, and made better in spirit and body by a day in the woods.

About three miles from our village is an orchard, which has been cultivated these many years by the widow of the original proprietor. It is the only one in the vicinity, and the old lady's name is therefore well known. And though no two words could be more unlike in orthography and sound than her own name and that of the fruit she sold, yet to me the former was always synonymous with apples. You could not hear or speak it without having your mouth water for the delicious fruit with which it thus became associated. The old lady was much patronized by our villagers and the settlers on adjacent farms. She lived quite neatly in a half-framed house, which you had to circumvent in order to enter it, there being three doors in the rear, but none on the roadward-side. (I avoid saying front, to be exact in the use of words.) The grounds contiguous to the house had at certain seasons of the year rare beauty and richness. A stream of some magnitude swept in a crescent form around the orchard-clad hill, on which it stood. Across the road this hill sloped downward to the stream in a smooth green lawn, dotted with trees. On either hand from the house and skirting the bank of the stream in front of it, was a dense grove of the peach, the apple, and wild-crab apple-trees. About the first of June these were in full bloom, and no perfume of Araby could excel their sweetness, no floral display, their beauty. As you approached the spot after sunset, when the light dews just moistened the blooming boughs, and the evening winds swept over them, the whole air was laden with their fragrance;

and when you gained the summit of the hill and looked down upon the nodding clusters of blossoms, set, as it were, in the tender green of the forest trees towering above them, nothing could be conceived more beautiful. Many a pleasant twilight ride have we enjoyed, lingering through the paths of this blossoming wilderness, inhaling its delicious odors, and gazing on its unequaled beauty. I remember one evening, when the sounds of bells seemed coming up from the grove below our path to greet us; they advanced slowly; and we almost stopped in admiration of the gorgeous sunset above and the wealth of the foliage lavished around. Presently the sounds became more distinct, and a large Pennsylvania waggon with a top of snowy whiteness emerged from the green wood. It was an emigrant family—a group of the happiest faces and the cleanest persons one often finds among them. This was a favorite camping ground,— and we lingered watching them till their supper fires shone in the advancing darkness, and then reluctantly turned our horses' heads homeward. How I envied those people!—to lie down there, bathed in the calm, pure air of a June night, the dropping petals strewing their place of rest, the clear brooklet murmuring to their sleep; who could submit patiently to imprisonment within four walls, as dull then as if nature were not doing her best in grove, plain, and sky to induce us to leave them!

But here lived the old lady of apple memory, and here amid all this beauty had she lived from time immemorial among the Yankee settlers. Her spirit had partaken of the scene. She lived neatly in doors, and there was an air of comfort about the exterior of her home quite in harmony with the feelings awakened by the surrounding scenery. How indeed could she have violated so beautiful a sanctuary, by a life altogether coarse and unlovely. But she was not proof against the pernicious influences which the possession of absolute power works in the mind which exercises it. Being for many years the sole dispenser of apples to a large region round her, she had grown capricious in her tastes, and now cared little to accommodate those whom she did not like. If you were one of her favorites, and called on her in the fruit season, either by way of compliment, or as a purchaser, she always presented you a dish of the choicest productions of her orchard to eat in her house, and made her happiest selection for your purchase. We were fortunately of this class. She regarded it as an evidence of kind and friendly interest, to inquire after the prosperity of her place, and usually tendered some hints gratis, on the cultivation of fruit trees. In one of these familiar lessons, she remarked that there was a way to make trees bear much earlier than most persons supposed they would.

"Prey how is that, Mrs. S——?"

"Why, when we was a settin out the last of our trees, them in the orchard down thar," pointing out of the door, "the man we got 'em of, told my old man that if he wanted 'em to bear early he must set 'em out when the moon was in *parrighee*."

"When is that, Mrs. S——?" said I, making a violent effort to preserve my gravity, for her keen eyes were fixed on my face.

"O, I reckon folks that's college larnt as you be, needn't ax me when the moon's in *parrighee*. I expect you can tell any time when you look at it."

"I am not college learned," I replied, "you know ladies never are, and I presume my husband has forgotten all about the *parrighee* of the moon long since."

"Well you can find it any time by looking in a *nalmanic;* that's whar we found it. Some folks," added the old lady, "don't allow there's anything in the moon about fruit and so on, but I reckon they don't know so much more than other folks as they think they do. I know a heap of things that does better when they're planted at sartin times o' the moon, and there can't nobody make me think 'tain't so, 'cause I've tried it. 'Tain't so much account about some things; I reckon taters does as well planted one time as another, and so does beets and so on, but cabbages and onions and all them 'dought to be planted in the new o' the moon, if you want 'em to be of any 'count."

Such edifying conversation usually occupied the time spent at the old lady's house. If you were particularly deferential and received instructions meekly, you were always rewarded by having your pockets or basket filled with the choicest apples for your own especial gratification. I know of no other way in which the good woman ever corrupted the morals of her visitors, but this was bad enough. Whose integrity could stand unshaken before a dish heaped with apples such as money could not buy? Who would venture to correct the friendly old woman's orthoëpy at such a risk? Certainly not one who had such a longing for the apple bins of eastern cellars as I had.

Such were some of the many excursions of autumn days which we shared. Then, as I intimated, the gentlemen more frequently went out in small companies to shoot the quail, grouse, hare, and squirrel. These parties were generally equestrian and very jocose among themselves, though the whole mass of female nerves in the village was in a flutter till they returned. Because it had been found that in the absence of game they shot each other! My husband had joined one of these parties and came home with shot enough in his limbs to make us count it quite a serious affair, though it only resulted in his giving two or three days' exclusive attention to books within doors.

Later in the season an occurrence under similar circumstances robbed us of one of our worthiest young mechanics, and produced a most melancholy feeling throughout in our little community. Two young men, intimate friends, had left the village together on Saturday evening, to spend the Sabbath at the house of a friend six miles away. On Monday morning they started for home, each with his rifle and game-bag, intending to search the groves and thickets on their way down for game. Near sunset they had reached the skirt of the grove about a mile and a half from the village, and discovering some quail in one of the hazel thickets which bordered it, they parted to "beat" the thicket. Stealing cautiously around, one raised his rifle and fired at a bird that was just tripping into his place of concealment. The bird fell, but a spring and a dismal groan at the same instant made his blood curdle. He dropped his rifle and ran to the other side. Judge of his feelings when he saw his friend lying on the ground, a crimson stream sprouting from his breast; and heard him exclaim in a faint voice, "C——, you have shot me!" In three minutes he was dead! The ball had passed through the heart! His remains were borne to the village on the waggon of a neighboring farmer, a coroner's inquest was held, and on the second day they were followed to the grave by the mourning citizens. The unfortunate man was a son of New Hampshire, the pride of his aged father and mother, whom he had left to seek a more promising home in the richer regions of the west. His friend, scarcely less an object of sympathy, took a vow never again to handle fire-arms; but so completely had the horrors of the scene fastened upon his mind, that he never recovered his former calmness. He brooded over the dreadful event with a morbid kind of self-accusation, abandoned his business, and at length wandered away melancholy, abstracted, miserable. This was a painful tragedy for our little community, and lasting and deep was the sympathy it created for the two unfortunate young men.

The reader will remember I informed him that our next door on the left was a grocery—(groggery would be the truer name, but what lady can ever make up her mind to write it). If he has heard nothing from this place before, it is not because I have not.

Many a day's tranquillity and many a night's rest did this horrid place destroy. All the influence which the respectable portion of the community could bring to bear upon it, failed to mitigate its character or check the abominations daily enacted in it. The sights and sounds of the poor wretches who frequented it often compelled me to forsake and close the front of my house; but it was vain to seek seclusion from them in my small tenement; their sickening shouts and groans reached one everywhere. Sometimes these diabolical orgies lasted two or three days and nights without pause, and then a time of comparative quiet followed. The master-spirit among those who shared in their scenes, was the individual who kept the shop. His ceaseless habits of drunkenness had made him one of the most disgusting of human spectacles. With a face enormously bloated beyond its natural proportions, eyes bleared and watery, white lips, parched and mottled with bright red spots, and palsied limbs, the miserable wretch, not yet thirty-five years of age, crept about, a warning, one would have thought, to those who congregated about him. But here they assembled, two or three miserably lost spirits from the eastern states, and as many Kentuckians of the lowest class; and here, hand in hand, they led each other to ruin. Sometimes the citizens would acquire influence enough over one of the band to keep him from the spot for a period, but they seized on him again at the first opportunity, and made him pay for his respite by a deeper plunge than ever. There was one unfortunate man highly connected in one of the principal cities of the east, where he had left a wife and two interesting children. He had fallen among these wretches soon after his arrival, but had several times been restrained, partly by his better feelings, partly by the remonstrances of his friends. Every one who knew him mourned over the waste of a man who possessed so many of the elements of usefulness and happiness. Early in the autumn, he received a letter from his wife, appealing to him, as her husband and the father of his children, to return to them or make provision for them to come to him. It touched the right chord in him; he resolved to become a temperate man. And he persevered in this resolution till the beginning of November with every promise of success. Accident at length threw him into the clutches of these fiends. They dragged him to their place of sacrifice, and compelled him to taste, nay, to drink; till he was again without self-control or reason. His friends, who had watched him with deep interest, seizing every opportunity to strengthen his good resolutions, called on the master demon, and begged that he would let him go; that he would not supply him with the means of self-destruction. He answered their remonstrances with curses, and assured them that as long as he had liquor and "Mac" had money, the latter should have what he wanted. On Saturday evening there was deep drinking in this miniature hell. The carousal held till morning opened, and at a late hour the various inmates set out reeling and stumbling toward home, or whatever lodging chance might bring them. The Sabbath opened clear and bright. A light frost had crisped the grass; the red sun came up the eastern sky, curtained with mist and smoke; soft winds crept over the embrowned forests and plains, and all nature seemed to be filled with a kind of sad joy. I shall never forget that morning. The holy quiet which rested on the earth contrasted strongly with the fierce and harrowing sounds of the previous night. I looked out just as the sun was rising. The smoke began to curl slowly upward from various chimneys, and a few early risers were abroad inhaling the air freshened by the frost which yet lay upon the grass. They looked as if care were dismissed, and man as well as nature was to enjoy a holy day. When the family who had sheltered poor "Mac," notwithstanding his many deviations, ascertained that he had not returned to the house, they dispatched a person to the grocery, to bring him home. But he was not there! The miserable proprietor reported as nearly as his half conscious state and drunken recollections would permit, that he left there about two o'clock.

"You'll find him," said he, "under some fence or the side of a house, fast enough, I'll warrant you; for he was drunk when he went away; he wanted to git off afore he took the last drink, but we made him go it!"

There was an unfinished house some distance below, and thither they went, thinking it probable that he had crept in there to sleep. But he was not to be found. They were wondering where he could have gone, when one of them, happening to pass near the open well, glanced into it, and was horrified to discover the figure of the lost man in the bottom, partly covered with water. He was immediately removed, and measures taken to resuscitate him, but life was utterly quenched. Another coroner's inquest was held. A rude coffin was nailed together, and the remains were deposited the same day in the earth. I see now before me the thrilling events of that day, faint as is this picture of them. I feel again the overpowering emotions we experienced when reflecting on the fate of this unwilling victim to the vices of others. The poor wretch, half conscious, notwithstanding the maddening potations that had been forced upon him, stumbling along in the dark night for a place of rest, thinking possibly of his broken vows, and of the faithful wife and children whose hearts would bleed could they know his situation; half resolving, perhaps, that he would still save himself, and never touch again the fire that had so nearly consumed his soul— all these thoughts and feelings, faintly recognized, passing through the mind that had bowed reluctantly to its renewed degradation, and all cut short by the brief and sudden plunge which ended in almost instant death! What an entrance into eternity! what a fearful leave-taking of the fair earth! what an introduction to the mighty future! For days my mind was busied with his last thoughts, and the fearful struggles he must have made to recover his hold upon life. I could not dismiss them.

If everything connected with this terrible place had been painful and disgusting before, it will readily be conceived that they were incomparably more so now. The groans seemed the dying agonies of fiends, the shouts their exultations. The reeling forms and bloated faces seemed more deeply lost than ever. But they did not remain long: public indignation was so roused at the destruction of a man who had naturally so much to win esteem and respect, that the grocery was doomed from the day of his death. Pity it could not have been before; but people require something which would startle the blind and deaf, to rouse them to action in such matters. Even now public opinion barely permitted individual action, but did not aid it. The license which conferred the power to do all these things was revoked, the shop broken up, and the miserable wretch who had kept it driven to seek another place of abode. He lingered about some time in his degradation, till at last one of his brother masons took him to his house in a neighboring town, and by some means induced his reformation. When I last saw him, I scarcely recognized him. But improved as he was, he still bore the stamp of a degraded, wretched man.

CHAPTER XIX

The reader must wish by this time to hear something of my housekeeping. It will be remembered that my only fire was in a small-sized Franklin stove; and as this had a grate in it, it will not be difficult for housekeepers to conceive that my conveniences for the multifarious operations of baking, boiling, stewing, and roasting, were somewhat limited. By the nicest possible adjustment of my tea-kettle to the middle of the arch, I could pass it in and out of the grate. The first task was by no means difficult, being generally performed when the vessel contained cold water. But to remove it, when the boiling liquid was bubbling from the spout, and every crevice performing the office of an escape pipe, to the utmost of its capabilities, was quite another affair. Nevertheless, twice, thrice, and even double the last number of times in a day, I wrought myself up to the effort, and what is still clearer evidence of heroism and genius, never failed, nor even met with any greater accident than sundry small burns on my hands and fingers. The greatest number of these agreeable little incidents of tea-kettle rescue, was four at one attempt, the average two.

Beside my tea-kettle, the largest vessel which I could use was a three-pint saucepan; and herein were performed all sorts of operations, from the fricasseeing of chickens to the boiling of corned beef and cabbage. Not to tax credulity too much, let it be borne in mind that I could use three of these at once—a priviledge which every dinner I prepared taught me to appreciate. The most troublesome of all my culinary operations was baking. It is true I had a good tin oven, but then where to place it was a troublesome question. If it had been possessed of any means of generating caloric within itself, so that, having placed the preparation within, I could have set it on the table or flour barrel, and left it to bake at its own pace, my troubles would have been sensibly alleviated. But my tin oven was like all others. Never taking into account the difference between a small Franklin and a wide fireplace, although it had looked the former in the face so often, and been times without number crowded and jostled from its position before it, it said, "Set me to the fire, and I'll bake your bread; if you don't, it shall stand here raw till doomsday." So I was always compelled to make some provision for it. The front feet could stand on the hearth, but the back ones were of the same length, and, of course, called for something to make up the difference between the height of the hearth and floor. Sticks of wood and chips—I had like to have said stones, but of these we had none—were the articles most in demand for this use. But as these, when piled loosely upon each other, are not the most stable foundation, it will not be wondered at, that my oven sometimes went over and poured out the half-baked loaves upon the floor.

But, beside these mechanical obstacles, there was another difficulty attendant upon baking, of much more serious import, and that was the making of the bread. I scarcely know how I should have conquered this, but for the kind instructions of the excellent old lady whose barrel of rain-water had been so acceptable a letter of introduction. The best of yeast from her own jar was always at my service, and the most patient directions for mixing, kneading, and rising. I had learned in the laboratory that it was a most pernicious thing to suffer bread to pass the stage of saccharine fermentation; and have no doubt that if any housekeeper, before I was one myself, had applied for instructions in making bread, I could have delivered quite a voluble lecture on the various stages of fermentation, and the changes attendant upon each. But theory is one thing, practice another; and though the knowledge I had derived from our lamented professor was by no means useless, yet it did not make my first nor my second loaf of bread as good as that of my neighbor, who had never read a page of chemistry. However, the mysteries of sponge, first mixing, moulding, and second rising, became familiar after a few sour experiences, till I could, with much complacency, set a plate of my own good bread before my husband. I had one other main difficulty; and that was to keep this last-named personage from making a private grocery and meat-house of my little place. Never man looked at the consuming powers of two common individuals through such enormous magnifying lenses! Those described by Mr. Weller to Sergeant Buzfuz, were nothing to them! Four dozen quails, and half a dozen rabbits, purchased in one day, it will be confessed, was rather a large provision, abating the innumerable fancies for salt-fish and corned beef, which one might take before these were consumed. We tried, under this profuse administration, the salted quail; and, I hesitate not to say, for the benefit of posterity, that they bear no comparison to the fresh bird. The same testimony will apply to the corned rabbit, of which we had a great abundance. I speak of these dishes, not to boast of the daintiness of our fare, but because they are, I think, anomalies in the gastronomic world, and because I wish that the young housekeeper who has never had so formidable a purchase to dispose of, may admire our ingenuity. Truth compels me to say, however, that a considerable portion of this game afterwards made its escape by the side door, without having seen the interior of my saucepans.

The period to which I looked forward with most trepidation, was the session of Court. My better half being in the legal profession, it would, of course, be incumbent on us to entertain some of the brethren whom this event would call together. Getting up a formal dinner was an affair quite beyond my comprehension. I had paid so little attention to the externals of the art, that I did not even know how a table should look when laid, to say nothing of the formidable detail by which it was brought about. The *first dinner*, therefore, was likely to be quite an event. While it was yet *in futuro*, Hal made his appearance at our little domicile. I laid all my troubles before him, but he bade me be of good cheer, promising to preside over the *cuisine* himself when the dreaded day came, and comforted me by asserting that he could prepare a handsomer dinner than half the housekeepers of the village, and that both of us together must make a brilliant thing of it.

Behold us, then, on the morning of the eventful day, all stir and earnestness. The moment the professional moiety of the household left, the consultation began. I was not in the condition of Elise, whom Mrs. Gunilla relieved, at a very late hour, with a pair of chickens. My purveyor had been at his large purchases again, and I had lamb, quails, chickens, and pig. In the perplexity of choosing I turned to Hal.

"Which shall I take? for you know it is impossible to prepare more than one."

"Let it be the lamb, then, by all means. It will be more substantial as a solitary dish than chicken or quail, and will not, on an average, compel so many of your guests to cannibalism as the other four-footed animal would."

"Be quiet, Sir Impudence. I don't employ cooks to make comments on my guests. But if you think the lamb will be better than either of the other meats, let us decide upon it. How shall it be cooked?"

"You have but one way—a leg of lamb will hardly go into a three-pint saucepan. You must roast it of course; and if you have dinner at two, it must go to the fire about twelve."

"But there is a difficulty," I replied, "about roasting which my limited practice has not yet enabled me to overcome. That is to tell when the meat is done! and a small degree of over or under doing, you know, ruins the whole for nice palates."

"Oh leave that to me," said my assistant. "I'll keep all that right. You make the various other things ready, and prepare the roast, and I'll be here in time to superintend it. I'm going over to see the Sucker court now."

"Well, don't fail of being here at half past eleven, for I shall be in a fever if you do."

"No, good by."

I spent the remainder of the morning in the subordinate duties of preparing potatos, turnips, tomatos, et cet. The narrowness of my apartment compelled me to restore everything to order as fast as I disordered it; I could not leave a utensil soiled, because there was no spare place which it could occupy. No vessel of water which had been once used could remain standing; for my hollow ware, beside the tea-kettle and frying-pan, was confined to the three saucepans already named. I had but one table and the three short shelves before described, and on, or about these, all my preparations had to be made. Such very limited conveniences for housekeeping duties drew the deepest commiseration from the neighboring ladies who visited me, and yet, strange as it may seem, I thought they were quite uncalled for. My entire unacquaintance with practical housekeeping, while it doubtless multiplied the few cares I had, rendered me unable to appreciate a more favorable condition, so that it was, after all, a source of much content. I had no better state with which to compare this, and was therefore ready at all times to pronounce it good. With a few alterations which I could have suggested, I should have thought it unexceptionable.

In the initiatory stages of the dinner, when doubts of my success would rise to torment me, I had one stronghold to flee for comfort. That was my dessert. There was no doubt about it. My pumpkin pies were as good as ever graced a New England thanksgiving, and the peaches delicious! And then, too, I was certain of good coffee. Mr. F. had taught me the Parisian mode of making it, and there was no chance of failure. So between the doubts and hopes, pretty nearly balanced (for what would the dessert be if the meat were spoiled), I got through the morning. Punctually, a little before twelve, came Hal full of marvelous things to relate about the court room, and the people, and the functionaries, more especially the judge. The personal appearance of this gentleman he declared to be very extraordinary. His wardrobe demonstrated that he had been on a long circuit and left his valise at the first stopping-place. One could scarce refrain condoling with him, and offering the loan of a change of linen. He patronized the never-failing uniform of a jeans coat and pantaloons; the latter so much worn, that really it was wonderful he had not remembered to order a new pair in place of those he must have left. So overflowing was the youth's mind with recollections of the Court-house, that I had some difficulty in bringing him back to the leg of lamb. But this was effected at last, and the earnest business of the day commenced. Boil and roast was the burthen of our song till half-past one. But the tribulation we were in! or rather I, for Hal was wicked enough to enjoy my perplexity. The lamb began to shrink as soon as it was thoroughly warmed through, and continued to diminish till he declared another half hour would use up its very shadow.

"It must have been killed when the moon was in *parigee*," said he, "for no position of the heavenly bodies, less extraordinary, could produce such an effect."

It was too late now to repair the consequences of this unaccountable freak; and its diminutive appearance when placed upon the large dish I had reserved for it, nearly made me desperate. What would my guests think of such a solitary piece of lamb! What a misery, I thought, that apologies have been so worn out by their unmeaning use, that one cannot now be uttered without the forfeit of self-respect. I can never explain the true difficulty here, for I should burst into an uncontrollable laugh over the wasting lamb. I can never tell them why I did not prepare another dish, because while I was expatiating on the inelastic capacities of a small Franklin, and three half-grown saucepans, they would be weighing some point in evidence or law, and wondering why women would talk forever about such small matters! There was but one way; and that was to be silent. The moment I made this discovery, I was at rest. If there be any excellence about my philosophy of life, it is that of adopting heartily, and at once, whatever way seems clearly to be right, no matter how much it may conflict with preconceived feelings or opinions. This disposition, ability, or whatever one may please to term it, has saved me many hours of indecision, complaint, and pining. It is so much happier, not to have one's energies and desires warring with each other—not to be debating between the right and the wrong—wishing to pursue the one, yet unable to abandon the other. If my moralizing over a shrunken bit of lamb seems out of place, the reader will remember that I had extricated myself from great tribulation by resolving to treat my dinner as if it were worthy, not only of my own respect, but that of my guests also.

My temperature, however, was a little raised by the sudden reflection that Mr. F. might double the proposed number of guests, if he could find, among his acquaintances, so many that were unengaged. He would forget the size of the house, the size of the stove, and the size of his wife's capacity as cook, and bring as many as if all these had been on the most extensive scale. Fortunately, the recollection of this indefinite hospitality did not seize me, until just as the tide of learning and law was flowing out of the white wooden temple, and I was soon after able to distinguish our little party, limited to the original number. Two of the guests were strangers

to me; the third scarcely otherwise. When the cermony of introduction was over, they were seated in the little front bedroom, and
I retired to dish up the dinner. Hal was missing, and I could not
call him; the partition was too thin. While I was externally busied
with the vegetables, and internally denouncing the friend who could
forsake one in the hour of severest trial, the popular half of the
great back door swung open, and the waggish face of my extempore
cook was thrust cautiously in.

"I say," he exclaimed in a whisper, "considering the lamb, I may
as well take a botanizing tour while you are at dinner, eh?"

"Be off," I replied, "and botanize, or do any other thing you
please, but don't come here to perplex me now, when I have so
many weighty matters to adjust."

"You don't call the mutton weighty? Just put a couple of quails
into one of those things there that never rest, and we'll have the
better dinner yet. It's a pity you hadn't something to lay around
that fraction of roasted lamb," returning provokingly to the sore
subject; "shall I get you a handful of greens from the prairie?"

"Oh, be merciful, Hal, and go away for an hour, if you won't
sit down to dinner with us. When you come back, I'll have a quail
ready for you."

"Well, good by;" but a moment after the face reappeared.

"Just allow me to suggest that you had better not take any of
the lamb. You need not look at the dish when you decline, but just
carry it off with a Graham air, as if you thought the less any one
ate of it the better."

"Now, sir, if you add another word to your impudent counsel,
you shall go elsewhere for dinner; speak only once again," said I,
seizing a tumbler of water, "and I'll—"

The door slowly closed, and my tormentor disappeared. I arranged my various dishes, unfastened my working-apron, and was
folding it, preparatory to inviting in my guests, when the face again
looked in.

"Shall I not come in and pour the water for you? It is rather an
awkward business."

"Nevertheless I am fully competent to it myself. Judge if I am
not," and away went the tumbler I had menaced him with plump
in his face. He was fairly rid of now, beyond a doubt, for the door
shut quickly, and a handkerchief was put in requisition on his
streaming face and head. When I had enjoyed the joke sufficiently
to be grave, I invited the gentlemen to take seats. One of them
was good-natured enough to praise the lamb, though it must have

been execrable. When they left it, there remained an abundant supply for a much larger company. But the coffee was indubitably good, the pie ditto, and the peaches and cream required no praise.

I got through the meal without receiving any very distinct impression of the characters of the party, except that one appeared a slow man, with heavy thoughts which came to the surface, somewhat as a load of coal comes up from dark mines, and seemed not a little astonished to find themselves there. Another seemed to be halting between two species of animate existence, his ears not being long enough to give him an undisputed position in one, and all other qualifications, except the power of speech, too short to entitle him to a place in the other. The third was a Kentuckian—a member of the legislature—an honest man of free but not elegant speech. A man who thought truly, but made some ludicrous blunders in giving utterance to his ideas. The character of a high public functionary came under discussion, and this gentleman testified to his being "the most indignant man" he had ever seen. I had before heard his honor spoken of as rather pugnacious, and supposed this to be the Kentucky style of expressing the same thing. "The most indignant man, madam," said he, turning to me; "he has no more dignity than a schoolboy!"

"Indeed, sir; if that be true, I think he has ample occasion to be indignant."

"Take some more of the fruit, major," said my husband; "help yourself, sir."

"Thank you, I'll *endeevor*," was the characteristic reply.

At last the dinner was over. What with law, blunders, and nonsense, the gentlemen adjourned to the court-room, and I sat like a feminine Marius looking over the ruins, when the face I had so recently washed without the consent of the owner, peeped in at a crack of the great door, and asked if there "was any mutton left?"

"Come in and see," I replied, "and look well to your conduct, or I shall try the virtues of cold water again."

"But this time I shall be able to return it, so it will behove you, madam, to look to your ways also. If you do me another such favor on credit, I shall feel bound to reciprocate both—with interest."

We, however, got through with no more hydropathic sparring; and when the house, i.e., the back room, was fairly set in order again, I felt no little ground of self-gratulation that my first dinner was so creditably over.

CHAPTER XX

As the autumn advances toward winter in the "prairie land," nature, as everywhere else, loses her benign aspect. Heavy winds from the west and north sweep over the immense plains, shaking their brown, crumbling herbage on the unburned regions, and howling with a sharper tone over the tracts that have been left naked and black by the fire. Much rain usually descends in the month of November, and slight falls of snow commence in the latitude of 41° about the middle of the following month. But they rarely whiten the ground till much later in the season. The roads are frightfully bad until the rains are over, and the frost locks up the surface of the earth. There is then rarely snow enough to make sleighing in the beaten tracks. The greatest depth seldom exceeds five inches, the average is about two and a half. Very few sleighs are kept. Occasionally a young gentleman who bears rich recollections of the moonlight rides of the east, possesses himself of a nondescript article of this kind; more, however, as a memento, than as a means of like enjoyment in the new country.

The farmers usually keep a coarse vehicle, on which they slide their produce to market and their wood home. When a ride is taken it is in this, rigged with the box of a farm waggon. They are pleasant rides, notwithstanding the roughness of the conveyance. A slight fall of snow on the long grass gives the sleigh an easy, flowing motion, and you glide as gaily over the prairies as you would along the fenced ways of the east, with a foot of snow beneath your polished runner. Away you go with nothing to restrain your motions. The wide domain is all unfenced; the frost has bridged the sloughs; and your excursion is bounded only by time and the capacity of your steeds. Dashing along, you start up a bevy of grouse that have been shrinking under a clump of tall grass or weeds. Away they fly, their steady wings cutting the clear dense air, with a scarcely visible motion, till they alight at no great distance, and seek a shelter similar to the one they have left. The small red wolf too occasionally crosses your path, but his gaunt form soon disappears behind some hillock or tree. If you turn into the barrens, you do not ride far before the tramp of your horses and the merry voices of your party startle some timid hungering deer from his browsing, and send him bounding over the snowy surface, with a tread almost as light and fleet as the wind that follows him. If a rifle has been clandestinely stowed beneath the buffalo robes, it is produced now in quick time, but the ladies one and all declare that it shall not be discharged at the fugitive. If it is leveled at him, they push it aside, or strike it up into the air, so that the sportsman, if he persist, sends his ball among the naked boughs, or if reasonable, lays it aside, and contents his savage heart with a promise to come out next day, unattended by "these foolish women."

The quail dodges about farm-yards, grain-fields, and woodland, and during all the winter months is trapped in immense numbers. I have known them offered in market at sixpence a dozen. No meat surpasses them for richness and delicacy of flavor. Broiled, fricasseed, roasted, or fried, they are incomparable. But one must have more stomach than soul to devour the little charmers, without some compunctions. The bare recollection of one of the cheerful, happy-looking little beings who has tripped along in the road before you when you were taking a summer ride or walk, the delightful feature that his presence lent to the landscape, and the charm of his clear voice, ringing through the copses and groves, must, if you have any love of these things, detract from the mere palate pleasure before you. Yet notwithstanding all these appeals to the higher sense of man, millions of these beautiful little creatures are every winter devoured.

The winters of these western regions are much shorter and less severe than those in the same latitudes in the eastern states. Indeed, this season scarcely sets in till the middle of December. After this the cold is often as intense as is ever experienced below the high latitudes of the New England states; but its period of duration is very short. Two or three days at most of such weather are invariably followed by fair, sunny days, often mild as those of June; the hard-trodden streets of towns become quite dry, and even dusty; soft, pleasant winds from the south prevail throughout the day; your fires die away in the bright sunlight that pours through the open doors and windows. Sometimes these days are attended by warm rains, which soften the soil and make the roads and streets almost impassable. It seems then as if spring were at hand. You almost watch for tender grass to spring through the dead herbage that covers the prairies. But these pass away, and presently the frost-king is down upon us again, his cold breath searching every cranny and chink of the rude cabin of the Sucker, and the unfinished house of the more ambitious settler. I do not mean to say that so mild a temperature as I have described is invariable at this season. Yet no person can spend a winter in the region to which I refer, without experiencing many such days. Farther south, in the latitude of

Vandalia and Kaskaskia, they make a considerable part of the season.

The most objectionable feature of the climate of all these valley states north of the Ohio, is the sudden and extreme changes to which it is liable. The mercury sometimes rises many degrees in a few minutes, and often falls as rapidly.

I remember one of these changes which occurred in the winter of '37, when the mercury fell incredibly in a very few minutes. There had been a slight fall of snow two or three days previous, which the warm sun had converted into water, and left standing in pools all over the surface of the frozen ground. The morning was mild, and the sun shone bright till a few minutes before eleven, when the air became suddenly chilly, and in less than ten minutes the whole face of the earth was locked as under a Lapland winter. Many persons lost their lives by the sudden and extreme cold. Travelers over the large prairies had no means of escape, and for several days tidings were continually coming in, of some unfortunate victim who had perished. An old gentleman and his daughter had left a little town north of us for their home six miles away just before the change, and never reached it. Three men on horseback were crossing a large prairie on the south, all of whom perished, with their steeds. One of them, in hopes to escape by uniting to his own the warmth of his horse, had removed the entrails of the animal, and crept into the cavity! They were all found the next day, a short distance from each other, stark and stiff.

In the northern part of the state the winters are longer, the snow falls deeper, and the cold, though not always more intense, is of longer duration. But the prairies here are divided into smaller tracts, and partially sheltered by copses of wood, so that the long winter does not rave so fiercely over them as it would over the wide savannahs farther south. The deep snow occasionally leads to dreadful destruction among the deer. It is often crusted over, so as to bear the weight of a man, while their long, slender limbs plunge into it, and sink them beyond the hope of extrication. In this helpless condition, the terrified creatures are overtaken, and often cruelly beaten to death, by barbarians whose only object is to destroy them. Sometimes they are not even removed, and at others only the choice parts are taken off and carried home for use. The unmitigated barbarity of these merciless hunters is more clearly demonstrated toward spring, when starvation has left the deer a feeble skeleton. In this state he can be of no value whatever, yet the ruthless butchery continues adding another to the many evidences that bloodshedding may become a pleasant recreation.

The fickleness of the wintry season greatly impairs the farmer's chance of success with fall crops. In those regions where the surface is not covered with snow, the small grains which the eastern farmer is accustomed to snow in the fall, have little prospect of coming to much strength of maturity; but this disadvantage is, according to all western agriculturists, compensated tenfold by the gigantic growth of summer.

One of the most trying conditions of western life is the first winter, which finds the settler moved out of his warm cabin into the new house which he has erected for himself, but not finished. The former tenement has afforded good security against the greatest degree of cold. Its thick walls, chinked between the logs with triangular bits of wood, plastered neatly in with clay, have been impervious to the biting frost. The wide fireplace has afforded abundant facilities for imparting warmth; and the heavy floor, if well put together, has protected the feet without a carpet. But since the last winter passed away, the new framed house has been erected. Boards split by his own hands form its thin outside walls, and these are generally for the first year the only thing interposed between the bitter elements and the shivering tenants. No wonder then, that the cups freeze to the saucers while they are at table, or that the chicken or grouse from which they have just breakfasted, is thoroughly frosted over while the housewife is setting away the remains of the meal. These are trying times. Quilts are put in requisition, in place of lath and plaster, the fire is kept on active duty, and food is abundant. Hope too whispers that such weather cannot long continue. A few pinching days, and the bright sun and the warm winds will steal in where the keen cold now enters, and be all the more welcome for the contrast. One, two, and sometimes three winters are worn out in this way. The material for finishing houses is scarce; labor is still more difficult to procure; and, most of all, the great length of the warm season and the thousand delights which the external world furnishes, relax the care and energy which under circumstances less favorable to other enjoyments, would prove a more efficient security against the rigors of this season. A like want of forecast against the inclemencies of winter marks the whole economy of the early agriculturists of these genial regions. Their cattle are no better cared for than themselves. No barns or outbuildings, except a small corn crib, are constructed for years after they settle on a farm. This neglect is doubtless owing, in part, to the scarcity of material for building, to the defective state of the mechanic arts, and nearly as much, perhaps, to the unsettled feeling experienced by these strange lovers of the freedom of frontier life.

Liable at any moment to be pressed upon in his chosen home by eastern emigrants, the western farmer feels that he must retreat from it. He has little sympathy with the living tide that is flowing over his beautiful plains from the land of the rising sun, and when it has passed and closed around him, he feels a stranger in his own home. The charms for which he loved the country are no longer there, the spirit which bound him to it dwells not in the thrifty growing estates of his Yankee neighbors. It has fled to the untenanted plains beyond, and thither he must follow it. Of what avail then were it to build, as if his life were to be spent here? He must be ever moving, ever in the van of civilization, pressing hard upon the Indian, whose footstep brushes the first dew from the face of nature in all these magnificent kingdoms of her richest wealth.

But I am departing from winter and winter life on the prairies. The firesides of many families present something of the aspect which those of our grandsires did in the eastern states. The small wheel employs the females in the hours not devoted to the cares of the family. The bunch of linen grows day by day, and by and by the sound of the loom may be heard from the chamber or the adjoining room, if there be one. The men look after their cattle, husk their corn at the shock in the field, and if preparations for building the next season are in progress, spend the remaining time in preparing timber, splitting boards, riving shingles, and in every other way making their own hands perform the duties of the various mills, machines, and instruments, which elsewhere relieve the cultivator of the soil of these duties. When nothing of this kind employs them, they fasten a horse to a little *"pung"* or jumper,* take a gun, and driving around the corn-fields of the vicinity, shoot grouse enough for one or two dinners, and return home to read or do whatever else seems good, until the return of evening brings fresh wants to be supplied at the farm-yard, or some social neighbor to chat away the hours at the fireside.

Navigation is suspended on the streams of the interior, and on the upper Mississippi, for a few weeks. It usually opens toward the last of January, seldom later than the first of the succeeding month.

* A miniature sleigh, each shaft and runner of which is made of one long bough bent up in front.

The ice bridge, however, is not to be trusted. While it remains, therefore, it is a serious obstacle to those whose business or pleasure leads them over unbridged streams; and some of the most painful accidents have occurred in attempting to cross them. I recollect one that took place during the last winter I spent in the country. A party of four or five young persons set out toward evening to cross the Illinois, for the purpose of attending a ball in the village opposite their place of residence. The river at this place is widened into what is, in this country, termed a lake. The width, at the point of crossing, is probably between half and a quarter of a mile. The weather had been remarkably mild for some days, and the crossing was considered extremely precarious; but their love of gaiety predominated over prudence, and the party entered on the dull, saturated ice. They had proceeded but a few yards from the shore, when it gave way, and plunged them all in. Fortunately, the water was shallow, and many trees and shrubs grew far out from the bank. They caught at these, and, with almost superhuman exertion, climbed into their branches, and were all saved; though they nearly perished of the cold before relief came. It was not until a late hour of the following morning, that their situation was discovered by some one passing near the water's edge; and then some time was consumed in getting a passage for a boat through the ice, which was now broken up and moving slowly off. One of the females, when taken from her perilous position, was stupefied and helpless. All, however, recovered.

The ice generally moves about the last of January. Navigation is then uninterrupted, till midsummer reduces the streams, and leaves the "bars," which occur at frequent intervals, too scantily covered with water to allow a steamboat of ordinary draft to pass them. This is true only of the tributaries of the Mississippi and Missouri. The latter streams are supplied with an abundance of water during the whole year.

CHAPTER XXI

It is always pleasant to resume communication with the world around, when the icy fetters of winter are cast off. Every one rejoices that the great highways are again open, even though he may expect to derive no personal pleasure or benefit therefrom. This feeling, united with the anticipation of the approaching jubilee of nature, makes the settlers in the vicinity of navigable streams rejoice to

hear of the "first steamboat." And as the sun wheels himself day
by day higher in our heavens, and the chill winds are followed
oftener and longer, by soft airs from the south, and the evenings
grow mild, and the frogs begin to pipe in the moist spots on the
prairies, one's very heart leaps to meet the benignant spirit of the
opening year.

How intense has been my enjoyment of such seasons in Prairie
Land! How entire the happiness, with which we have stood by our
door at a late hour on some mild March evening, when all sounds
of human life were hushed in our little village, and listened to the
thousand minute and gentle voices by which nature announced her
emancipation from the grim rigor of the hoary winter! Millions of
the little creatures just named, tenants of the sloughs and low
grounds moistened by the rains and melted snows, send forth their
cheerful chorus to the night. The moon shines faintly through a
veil of mist and smoke, accumulated from the slow fires that have
all day crept lazily through the saturated grass. Delicious breezes
press gently over the vast plains, with a solemn ceaseless sound,
that subdues and yet gladdens the soul! In such an hour the mind
is all unchained from its material fetters—free—its conceptions
large as nature herself. It floats with the evening winds over all
the dim region, searches, like them, every recess in plain or grove,
teeming with young life, and ready, when a few more sunny days
shall have passed, to burst into visible and joyous beauty. Sympathy,
thought, emotion, when nature is in such a mood, scorn all laws
of time and place, and career through every period, and over all
the regions of space. What are nations and empires the most potent,
to the existence of which mind is conscious? The mightiest events
of earth sink into insignificance before its own exulting sense of
being. It asks no power but that which it can achieve for itself. It
sees neither joy nor pain, in the definite acts of life, whatever be
their nature. It asks only to go abroad with the unfolding of the
omnipotent spirit that breathes around it, of which it feels itself a
part. All its past is but a point—all its future eternity! It inquires
not how or whence it came, cares not for the circumstances in
which it finds itself, but rejoices in being—itself the most wonderful
of all the mysteries which it cares not now to solve. Nature, in all
her vast extent, her manifold operations, is within its grasp. Clouds,
volcanos, oceans, tempests, mountains, deserts—the secret work-
ings of the vital and physical laws, the innumerable forms of life
and matter; all the beauty of the world which is just bursting into
life; all the glory of the millions that have passed away, become

only sources of exquisite pleasure. They waken no inquiry, they seem no mystery. We live in the past as if it were the present; we are tenants of all time. We seize, for a moment, our place in the spirit world, and look upon material nature as if we were no longer a part of it. What are such reachings of the mind but a lengthening of the bonds by which it is allied to Omnipotence? Are they not foretastes of its unshackled future, glimpses of its eternity—faint and brief, surely, yet sufficient to make us rejoice that it is not destined to reside ever with matter? Who is not richer for such a moment? Whose soul does not thrill with a joy unutterable, when this chord has been swept by the breath of nature, to find how deep and rich are the tones it yields, in making up the harmony of his being? Who does not descend to earth, from such ecstatic flights, happier and better for the exquisite sense which has been kindled by them! His love of the material beauty and harmony which has summoned him from himself is a thousandfold stronger. They are no longer regarded merely as objects of delight to the faculties which perceive them, but, as links to draw us higher, as incense laid on the altar of our hearts, to kindle therein brief but angelic light. Blessed be nature—beautiful, life-enkindling nature! Blessed be the thousand arts by which she appeals to our love and reverence. Bud, leaf, and tree, raging tempest and gentle life-distilling dew—fathomless ocean and clear, moss-bound spring—blessed are ye all. And thrice-blessed and adored be the wisdom which has enabled us to see all these, and feel ourselves partakers of their being, their beauty, and their power.

The majestic silence (for the rich music of nature is silence to the soul that harmonizes with it) in which such emotion can alone live, is deep on the dark plains around us. No discordant sound of life—no jarring stir—no hum of art or toil, breaks on the soul. Its pinion soars untiring—its keen sense is drawn ever onward, but only by the voices which Omnipotence has called forth. The human world is all absent, gone, faded away in the immense distance. What sound is that which recalls the ear to its mortal sense, at this deep hour? A slow, measured march, which you deem for a moment might be the deeper bass of the universal choir—the cloud voice answering to the solemn spirit of the night. Whence comes it? It is distant, but belongs to earth. It dissolves the spirit fabric in which we have been enshrined, and leaves the keenly sensitive soul unshielded, until it again enters the mortal, and adapts itself to its old abode. Earth is here again, with all its forms of beauty and notes of harmony, to waken admiration, wonder, and

love. The vision is past. Sensations and emotions belonging to the
mortal, come again, all summoned from their slumbers, by this one
note from the human world. What is it? A moment's attention tells
you.

Far off in that forest, behind whose leafless boughs the sun set,
and the twilight faded, lies a stream—a river. Its dark waters flow
slowly onward, between rich banks, wooded with the gigantic black
walnut, the graceful elm, the slight and mobile cotton-wood. Nearer
the margin the redbud already begins to swell, and close beside it,
the pure white blossoms of the dog-wood are unfolding. So that
even now, before the trees are clothed with their young leaves,
these beautiful shrubs enliven long lines of the dull, brown forest
with chaste and exquisite colors. As the winds career along the
surface of the waters, they bend and dance above them; and when
their more majestic neighbors shall put on the vernal garb, they
will fling their petals to the stream, and mingle in the common
world of leaves about them. In all the still, currentless nooks of
this stream, myriads of wild fowl are now engaged in preparing
for their young. Occasionally a scream overhead, and the sound
of swift wings cutting the air, announce that another party has
arrived from the sunny south, to join them. If you were near that
river, you would hear their small talk all the night, as they glide
about in the water. And sweet music it is, to one who loves the
wild and unrestrained in nature. Here they have built their temporary homes and reared their young, from time immemorial. And
here, long years ago, they were unmolested in these cares and
pleasures. The wild tenants of the woods and streams passed them
by, without harm, and if man came there, he came silently. The
slight canoe shot through the waters with a sound that scarcely
struck their ear till it was gone. The night was profoundly quiet—
the day brought no harsh sounds, no waste of joyous life, no giants
rushing through the still waters, casting their waves far up on the
shore, to return laden with mire and earth. Now, how changed!
Monsters plough the bosom of the river, whose hoarse voices ring
through the silent valley for miles; whose eyes are fire, whose breath
is destruction. Long before they approach, their measured march-
ings terrify these feathered dwellers in the wilderness, and long
after they are past the sound returns, and the disturbed waters roll
ashore with an angry splash, as if they would signify their displeasure
at such intrusion. It is the note of this almost living thing that fell
on our ear just now. Though nearly nine miles away, it may be
plainly heard in peculiar states of the atmosphere. Its first few puffs

are faint, but as it approaches nearer, they swell louder into the silent air, till you almost fancy you can hear the wheels dashing into the foamy waters. Then they die away. Fainter and fainter grows the sound, and at last it is wholly lost. Silence, profound as before, reigns around us, and the mighty creation, that called us back to earth, is gone, to break the solemn repose of the wilderness beyond.

One of the most impressive features of this magnificent land, is the magnitude of its streams. One can form no adequate conception of the effect which these water-courses have on the mind: the smallest of them that is ever entered by steamboats, longer than the most vaunted rivers of the east; the largest, half spanning a continent.

To float along on these majestic waters, through regions whose fertility and beauty we can scarce imagine to have been surpassed by Eden itself; to travel thousands of miles through forests whose deep aisles reëcho to no sound save the monotonous breath of your own steamer, and plains which stretch away from the waterside to the sky! millions upon millions of acres, sending forth no sound or sign of life; silent, tenanted only by wild animals and at long intervals by the solitary wood-chopper, whose "shantee," hidden among the trees, is indicated by the smoke which curls up from its stick chimney; or possibly by the shouts of children around its door: to travel thus for days and even weeks, your steed never tiring, your speed never flagging, is to gather an idea of vastness, unparalleled except upon the ocean. Firm, inhabitable vastness, every foot of which is teeming with the energies that support life; every acre of which would yield an ample subsistence to large numbers of the famishing and perishing thousands of the crowded old world.

To set out on one of the tributaries of the mighty stream which has given name to this immense valley, to follow this comparatively insignificant one till it is lost in the larger, and then to float on amid waters that have fallen upon the mountain peaks an interminable distance toward the setting sun, and made their devious way through the myriad windings of forest, cliff, and plain, bearing messages from all these to the distant ocean, awakens a perception of extent which it is impossible to realize elsewhere. There is a sublimity in journeying on these great waters which language cannot describe. You feel it from the first moment you find yourself afloat. It is not in looking out upon them. To the mere optical sense they are often less impressive than the puny streams of the east. It is in the association—the idea that the water which ripples at your side has come from a far land, a land full of unexplored wonders and beauties. The reflection opens an immense field of thought and inquiry, and makes you long to be transported to the region where all these exist.

But you must love nature, to enjoy this sentiment. There must be a chord in your mental existence that will vibrate to the potent wand which summons life, beauty, and majesty to these vast solitudes.

Oh, I love nature. The old world, burthened as it is with the sublime and exquisite products of human energy, enveloped as it is with the associations of tumultuous ages, and glorified with the light of mighty minds, is interesting. It tells many a tale to subdue and to enkindle the soul; it opens many a volume to delight, to astonish, to agonize. It offers a continual spectacle of warning, exhortation, and instruction to him who will gaze thereon. Wiser heads may prefer this, but give me the free untrodden empire of nature! Give me her piled cliffs, her forest aisles, her chant of rushing winds and waters, her untrained songsters, her exquisite forms and hues of beauty, and I will ask no other. The lofty edifices which art, directed by the religious feelings, has wrought and piled, may waken devotion in others, but my cathedral should be the overhanging cliff, my temple the eloquent shades. My worship is kindled by these into far more intense life than by the displays of human power. Living much with nature, makes me wiser, better, purer, and therefore, happier!

CHAPTER XXII

The spring of '37 opened with delicious beauty on the prairie land! The growing world, both animate and inanimate, seemed to rejoice in the departure of an unusually rigorous winter. The showers fell more lightly than those of the previous year, and the earth, moistened with gentle rains and bathed in genial sunshine, seemed more willing than ever to enrich man. Happy would it have been for the inhabitants of these fertile regions had they obeyed her summons, and turned from the alluring uncertainties of speculation to honest, productive labor! But they had not then learned the bitter lesson which the few following years taught them. Men had resorted to the west expecting to coin the rich soil, not be expending patient labor to convert its energies into products useful to man, nor by erecting upon it homes which should increase the amount of happiness there enjoyed; but by dividing it into small fractions and setting an inflated estimate upon them—an estimate not authorized by its capacities, or the condition of the country; but dependent on the extent to which they could deceive each other and themselves. So the growing population of the rich savannahs disregarded all the strong inducements which the earth held out to seek legitimate wealth and happiness, and left the fertile acres untilled, to scour the country for "town sites," which no one of their generation will ever see occupied. Time and energy were spent in these fruitless labors, that, well directed, would have enriched the state. Men seemed to have forgotten that wealth has natural sources, without drawing upon which, it can never be obtained except in few and rare instances. And, forgetting this, they plunged deeper and deeper into the mazes of speculation. The cloud of distress which had risen over the eastern world had not yet cast its shadow on these favored regions. Money was abundant, and hope high. This was the year of the "crisis" in the west; and the change which succeeded it was terrible.

But the country was now full of life and energy. The human, the animal, and the vegetable world seemed alike rejoicing in the superabundant vigor of the season. Happy and joyous life smiled everywhere! Our little village had received many valuable families the preceding autumn, and with the first flowers of spring came several others, who had been long expected and were joyfully received. Among the former was one which I shall introduce here, as well for the interesting character of its members, as because there is a tragical sequel to be told, by and by, of the husband and father. This family consisted of four—father, mother, and two sons. They had emigrated from the metropolis of the east late in the preceding autumn, and spent the winter in a neat little dwelling on the southeastern border of the village. They were members of the Society of Friends, and if their form of faith were to be accepted as the origin of their many and exalted virtues, one could wish it universal. Nowhere else were such peace, harmony, gentleness, and affection found! The father was a middle-aged man, with nothing extraordinary in his personal appearance till the expression of his face, and the contour of his head, arrested attention. The latter would have delighted the phrenologist, the former would have won the affection of the most timid child. Benevolence, kindness, mingled with justice, and proper degree of self-respect, were the leading characteristics of both. His high, open brow, and mild yet intelligent eye, the noble development of the upper portion of the head, and the thinness at the base, were delightful assurances that a spirit every way worthy the name of man dwelt within. And so it proved. No person was more respected, more beloved, and it is a rare combination that commands both these tributes from our fellow beings. Endowed with a fine taste, and good powers of mind, he had been ever a devoted lover of some branches of natural science, among which ornithology claimed preference. Much delight therefore was in store for him in the new varieties of birds to which western life would introduce him. And great was his pleasure when a leisure day came, to sally forth, gun in hand, and return after a few hours' ramble, with some of the feathered tenants of the new country for preservation. Many beautiful specimens of his preparation are still found among eastern collections, and in the homes of his friends. Such was the husband. The wife, though differing widely from this, was not less respected and beloved among those who knew her. Plain and exceedingly neat in personal appearance, soft and quiet in speech, gentle and tender in her deportment, kind and dignified in her treatment of strangers, and unaffectedly loving in her family, she was an object of just admiration and warm regard. Between these persons there still existed that lively affection which poets sing as belonging only to the fresh and glowing days of youth. Their intercourse was marked by the tenderest consideration in each for the wishes of the other. Their language had still the warmth of youthful feeling, chastened by the purifying influences of parental love, and the higher moral sense which well-spent years produce. The happy children of these parents were two sons, well advanced toward manhood—such sons as one might expect would grow up at a fireside adorned by so many virtues. And beautiful it was to see this family gathered in their neat and simple home; each a bond to the other, and all to him. They were the model which many of the young beginners in our village set before themselves for imitation. Happy will they be who shall ever reach its perfect semblance.

When the spring came, the father and sons began to open their farm about two miles below the village on the prairie. It was a beautiful spot. The plain around was diversified by high swells which fell off into pleasant hollows, where the large, luscious strawberry, concealed by the rank grass, clustered and ripened much later than on the adjacent elevations. Groves bordered the prairie at no great distance from the house on the south and west; and on the northwest lay a bold eminence, on the summit of which stood the cabin of their nearest neighbor. In due time, the little cottage in which they were to find their future home, was completed and entered. Trees were set about it, outbuildings constructed, and the farm began to wear a cheerful and inviting aspect. The health of the mother, which had been extremely delicate in the east, improved very much. The cares of her family were no longer burthensome to her, and every source of enjoyment seemed opening before her, as if youth were returning, instead of passing away. And here, giving and receiving happiness, we leave them for the present.

Meantime many farms began to be opened in the vicinity of our village. Riding over the prairie you would see the heavy team of three and four yokes of oxen traveling slowly over a tract, dragging after them a plough, which if you have never seen "*breaking*" done, is an entire stranger to you. The forward end of the beam runs on two wheels, to the axle of which the team is made fast. One of the wheels, that on the right, is larger in diameter than the other by about three inches. This runs in the furrow; and as the machine advances, a belt of turf, from eighteen to twenty-seven inches broad, and two or three deep, is cut off, and turned smoothly over into the space from which its neighbor has just been ejected. When the turf is well broken, these strips lie as smoothly in their inverse, as natural positions. The uniformity of the surface renders it unnecessary to hold the plough; so that one man can perform the labor alone. If the track be fenced previously to breaking, a very respectable crop of corn, called by the farmers "sod corn," may be raised on the broken turf, with no other preparation than this. It is usually planted at the time of ploughing, a few kernels being scattered along the edge of each furrow, and left to spring up between the contiguous belts of sod. I have often seen this "sod corn," thus planted and never afterward aided by cultivation, attain a larger growth than the most cultivated fields of the east. It is principally used as fodder.

June is the month generally preferred for this process of breaking. The turf, once fairly turned, the overlaid vegetation decays during the summer, the roots below "die out;" and by the next spring a pair of horses will easily turn a furrow four inches below the first. After this, nothing can exceed the ease with which the soil is cultivated. So mellow, soft, and free from obstructions is it, that a child could almost work it. Breaking the turf is, to the prairie agriculturist, what clearing the ground is to those of wooded countries: the difference being that one man with a good team and plough will break three acres of the former in a day, while the same force employed in the forest would scarcely prepare a like area for cultivation in a year.

The fertility and inexhaustibleness of the prairie soil are other sources of pleasant congratulation to its cultivators. From three to six and even nine feet of the richest black loam cover millions of acres. No wonder that an English gentleman, on riding many days over such rich grounds, and seeing them lie along the navigable streams for thousands of miles, exclaimed in astonishment, "It is wonderful that your farmers do not cultivate these rich lands!" One might easily have told him that we had not a sufficient number grown yet! There are spots in the prairie country which have been planted with wheat annually for two hundred years, by the early French settlers; and yet no signs of exhaustion are visible. The growth is apparently as rank, and the maturity as vigorous, as in the first year of its culture.

These slow-moving teams and the brown surface around them are pleasant sights to those who love to witness the growth of a country. Then there are other features indicative of the same thing, which one rejoices to look on. Houses spring up in various parts of the prairie, with fenced fields about them. The road on which last spring we could ride three miles north from our village without seeing a dwelling or any sign of cultivation, has now within that space two houses, one of which has a noble farm look. The other is the residence of a worthless mechanic, whose home might be a princely one, if he would use his time and skill in that manner, instead of spending it in lawless carousals, and spreading ruin and degradation among the families of his neighbors.

Fence-making is an important item in prairie agriculture. Where farms are opened at a considerable distance from timber, the expense and difficulty of procuring rails are insurmountable; there is no stone to supply their place; and the next expedient is to use the turf. This is sufficiently firm, and when properly "laid up," not only serves admirably for purposes of utility, but often lends much beauty to the face of the landscape. Hedges surmounting these walls of green have been tried, and I believe sometimes with tolerable success. There is no doubt, if sufficient pains were taken, they would succeed to perfection, and nothing can be imagined more beautiful than a densely populated prairie, divided by such hedges, the broad rich harvest waving between, and the luxuriant orchards bending their laden boughs over them. I have seen some sections of these turf fences surmounted by a lofty border of the late yellow flowers, so that at a little distance the earthy elevation was perfectly concealed, and the field looked as if it were inclosed by a floral hedge six or eight feet in height.

Another and a still more delightful task to the person of taste is setting out trees. Early in the spring you will see an occasional waggon, laden with the young members of the forest, going to some cheerful-looking farm, or rolling into the village with its choice cargo, for the public grounds. In the season of which I am now writing, the square of our little town was surrounded, and many private grounds were similarly ornamented with them.

No enterprise, public or private, produces more chaste and un-selfish joy than this. Every body loves trees, and every one feels a thrill of gratitude toward the man whom they see planting one. A tree is unlike any other ornament. Though set on private property, it is a public blessing. It is not like a piece of statuary or painting, accessible only to the few. Its beauty may be seen, its glory appre-ciated by all. But not for this alone is it prized. Every leaf-laden bough that dances before a prairie house, invites the merry song-sters of the woodlands to come out and cheer its inmates. And the rapid growth which the locust, cotton-wood, aspen, and some other species have in the strong soil, leaves no excuse for living long in a treeless and birdless home. While the more beautiful and stately specimens are coming forward, these will give the bobo'link, brown thrasher, robin, whip-poor-will, &c., ample encouragement to visit you. They will not come without them.

CHAPTER XXIII

As the spring advanced, we forsook our little toy-shop, and, after boarding for a few weeks in the family of a very dear friend in town, I found myself once again domiciliated within the beloved walls of Prairie Lodge. The earth, I think, holds no spot, the memory of which will ever be so dear to me as this. Even at this long distance of time and space, and with the wide chasm which succeeding events have opened between the *then* and the *now*, I remember its every feature, its every charm, as if they had been seen and enjoyed yesterday. The little stream, and the willows which drooped over it; the profusion of roses, which drew, daily, excla-mations of delight from Mary; the rich grass about the house, which she had so carefully watched and defended against the encroach-ments of its wild neighbors; the tall old oak before the door, and the vigorous growth of the shrubs and vines which had been set in the garden the preceding spring, and which every evening found us admiring; the rich foliage of the barrens and groves around, and of the tract covered with the shrubby oaks where the solitary graves were made, seem as fresh as if objects of the present hour. The latter spot more particularly won much of our thought and admiration during the summer. It lay in front of the room in which most of our time was spent; and, in the warm afternoons, when the sun left the door shady and cool, we used to gather near it or even upon the sill, and sit and look at the bright leaves glancing in the light, and talk of such repose as might be enjoyed beneath them, till it seemed as if to lie down there would be no terror. In June, when it was in the height of its beauty, the whole tract was thronged with locusts. Myriads of these busy insects reveled in the rich foliage; all day the soft air resounded with their ceaseless hum, and we used to listen to it with a kind of charmed feeling, and wonder over the mystery which unfolded itself in visible forms only at such long intervals. Toward the close of July their song and revel ended. Their feasts had been principally confined to wild vegetation; the fields were scarcely touched, and the abundant harvest yielded a generous reward for the labor which had been bestowed upon it. Day after day the creaking wain came slowly in from the sunny fields, and its rich burthens were transferred to the noble barn which the farmers had reared and finished with their own hands. The labor of the season was severe both in doors and out. But Mary had passed through five such, performing toils infinitely multiplied during some of them, by sickness in her own family or the neighborhood. Still I wondered each day, as she moved about to her appointed tasks, how so slight a form could endure so much. Yet she rarely complained of fatigue or indisposition. But I looked with boding anticipations at her small chest, and thought of our mother who had died long, long years before, of the disease which this figure too surely signaled. And yet we were happy; no word was ever spoken that defined these thoughts. Indeed they had but a dim existence in my own mind. We laid plans for finishing and ornamenting her house; we formed schemes for revisiting the scenes of early childhood, discussed systems of education for the promising boy in whom we all delighted so much, and, in every expression and thought, looked forward to sharing a long life in the beautiful country we so loved, and to many years of happiness and comparative ease for her in the home she had so hardly earned. But as summer drew to a close, she began to droop, and a cough, so slight that we scarcely noticed its existence, began to hang about her. There was no pain, apparently no disease, and yet the limbs, that had never before tired, now refused, at times, to obey the energetic mind! "What can be the matter?" she would say. "It must be indolence! It must be that the event which I have so ardently desired, the arrival of my friends, has wrought a desire for relaxation from the severe labors which I have never abated before, since we came to the new country."

We were accustomed to repel this half-playful self-accusation, and it was often said that she needed repose; that she had exhausted her energies by incessant labor, both of body and mind; and that they would return fresh as ever after a period of rest. In any other case we should have known this was a glaring fallacy; but we wished it so, and therefore believed it. But when the repose came, the result we had hoped for did not follow. At times, it is true, there was a little recruiting, barely enough to balance our fears, with the hope it enkindled, but the gain would be all unaccountably lost in a few days; and then our ingenuity was vainly taxed for a reason, and for some other resource in which to trust anew. Thus it went on. The last of August brought an event which quite diverted our attention from all previous objects—an event fraught with emotions at once the most joyful and solemn to me—one which ever opened the deepest fountains of feeling in the female heart; which added to my other sources of happiness the charm of maternity. Absorbed as I was in this new relation, as we all were in the little being, whose charms and wants claimed our attention, we forgot, in a measure, the previous object of our solicitude. She seemed to be better too, and when we left her late in the autumn and returned to our little village home, we had the most ardent hopes of seeing her quite well before the winter set in. When the calm mild days of the Indian summer came, she rode down, and spent a considerable part of a week with us. Our boy grew nobly; and what with the delight this gave us, and the hopes which occasional periods of improvement in Mary kindled, the short winter wore nearly away without startling us from our fancied security. But the time came when we could no longer delude ourselves! The invalid herself was the first to show us how much we had been deceived. We were frequently together, and one day toward the last of February, when we all were seated in her room, she took occasion to express her wishes in regard to the disposition of affairs when she should no longer be with us. She spoke as calmly as if preparing for a journey to some pleasant land from which she would soon come back restored and happy. We were plunged in the deepest grief. I can never forget the effect which this conversation had upon my feelings. It seemed the opening of a dismal gulf before me, whose hungry depths were going to devour the form, the affection, and the noble mind I had been so long denied, and had but now just come to enjoy. I had nothing to answer, not even tears. To utter words of hope, with that wasted form before me, and those dark eyes fixed upon my face, their deep, intense, unearthly light piercing my very soul, was impossible. To unite with the resignation she expressed, equally so, and thus I was compelled to listen in silence to her feebly uttered words, every tone of which struck upon my heart like the voice of a burial knell! I have seen few bitterer days than that. It broke down the barrier of hope which I had almost unconsciously reared around us, and left nothing whereon to lean. I felt then that the reality could scarcely be more agonizing than the certainty which placed it before me.

My sister's disease thence onward took a more active and complicated form. But it wrote itself in strangely deceptive characters on her person. In her days of early girlhood, she had possessed what a few persons call beauty. Her figure was always slight, and the bust too thin for mere physical beauty. But there was a grace in all her movements which few could see and not admire; her finely proportioned head was covered with a profusion of glossy chestnut hair, which flowed halfway to her feet. Her high, broad forehead surmounting a small lower face, indicated the presence of a mind of no common order. There was something quaint yet sweet in the expression of the mouth—something which gave assurance of the predominance of earnest and grave thought; and yet betrayed the presence of a humor which, upon sufficient provocation, would break forth into irresistible laughter; and a merry laugh it was, when it came—a laugh to which no one could listen without responding. But the finest feature of her face was the eye. It was dark, darker than the hair; and though not uncommonly large, was at times dilated and lighted up with such an expression that one would not hesitate to pronounce it of extraordinary size; it was a bright, clear eye, that one could look into, as into a shady spring, and seem to see all that lay beneath the surface. In my early admiration I had thought it exceedingly beautiful, and my ripened affection was scarcely likely to correct my judgment if it erred. Beside, it had gathered a richer expression from all the stirring duties, pleasures, and trials of her new life. It was now the eye of a mother, a wife, a high-purposed, thoughtful woman. On her sick bed how changed were all these things; the thin form was now so

wasted, that we could bear her in our arms from one place of rest
to another; the face seemed more than ever disproportioned to the
heavy forehead—the complexion was pure, and the cheeks had
each a color like the deep blush of the roses she loved so well. But
the eye was most changed of all; it was dilated, apparently to twice
its usual size, and was indescribably bright and clear.

As the genial days of spring drew on, and the balmy air floated
in at the open doors and windows, we used to lift her from the
bed as a mother would a pining infant, and lay her, half recumbent,
in her pillowed chair, where she could look abroad upon the opening
world. Oh, it was bitter then to sit helplessly down beside her;
when her large spiritual eyes were wandering over the reviving
plains and awakening groves—when every shrub and tree that she
had so loved and cherished around her home, was putting on its
richest charms to fascinate and bind the heart; when the birds,
whose joyous notes had cheered the solitary hours of so many
similar seasons, were returning to their olden haunts full of life
and music, and the vines and roses that her own hand had trained
were unfolding their young tendrils around her casement, and the
brook which she had so gaily challenged me to arrest, under the
clump of willows, was coming down with its freight of vernal waters,
babbling and murmuring the same song to which she had listened,
through long years full of vigor and hope; and feel that she was
passing irresistibly away from all this; that a hand was upon her
which neither skill nor affection could remove; that by and by she
would depart, no more seeing nor seen: this was the agony which
never finds utterance.

To feel that in this spot, made beautiful by her untiring industry
and little arts, she had spent so many years of loneliness and toil,
pining for those far-off few, for each of whom her faithful heart
so yearned; anxious to perfect her home, that if they came they
might be happy in it; and that now, when this was nearly consummated, and the fond ones were all gathered at her side, she was
going from among us, and we were impotent alike to save or detain
her, was insupportable. Yet this was my task on the anxious days
that ushered in that memorable summer.

The solitary resting-place of her friend lay directly before the
door, and though the graves were hidden in the rich foliage of the
shrubbery around, the spot claimed many of her thoughts. They
sometimes found faint utterance in words.

"It is beautiful," she said one day, while looking out upon it, "it
is beautiful, that dancing foliage! How many days I have watched

its blended light and shadow from this door. But the feeling with which I have done so, has wonderfully changed since the grave was made. Before that, I used to wonder when the bushes would be removed, and delight to anticipate a luxuriant orchard growing up there. I have had fair visions of trees laden with the red and golden stores of autumn, such as I used to love to wander among, away in the land of our nativity. I was always a lover of autumn. When I lived in the great city our friends used to visit the country in the spring and summer; they especially loved the joyful spring-time. But I chose nature's solemn autumnal days. I loved then to steal away to the silent wood, or ramble under the drooping boughs of the orchard trees. And here, I anticipated many sunny days in advanced life, when I should find that pleasure on this spot. But when the grave was made, this feeling changed. I would not have seen a shrub removed, nor a tree felled, for the world. It is so quiet now, so far removed from the stir and toil of the farm, and the large, glossy leaves of those low oaks are such fit drapery for one's final couch! See, when a slight breeze rustles them, how the light and shade mingle on their polished surfaces. Those tall trees that stand beside the grave, and mark the spot in the wilderness of leaves below, must never be cut down. They are dear to me, and will, I trust, be so to you all by and by. Do not weep for me. It is true, I little thought to have been laid beneath them so soon myself; but it is the tomb I have always wished I might rest in. When I used to see the dead borne through crowded streets, and deposited in populous cemeteries, I prayed for a grave in the deep wilderness, with the rich foliage above, and solemn silence around. I have reached it sooner than I then wished—my autumn has come before my summer has reached its full dawn; but what then? except," she added with moistened eyes, the mother rising superior to the submissive christian, "except for my boy, who needs his mother's care these many years yet—except for him, much as I love you all, I could go willingly to the greater peace that lies beyond. But it pains you, and I will say no more. Look," she said, after a pause, "there is a bird that has built her nest every spring, in the tall tree over the grave. It is a little pe-weet. They are not so fine singers as some others, but I have always loved them, because they belong to our earliest associations. When I used to lead you to school, up the hill-road by the Friends' Meeting-house, those birds would greet us from the fences and trees, every dewy morn-ing; and I remember so well the delight you used to express, when I could succeed in making you see that it was, indeed, no other than a little brown bird that had spoken the name of our elder sister so plainly, that they have ever since been associated with my pleasantest reminiscences of our childhood. What a blessed privilege to pass one's childish days in close communion with nature. The heart is so susceptible then to impressions of beauty—so free from everything which afterwards engrosses and lacerates its sensibilities! One gathers then many a gem to bear through life, many a bright glance from the benignant face of nature, to beam on the stormy hours of after years. I would not barter the recollections of my early childhood, for the united display of the cities of earth. I would not lose the delicious memories then gathered, of the deep wood, the running stream, the mossy rock, the valley, mountain side, and verdant plain, for all the wealth which art can boast. I value the exquisite productions of the sculptor and painter, but I *love* the works of God. One affords the highest pleasure to the mere human faculties, but the other exalts our affections to the angelic! When I hear mothers, who have come from cities to this glorious country, regretting the change on account of their children, I long to lead them forth, and show them the magnificence in which they may revel here. Feeble minds! that can compare the puny works of man to those of his Maker. I could better educate a child here, with a great volume of nature to expound to him, than in the pent city, with all its dusty libraries and elaborate preparations. I could draw his soul upward—I could purify his aspirations—I could instil the love of enjoying and creating beauty— I could teach him those great truths which ought to be the foundation of all education, better here, alone with nature, with a few choice books, and enough of society to call out the natural affections, than the most learned professor could, shut in his cloister. I count knowledge of things as they exist; I count a high reverence for the right—a strong reliance on truth—just perceptions of duty—a keen sense of the beautiful and harmonious, which God has created around us, and a profound adoration of Him, superior to the gross ideas, related in the languages of nations long extinct— to their corrupt mythology—their feeble attempts in science— their sanguinary wars. I would rather my son spent years, roaming among the sublime solitudes of the mountains and plains, studying the secret labors of nature, and her grand and beautiful productions, the Bible his only book, than the same length of time in becoming acquainted with the Greek or Latin tongue. I wish his affections drawn out thus, when I am gone, It will soothe the hardest pang of my early death, to know that he will love what I have loved and derived such happiness from. But you say I must not talk. Indeed, I feel that I cannot; let me lie down; the shadows of those tall trees are lengthening on the miniature forest below. If I could walk out with you an hour hence, we should look upon a sunset, gorgeous enough for the skies of Italy. But go you alone, and when you see the golden, purple, and crimson tints, changing and blending, fading and deepening, and feel that you can scarce restrain the emotions which the scene kindles in your bosom, think how often I have looked upon such, and wished that you were here to enjoy it with me. Draw the curtain, and let me look out upon the grass at my little elm. How gracefully it bends! I once thought to have seen it a majestic tree; but that will be for other eyes than mine."

CHAPTER XXIV

Such, and so heartwringing, were these last communions. I had never seen her so beautiful as she was in those days. Her mind, too, seemed to act with more than its usual strength of reason. It was thronged with images of beauty which took the most appropriate and eloquent forms of expression. There was a kind of painful pleasure in listening to these feebly enunciated thoughts and sentiments, which I could not deny myself.

I remember one bright day, when she felt unusually well, she was sitting up in the bed supported by pillows, and looking upon the growing world outside. She had just heard her little boy recite the Lord's Prayer, and dismissed him to play, when she turned suddenly to me, and said "To-day is the eighth anniversary of my wedding."

"Is it possible?" I said, struck by the painful thought that it must be the last she would ever see; but as we were accustomed to suppress our feelings in her presence, I remained silent.

"Yes, it is eight years to-day, and just about this hour, too," glancing at the clock, "since I stood by my husband's side with a heart overflowing with strength and hope. We were both young; I was but seventeen, and he some four years older. We had health, energy, intelligence enough to enjoy the highest pleasures within our reach, and, above all, that affection for each other, without which all these blessings would have been of little avail to secure happiness. Eight years! I spoke of it this morning, but it was so painful to John to recall the pleasant recollections of that day, that

I forbore. I feel strong now, and you must let me talk. Do you know we have never been acquainted since we were little girls?"

I looked up in surprise.

"I mean," she added, "that we have never enjoyed that full revelation of thought and feeling, which alone can constitute acquaintance between sisters. There has never been an opportunity for this till since you came here, and you have thus far been too much engrossed with other affections to admit of it. Do not think I speak reproachfully; I have rejoiced in your happiness, but the young wife and mother could hardly find time and affection to bestow, in those deep, heart-searching communings, which should make each thoroughly known to the other. There have been long years of event, and ages of emotion in the life of each, since we lived together unengrossed by our love for others. Now you must listen, and let me tell you something, such as my weak memory and weaker powers will permit, of those many years of separation.

"You remember the little home in the little village surrounded by mountains, where we first found ourselves. You remember one chilly, dark afternoon, when we returned from the small schoolhouse in the woods, we were met at the gate by an older schoolmate, a relative of the family, who told us to come softly in, for our mother was dying! You remember the awe which these words inspired, and the solemnity with which we were led through the tearful crowd collected in the room, to her bedside; and how we gazed with bursting hearts into her dim eyes, to which the full day already seemed faint twilight; how we took timidly hold of her hands, that were wandering in air to grasp the children she could no longer see. You remember how next morning, when you asked to go in and see her, she lay upon a hard board, straight and cold, and how we turned away from the pale face and leaden eyes, and refused to believe that it was our dear mother; how we stayed home from school, and wandered all that day about the silent house, scarcely speaking above a whisper, and occasionally peeped fearfully into the dark room; how the next day, mourning garments came; and a coffin that struck us with such dread we could not be brought to look on it, till a great crowd of people gathered about, and our father led us up, and asked us to look once again at our mother, before she was put in the cold earth. I recollect you were not tall enough, and he raised you in his arms by my side, and little Henry, still younger, looked down from his uncle's arms and lisped coaxingly to her to get up and take off her cap. A few minutes after, the coffin was closed and borne away! We followed it, and when it was covered in the grave, returned home, scarcely knowing what had happened, but having a dim impression that some great sorrow had come upon us.

"From that day we had no longer a home in common; when we met, it was as visitors. This was a great affliction to me, for our continual companionship had ripened in my older mind to warm attachment, and I was grieved to be denied its object. You were more easily satisfied with little Henry's company; though I remember no one's arrival ever gave you so much pleasure as mine. All your most charming resorts were shown me, all the choice mementos that had been laid carefully away since my last visit were brought forth, and many little things exchanged by way of remembrancers. Those were delightful visits that I paid you at grandfather's. The dark pine-tree that stood before the door used to play music that held us spell-bound many an hour, while we sat beneath it. I remember at these times, and when we lay in bed, while the rain was pattering on the roof close to us, you always began to talk of "ma," and expected her return. You used to ask me if I thought she would come back in the cap and night-gown she had on when she went away; and where she would stand when we first saw her. At last these visits ceased. We were wholly separated. You went many hundred miles from us all, with strangers, and the remaining four gathered once again under our father's roof. But no longer in the little village; we were now in a great city, and I was old enough to begin to learn that life had more painful realities than had come to us, when we were together. Seven years! what may not seven years — from nine to sixteen, from seven to fourteen — do for children such as we were? What did they, till we met again, bring us? what sorrow, keener than all that had gone before, in the loss of our last parent! to you, what oppression and bondage among heartless strangers! Those were dark volumes to be opened by gay-hearted girls, that we learned to read during those seven years: gloomy commentaries on the world in which we were left to make our way to happiness or ruin. Mine taught me to shrink continually from the world, to regard it as an enemy ever on the watch to destroy my peace, ever waiting with lies and deceit, to lead me away from my true path. The greatest blessing was, that I had a pretty clear perception of what this was. Many a poor girl who started under fairer auspices than myself, has made a total wreck. Since I have come to years of maturity, I have learned that our mother was gifted with a superior mind and great depth of purpose and feeling; and if we have struggled successfully against tides that have borne others to ruin, we owe praise and gratitude to Him who gave us such a parent. But I had some terrible trials in the great heartless city during those years! I remember one fierce conflict of four days, that came near destroying my reason. I have never been able to look back upon it without a shudder. On the one hand, misfortune and suffering among those who were dearer to me than my own life; on the other, ceaseless labor by day and night for a pittance which I tremble to think is now lessened by nearly half to thousands of unfortunate females, similarly situated. How could I escape the tempters, who never tired in spreading their diabolical nets for my weary feet? I will tell you the nature of this fierce trial some other day, when I am stronger. Let me hasten on now. When I was little more than fifteen, I received an offer of marriage from a young man who had shown himself an honest and firm friend from the first day of our acquaintance. He was several years my senior, the son of wealthy parents, and bore an unexceptionable character. All these things made him what the world calls a 'very desirable match.' Our friends thought it almost heaven-sent. Everybody was so pleased with my fortune that I too thought it must be good, and with much encouragement from others, and sanguine hopes of the increased happiness I should be able to afford those I loved. I finally entered into an engagement with him. But it did not require much reflection on my part, after this relation was established between us, to discover that the affection which should be the first and holiest motive to marriage, was wanting in me. All the other requisites of happiness — wealth, integrity, an agreeable person, and certainly as high an order of intelligence as most girls of fifteen look for, were present. But I soon saw that these would not do. Poor as I was, and welcome as would be the means of ease, and the opportunity of intellectual pursuits which I most craved, I could not perjure myself to obtain them. Better my two hands and a subsistence daily earned with them, I thought, than wealth, and a spirit oppressed with so great falsehood! So I told Mr. H. that I was convinced I should consult the happiness of both, by begging him to release me from the engagement. After many conversations and much reasoning, which continually strengthened my previous conviction of the right, I prevailed, and turned from the high anticipations of those few weeks again to my needle. But I must not linger over those days; in less than eighteen months I entered into the engagement which was fulfilled eight years ago to-day. It will soon be severed now. This was one of the heart. There was no wealth, no position superior to my own, but only those personal qualities which assured me that, without these, our happiness would be enhanced by a union. I loved my husband, and that was a stronger motive than all that had operated in the other case combined.

"During those eighteen months I had found another source of tranquillity, in higher and more clearly defined perceptions of religious duty than I had ever before experienced. I had found that there was positive and exalted happiness in approaching my Maker as a tender father and friend. And thanks be to Him, who deserves our most elevated affections, this never failed me in my hours of severest trial. It was a safeguard and shield. Armed with this newly awakened sentiment, I felt secure and quiet amid all temptations. Most young persons think their enjoyment of life will be diminished by an allegiance to the laws of christianity, but I think they are in error. Mine was infinitely increased! I wished every one to feel as I did. It was in this state of mind, and just after I had formed the engagement with my husband, that I met you after the lapse of those seven eventful years. Such a period, spent as that had been by you, not only in a natural but moral wilderness, away from society, away from schools, away from everything but the tyranny of a selfish, passionate woman, and that woman—oh most wonderful phenomenon!—that woman an Atheist—a defier of her God—had wrought startling changes in you. The timid, inquiring child from whom I had parted with such agonizing tears, met me almost a woman in stature, and with more than a woman's boldness of thought and speech;—they were an atheist's! Judge now—but no, you cannot; you never can until you are similarly situated, of the anguish I experienced on the first evening of our reünion, when, as we all knelt down, my heart overflowing with a gratitude which God alone could measure for your restoration to us, you walked away to the door, saying you wanted no part in such delusive mummery! I never remember to have felt a keener pang; and when, after much persuasion, I induced you, through your affection for me, to rejoin the circle and wait while thanks were offered and petitions put up for yourself, you turned impatiently away and requested that you might be made the subject of no more prayers until you saw the necessity of them. You remember, that our conversations almost always took the form of controversies; that I found you conversant with the works of Paine, Volney, Voltaire, and nearly the whole school of infidel writers, modern as well as early; that every consideration which I proposed was instantly gainsayed by an appeal to them, or by some fearless suggestion of your own mind. You had not only made these men your standard, but even exceeded their impiety, and by your impious reasoning, made up of the boldest conceptions and the most unshrinking conclusions, led yourself to renounce all belief. I was at last compelled to give up in despair, trusting to time and better influences to eradicate these frightful errors.

"A few weeks parted us again. I have sometimes, when looking over our past lives, compared ourselves to two helmless, rudderless ships, floating on the storm-wrought ocean. For a moment they approach each other, and seem as if they would journey on together, but the next, they are parted and driven about on the waste for years; perhaps never to meet again till they decay and sink into a common sepulchre. It has been almost so with us. We parted; you to seek the education and mental culture which should have been the work of earlier years; I to make such preparation as I might, for the great event before me. The next spring I was married. You know my husband had meantime visited this country, and returned a few weeks previous to our union, with such glowing descriptions of its beauty and advantages, that his father gathered the little means he had, and proposed that we should all start west together after our marriage. We did so, and it will be eight years in a few weeks (I may live to see the day), since we bade adieu to our friends and commenced our journey. This state at that time was thought, among the stable population of our mountain region, to be almost beyond the knowledge of civilized man. Our friends bade us farewell as if we were about to plunge into the deserts of the old world, instead of the richest and most beautiful region of the new.

"I rejoiced in that journey. It was the season of life fullest of hope and trust, and all nature seemed like me, to be exulting in the future that was opening before it. We journeyed several weeks through the blooming orchards and fields of the cultivated country, and at last plunged into the heavy forests of Ohio and Indiana. Here we sometimes slept in our waggon or on the ground, and took our meals in the woods. At last we emerged upon the great prairie which extends from the Wabash, west and north, nearly three hundred miles. Here the magnificence of the country to which we were bound began to appear. I remember, as we journeyed day after day across its heaving, verdant bosom, that I seemed to be living in a new world. All the noise, all the selfish hurry and turmoil in which my past years had been spent, faded away. They seemed as remote as if the barrier of eternity had been placed between me and them. A new creation was around me. The great, silent plain, with its still streams, its tender verdure, its lovely flowers, its timid birds and quadrupeds, shrinking away from our sight; its soft winds, its majestic storms—was a sublime spectacle! Occasionally a herd of deer bounded across our path, or a solitary pair of grouse, startled from their parental cares, rose and cleft the air like the arrows of their old pursuers; but save these we were alone, in silence broken only by our own voices. I thought how many ages that plain had been spread out beneath those soft skies and that genial sun; how its flowers had bloomed and faded, its grasses grown and decayed; how storms had swept over all its wide expanse, and the thunder echoed from its bosom; how the solemn winds of autumn had sighed over it, and the raging fires marched in unrestrained fury from one border to the other; how long all this power and magnificence had displayed itself unseen of any eye, save His who made it! How long all these mighty and beautiful phenomena had followed each other, and awoke no human emotion, appealed to no enlightened *soul*. Nature disporting with herself, frolicking in merriment, fading in sadness or raging in anger; the sole witness of her own acts!

"Then as we crossed the narrow, deep-worn trail of the dark people who had traversed it so long before us, I thought how much emotion had dwelt here; how much love, hospitality, friendship, and fierce hatred had grown, matured, and been extinguished here. How many fearful war-shouts had resounded; how many death fires had been kindled in the distant groves; how many wailings for the lost had mingled with the solemn winds.

"In imagination, I could still see files of dark warriors stealing silently along, unmindful of the flowers and the bright skies, the gay birds and the happy creatures who reveled in the rich world of vegetation around them; intent only upon the fierce butchery to which they were marching. And my blood used to chill under these fearful visions. But my husband enjoyed them. He had more sympathy with the stern and implacable in the Indian character than I, and he delighted to think of the free warriors roaming, fearless of their foes, fearless of storm or tempest, in search of their enemies. Later years have quenched much of this feeling in him, but he still loves those legends of the olden time.

"As we advanced into the midst of this immense prairie, our horses were tortured by a large fly that gathered in great numbers upon them, and drove them almost to madness. At length we were obliged to stop during the day, and travel all night. There were houses at long intervals, situated sometimes in the points of groves that projected into the plain, and sometimes several miles from the woodland. These were usually our stopping-places, where we remained during the day and then traveled on. My heart ached for the men. They could sleep little during the day, and two or three (there were five of them, you know) were obliged to be continually on foot at night to guide the horses. Their fatigue was almost insupportable. My husband has told me, that he was conscious of having often walked several rods at a time when he was asleep; that his eyes closed in spite of all his efforts to keep awake, and at length a stumble or a word from some of the party would startle him, and he would find himself walking along beside the team as usual. They were faithful creatures, those horses. You have caused and enjoyed many a hearty laugh at their expense; but if they had borne you patiently over nearly two thousand miles, of roads without bridges; traveled night and day with you, you would feel something of that sentiment which has often restrained me, when Tyler's peculiarities have set your powers of ridicule in operation.

"But we left the prairie at last; I was not sorry; neither could I rejoice, except for those who suffered more than I. But the long journey, the excitement attendant upon the strange features of the country, and the broken rest, were too much for me. When we reached the crossings of the Mackinaw, about thirteen miles from here, you know where it is, I was in a raging fever. We traveled on, however, for there was then no house where we could stop. Our people heard in some way that this 'claim' was for sale. They wished to buy an improved one — that is, one with a cabin in which we could live till a house was built, and with grain enough on the ground for the season's use. I have pointed out to you the very small, low cabin which we found here. There were also several acres of grain growing. We all liked the situation, and so a bargain was soon made with the owner, or the 'squatter,' as he termed himself, for his place. But there was one circumstance which was very awkward for us. He could not leave the larger cabin till autumn, and we were therefore obliged all to live in that little pen until our people could build another. I scarcely know how things went on those few weeks. I was sick and wretched in person; but at last the other cabin was finished, and we felt ourselves very comfortable in it. When the family of the 'squatter' left us, John and I moved into the old one, and lived there until the framed house was built. That was our first introduction to cabin life. The summer was considerably advanced when we arrived, and our people were soon engaged in the harvest. The grain was stacked in the cow-yard, for there were then no barns or outbuildings of any description. When the harvest was over, they began their preparations for carrying on farming more systematically the next year. They made fences, ploughed and sowed, and built a small log stable for their horses.

"I remember the whole land seemed to me a paradise that summer and autumn. The profusion of late flowers and wild fruits, the abundance of game, the richness of vegetation, the mildness of the climate, the sublime storms, and the soft musical winds, delighted me. Our men worked much in the woods, and I used at noon to take a small basket of dinner to them. The sound of their distant axes, and, as I drew nearer, of their cheerful voices, contrasted delightfully with the silence of the sleeping grove.

"We all had good health so far, and appetites that led to many jokes between ourselves about famine, et cet. You have now learned by experience how this climate acts on the appetite, and you may judge of the amount of food which nine persons, in this stage of acclimation, would consume. But we had plenty of grain stacked, and meats more delicious than the daintiest markets of the east afford, were abundant everywhere, so we only exulted in our fine health, and pursued our labors joyfully.

"The prairie below us where there are now so many pleasant farms, was then unsettled. There was no house on the south between us and the Mackinaw, and at the crossings of that stream was the only family whom I visited for the first two years. You ask if those were not lonely years. I answer that there were many, many hours when John and I talked of the friends we had left, when the cheerful social circles where we had sometimes met, were named with moistened eyes, and yet there was no day of them all when we would have returned and forsaken the land of our adoption. Much as we wished for the society of our absent friends, we could not have consented to exchange for it, the joys we had won in the new country. We loved everything in the new land too much for that. But I was telling you that the prairie was all unsettled when we came. I believe it remained so two years. The autumn fires raged then much more fiercely than now that they are trodden or partially fed. You cannot estimate, from what you now see, the sublimity and fury of those early conflagrations. One afternoon late in October, the prairie below us took fire by accident, or was set on fire by some one on the other side. There was little wind, and the flame came lazily over the grassy surface; it seemed as if a breath would extinguish it. It was a fine spectacle, however, to us newcomers, and we watched it occasionally, almost wishing that it might show a little more energy. No one thought of danger. Toward sunset the wind rose slightly and the fire increased; as darkness came, the breeze freshened till it became almost a tempest, and the plain around was a sea of roaring flames as far as the eye could reach. It daunted us a little, but was too sublime a spectacle to turn away from, till one of the family suggested that it came with such fury the stacks might be in danger. The thought was instantly acted upon, and every precaution taken to secure them, but vainly! The fire came on with such irresistible energy that, like the wind itself, it overleaped all barriers. In less than an hour, our grain was burned to ashes! The houses, farming utensils, et cet., were barely saved, and we were left in this thinly inhabited region with but a mouthful of bread stuff! It was a severe blow to us with our small finances, and the difficulty of procuring grain, independently of that.

"But I enjoyed that fire. The finest spectacle was when the danger had passed. While the stacks were burning more slowly, the flames swept furiously onward through those shrub oaks. That was a magnificent sight. They mounted quite to the tops of the tallest trees, and went roaring and cracking through the silent barrens with a noise that contrasted strangely with the usual stillness of the hour. The blackness and desolation of the following morning, and the reflection that we had lost all our grain, were painful consequents of such an entertainment. There was, however, no danger of real suffering. The greatest abundance of fine game abounded in our vicinity, and it could not be impossible, so we thought and said, to find something whereof to make bread. Our houses and other property were spared, and we were thankful.

"By the next summer the unnatural appetite which had beset us all, disappeared, and the succeeding stage of acclimation came on. Part of our number were prostrated with bilious fever, which in almost every case was followed by ague, and the others were visited with that cutaneous disease which you know sometimes takes the place of prostrating fevers. It is the safer process, but scarcely the more agreeable. Some of our people suffered extremely with it. Their arms and hands were perfectly denuded of skin, and in such a state, that, for two or three weeks, those who were not so afflicted had to feed them as if they were infants. My husband and I both underwent the severe ordeal of a long fever, succeeded by ague, but we came through, apparently with unimpaired constitutions. All recovered in time, and there has been little sickness among us

since, except the poor invalid sister, who seems to have been born
to suffer.

"Still we have had many seasons of trial. There has been more
or less sickness in the country every summer, and we cannot sit
down in our own homes in peace when our neighbors are afflicted.
I have sometimes rode one, two, or three miles every day, or every
alternate day, to visit a sick neighbor; and here our visits are not
calls. We go to perform the duties of nurse for a day or night, and
having no servants at home, are obliged to return as soon as possible,
and, notwithstanding our weariness, proceed at once to the cares
of the family. We had beside, as I have already informed you, many
strangers in our homes, some of whom were long and dangerously
ill while there; and these circumstances increased our burthens:
nevertheless we were happy. In the fall of the third year our little
boy came to cheer us with his beautiful presence. Oh that was a
happy day when I first heard myself spoken of as a mother, and
happier still were those that followed, as our darling grew under
our care. He is a brown boy now, since he has gone abroad so
much, but he was a beautiful babe. He had dark eyes and hair, and
a clear skin, with cheeks that deepened like the heart of the rose
whenever he slept. We moved into this house the next spring. I
had a great deal of labor to perform, and the dear child used to
sit and creep on the floor from morning till noon. Many a time,
when I have been too much engaged to attend to him, my ear has
been struck by the cessation of his prattle, and I have turned to
find his cheek pillowed upon the naked board, and his wearied
faculties lost in profound sleep. I have laid him on the bed, sometimes with smiles, sometimes with tears. I was seldom lonely now,
even when his father was away all the long days in the field or
wood. He was a world to me. Our society increased, too, about
the country. Many intelligent and excellent families came into our
neighborhood, and the little towns that had grown around us,
improved our social life very much. Still we were not so dependent
on society as you might suppose. The charms of the country, which
never tired with us, the delights of building a new home and
beautifying it ourselves, of having everything grow from nature,
under our own hands, and the pleasure we began to anticipate in
your arrival, were ample sources of happiness. Every tree and shrub
which we planted in our grounds was a companion, whose growth
it was delightful to watch. Every strawberry-bed that I discovered
about the house was counted on as a means of enjoyment when
we should all be once more assembled.

"I must be a dreamer, for I have had delightful visions of our wandering together long years hence, over these little spots, our children gathering the fruit, while we looked on and applauded their kind zeal. But that is all past now; I have striven to make my home pleasant. I have wrought within and about it harder, perhaps, than will ever be the lot of another. I have loved its natural and its cultivated beauties better, perhaps, than any one else can, and now I must leave them! It is hard, but hardest of all to leave my husband, who has shared these pleasures and tasks, and my boy, for whom we have most rejoiced to perform them. Yet I desire not to remain. The solace which, under lighter afflictions, I learned to draw from divine sources, is more precious now than ever; and though, to the human eye, I seem to have toiled through these twenty-five years to gain this spot in life, and my blessing is yet unenjoyed, still, I doubt not, it is best so. I have, perhaps, had my share of happiness. If I have endured bitter griefs, I have enjoyed intense emotions of pleasure. If I have buffeted storms and tempests, my sunshine has been proportionally bright. If I have been oppressed with cares and labors, my rest and freedom have brought delights enough to compensate for them. If I have been repeatedly and long separated from those I loved, I have felt the most unalloyed pleasure in meeting them. I would fain persuade myself that the two years have repaid all the ardent prayers I offered for the presence of my brothers and sisters, and that I am ready to depart and leave you all! Once I should have felt it my duty to bow with unqualified submission to my fate, as to a special expression of my Master's will. I should have attributed no part of it to the effect of natural causes which were left to human control. Now I feel otherwise. I have learned within the last few years to be wiser, though I humbly trust not less a christian. If my resignation is not entire and blind, it is because I feel that the responsibility of my early death rests on human beings, and that the will of the Almighty is expressed in it only so far as to remove me in kindness when repeated transgressions of His law have placed it out of my reach to be longer happy and useful. Do not weep. I am tired now; take away the pillows, and let me lie down. I have talked long, and yet have failed of relating half that I desire, or expressing what I feel. Bring me a rose from my favorite bush. I would have something fresh and beautiful to win repose after this long effort."

CHAPTER XXV

I never saw my sister so beautiful as she was at this period of her illness. But we knew it was the beauty which ushers in decay — the rich sunset which is soon followed by blackest night. And even so it proved. The last signs of emaciation began to appear as spring passed away. When the full strength of summer came, the beauty had departed from the wasting frame, the cheeks no longer wore the hectic hue. They faded and grew thinner each day as we looked upon them, till it seemed, when she slept, that mere emaciation must forbid her ever waking.

The summer began also to grow gloomy abroad. Tidings of disease came from every part of the great valley. Strangers from the states, south, east, north, and west of us, spoke of the suffering and death they had left at home, and witnessed along the way; and an unusual solemnity rested over the whole country. The heavens seemed no longer propitious. The sun poured down his scorching rays upon our great prairies; but no rain fell! Vegetation began to parch; the heavy dews grew lighter and the heat more intense. My sister's sufferings were greatly enhanced by the hot and unrefreshed state of the atmosphere. She pined for showers, for the freshness, beauty, and odors which they used to awaken in the world around her. She grew weaker daily, and expressed a clear conviction that she should not live to see the month of August. At her request, a large Bible was procured for her son, and a letter which she had addressed to him while she was yet able to hold a pen, fastened among its leaves. There was something deeply touching in the hope which led to this act. She trusted that this voice speaking from a mother's grave, to a son whom she had so dearly loved, might link his affections to her in after years; might be as a spoken admonition to him when temptations crowded his future path. The beautiful lines beginning with

> "Remember, love, who gave thee this,
> When other years shall come,"

were inscribed by his father on a blank leaf.

She loved the scriptures, and frequently asked to hear the sixteenth chapter of John read. Its exalted and earnest promise cheered and strengthened her. The month of July drew toward a close, and we could not but see that her days were numbered. The form that had once been so elastic, was wasted to a shadow; the limbs that had never tired were feeble as an infant's; the wan face with its large, sunken eyes, and passionless expression, all told that a period would soon come to her sufferings and our fears. She was restless; she pined to be abroad, where she could see the face of nature and the familiar objects she had so cherished. Her husband would bear her in his arms to the shade of the old oak before the door, where she would sit while the soft air played over her pale brow, and look upon her favorite shrubs and flowers with a kind of mournful affection as if she would fain linger yet a little while among them. There was one young rose-tree which she had set with her own hands the year before in the corner of the yard. It was luxuriant and full of vigor; she begged it might bear her name and never be removed. "You cannot think," she said one day, "how much I have loved these flowers. When the beautiful wilderness lay about our home, they were like friends of the olden time to us; familiar voices from a far land. Everything was new to us here. The trees were not such as we had played beneath in childhood; the flowers were strangers; the very grasses seemed to belong to another clime. It is true there were glory and beauty in them all, but the heart cannot rejoice in what is altogether strange. I have often thought if I were placed in a world where nothing but exquisite loveliness and forms of beauty grew around me, I should still crave some familiar object, however plain; something which would be a visible link to the bygone. These flowers were such; many a long day, when I have been all alone, I have stolen out in some leisure moment, and stood by them and dreamed pleasant dreams of the years long gone. Here was the same rose which I had thought it such a privilege to pluck and carry to school or to praying. It had the same odor, the same clustering petals, the same deep tint nestled in its dewy recesses, and why should I not love it! It was a pleasant remembrancer of the past; the only one I had in all the world of nature. I nursed them as children, watched their growth and exulted in their beauty, and the love of them will go with me to my last resting-place.

"It is a strange thing," she added after a pause, "this undying desire of the heart for something which it has before known and loved. I have thought much of late, whether it does not prefigure a renion with the objects of our earthly affections in the spirit land! Those who have loved strongly here must be changed in their whole nature, if they enjoy the happiness which we picture, and yet find there none who have shared their human affection. I sometimes feel convinced that we shall know and love each other there; but then—*if we found not all!*—if some whom we have loved and pitied; some for whom we have struggled and prayed, for whom we could have laid down our lives, were not among the rejoicing throng! Oh, it is a terrible thought! it is the one which most pains me now, till I reflect that whatever is, is best. It sometimes occurs to me that the beatification of the just made perfect will consist principally in arriving at such wisdom, such an exaltation of mind over feeling, that we shall recognize all things in the economy of the Divine ruler to be right. If the mind be thus elevated over our present affections, we shall feel no pain in the absence of those whom we have loved on earth. But it is difficult to conceive such a state while we are here."

Such were some of the conversations of these last days. They were uttered in so low a tone, that the rustling of the leaves or the chirping of a bird would drown their sound. But we had listened so long, with all our senses sharpened; had become so accustomed to gather the import of her speech, from the play of the wasted lips, and the expression of her languid eyes, that it was no longer difficult to understand her perfectly. One day, when her husband was sitting alone by her couch, she asked him for the hymn book. Her hands had scarcely strength to support it while she turned the leaves slowly, and, at length, opening to that sublime burial piece, commencing

"Unveil they bosom, faithful tomb,"

she handed it back, with a request that it might be sung at her funeral. "It is an impressive poem," she said, "and expresses the hopes in which I die. I pray daily that they may become yours, and that you may bring our boy up to entertain them." Her last hours with her son were very touching. She felt an anxiety which was intensely painful to us, to impress a recollection of herself upon his young memory. Sometimes she despaired, and her lamentations were the only words of murmuring we ever heard. "He will forget me," she would say. "He is too young! Oh if I could but have lived long enough to be assured of a place in the affections of the man whom I have borne. If I could feel that during his life, the rec- ollection of his dying mother would be to him what mine has been to me, a safeguard against temptation, a shield against the unholy allurements of a world in which so much that is evil must be resisted! But I fear he will lose it! his mind is too elastic. Yet I must submit to it. I only ask that you will all aid in the execution of my wishes after I am gone. You will have many opportunities to speak of me, and recall his young faculties to the effort of remembering me, as

I have been for the last year. I would rather his memory bore its impress from my well and happy days, but that is impossible."

The last days of July were now drawing on; and though there was no change, other than that which had been manifest from day to day, for several weeks, still our beloved invalid assured us that she should not live to see August. The thirtieth of July was Sunday, and a solemn day it was with us. The angel of death seemed visibly hovering over the silent house. Our babe, usually a lively, happy little fellow, full of laugh and prattle, was somewhat unwell, so that even his pleasant voice was seldom heard in the silent rooms. The few words that we spoke were uttered in low tones; the table was laid very quietly, and its contents removed each time almost untouched. The day was excessively warm and dry. "Oh!" exclaimed the suffering invalid, "shall I never see another pleasant shower fall upon the fair earth? shall I never again inhale the delicious odors of reviving grass, and flowers, and trees; nor hear the happy songs of birds when the clouds are fading away in the distant sky? How much I long for this once more. Take me out, John; let me breathe once more beneath the open sky!" Towards night a slight dew began to gather upon her forehead. It chilled me, as if a mountain of ice had fallen beside me. It was a sign which I knew too surely foretold the fulfilment of her painful prophecy. I passed my hand softly over her brow. It was cold and deathlike. Then I knew the dart had gone forth—the struggle had commenced. Death was among us! She smiled faintly as I removed my hand.

"Is it moist?" she whispered. Tears were my only reply. "Then I have not much longer to suffer. Let them all go to bed; I shall see them to-morrow morning." I sat at her side all night! As the dark hours flew by the death damp gathered in cold drops upon her brow, her large lustrous eyes grew dim, and her breath came more hurriedly. She was restless. Many times during the night I raised her from her recumbent position; but she soon returned to it, weary and exhausted. Oh, that was such a vigil as I hope never to keep again! When morning came she was apparently the same. Breakfast was set, but it was a mere form. Our boy seemed more unwell, and claimed much of my attention; still I scarcely left her couch. She spoke little. About nine o'clock she said to her husband, "Between eleven and twelve I shall cross Jordan." It was even so. She was conscious when the last moment approached, and turning her dim eyes toward the clock, with a faint smile, extended her hands to us. Her face suddenly blanched—her white lips parted an instant—and all was over! Our long-dreaded trial had come.

The patient spirit, to whose wants we had ministered so anxiously, had fled!

Fond and faithful sister! How often thy memory steals on these distant hours! How often thy griefs and trials rise in painful array before me! How jealously memory treasures every unkind word or look I gave thee; and how faithfully does she set them before me, now, when to recall them is impossible, when the wound which they inflicted is no longer within my healing, when all the arts which the tenderest affection can suggest are impotent to procure the forgiveness that could alone silence regret. Thy tomb is far away from me! The silence and beauty thou so much lovedst are around thee! The winds of spring bear the same delicious odors over thy couch that played around thee years ago; the foliage is as bright as when it danced before thy rejoicing eyes, the stream winds as softly by, as when thy light footsteps trod its verdant bank.

> "There, through the long, long summer hours,
>   The golden light doth lie;
> And thick young herbs, and groups of flowers,
>   Stand in their beauty by.
>
> "The oriole doth build and tell
> His love tale close beside thy cell,
>   The idle butterfly
> Doth rest him there, and there are heard
> The housewife bee and humming-bird."

The solemn winds of autumn moan around thee, and bear from thy overshadowing canopy of boughs, rich offerings to thy tomb! We buried thee with many and bitter tears: we trust in the faith which so exalted thee above thy trials, to meet thee, where tears are all wiped away, where there shall be no more sorrow, neither any sin, nor any pain.

CHAPTER XXVI

My sister's death was a severe affliction to me. Much as we had been separated by the events of our early years, our hearts had grown together by the strongest bonds of sisterly love. We had looked forward to an unbroken union, in the beautiful country whither she had led us, and now I was there, but she was gone forever. Much and bitterly did I grieve over the dreadful void left in our circle by her death. But our little boy's health soon claimed attention. He did not recover, as I had trusted he would, and when the first few days were past, he seemed so much indisposed, that a physician was summoned, and all our energies directed to his restoration. I was too ignorant of children to appreciate his true condition, and the blow which had just fallen, instead of preparing me for a heavier one, seemed rather to be a security against further affliction. While, therefore, I hovered around the sick couch of our babe, sorrowing over his sufferings, which my ignorance did not permit me to appreciate, and anxious beyond the power of language, to see him joyous and happy again, and hear his musical voice, breaking upon my silent hours of grief, I never dreamed that it would not be so. True, I saw him waste day by day. I saw the fair face grow thin, the vigorous limbs feeble and tiny, the bright red lips pale and distorted with suffering. His large black eyes, in which love, delight, and wonder were used to reign alternately, now wore only the sorrowing look which tells of pain; and his fair brow was contracted to a slight frown, as if he would fain resist the infliction. Yet notwithstanding all this, I never dreamed that he could die. It was strange, it now seems incredible to my own mind, looking back upon that awful period, that I could have been so blind to a language which afterwards seemed to have inscribed itself, in letters of fire, upon my heart. Yet so it was; and many a young mother, who has entered upon her holy office, as I did, with no acquaintance with infant life, either practical or theoretical, will bear witness, that even a mother's instincts are all too feeble, to be trusted without knowledge. Our boy never grew better; he sunk from the time of my sister's death, and spite of all that skill and tenderness could do, just two weeks from the day on which her life closed, he yielded his, and we were wholly bereft. Even to the day of his death, I did not anticipate the event. It is true, I had fears, anxieties, sympathy, which only a mother can feel, but preëminent over all these, there was a *hope*, so disguised by its very strength, that I did not recognize its true character. When, therefore, the kind doctor, who had stolen an hour from his arduous duties, to spend it with us, said to one of those present, that "the little sufferer would soon be released," his words seemed to dry the very springs of life within me. I had no word to say, no tear to shed, but I gazed upon the little panting form, and glassy eye, with every faculty suspended by that dreadful sentence. In half an hour, I was a childless mother! Such alone can judge my feelings!

My previous affliction was utterly forgotten.

Who shall ever tell the bitter, the agonizing pangs, that rend the very bonds of life, when a mother stands by the cold clay of her only child! What thronging recollections come of happy hours, and shouts of joyous laughter, and peals of merry music, which earth will never again afford her ear; and then, oh agony beyond comparison, of pain which she has not alleviated, or perhaps has caused, of grief which she has not soothed, of sadness which she has not cheered, of words spoken in impatience, when they should have been uttered in love, of little pleasures denied, when they should have been granted, of mortal agony which she could not share, and Death descending in grim tyranny upon the little sufferer, who is all unconscious of his approach. God grant I may never see another such a night, as that which closed the life to which my own was so closely linked! There he lay, in his little crib, where I had so often frolicked with him, the lips now all cold and leaden, which, in his last agony, had called imploringly on me, by the dearest name to which the heart of woman ever responds; the eyes, which had so often looked into mine, overflowing with merriment, with silent wonder, of appealing tears, closed forever. What could I do? How impotent is every form of expression, which grief can take, to relieve the heart oppressed with such a burthen.

Again the spot where we had stood so few brief days before was visited. The little coffin which seemed to carry my very heart into the earth with it, was lowered close beside my sister's grave; but the latter had not now power to call forth a single tear. We turned away. The deserted house stood before us: its doors were closed, its windows all silent, its neglected vines climbing in untrained profusion over the silent walls. At any other time it would have unsealed all the fountains of emotion within me; now I scarcely recognized it as an object connected with my feelings. The deepest chord of my heart was vibrating to the last fierce blow, and no lighter touch could waken its other strings.

But the home whence our darling was forever gone! Oh who shall describe its desolation! who shall ever tell what a mother feels when she returns to her silent house from the new-made grave of her only child? How the practised ear will listen for the accustomed greeting; how the eye will wander to the door for the merry face that was wont to come peeping in; and then what agony, when some favorite toy is turned from the place where it was hidden by those little hands which you never more may clasp, which will never again wander in playful affection over your face and neck! The little garments which you have not had the heart to put away from your sight, hang about your room as they did in happier days. Here is one perhaps in which the little departed breathed away his life, and there another whose bright colors and tasteful fashion carry your aching heart back to the days when all was blithesome promise and intense happiness. I shall never forget the pang that wrung my bosom when one morning, two or three weeks after we were alone, I found a toy of pine wood indented all over with the print of small teeth. The last hand that had touched it was my babe's, its familiar form and bruised surface brought the happy little owner so strongly before me, that I seemed to live the terrible parting over again.

CHAPTER XXVII

The close of this summer found our home a melancholy one. Days of agony, and nights of delicious visions that made the morning sorrowful, wore slowly away. Abroad, the gloom still deepened. The sickness which had begun early to prevail in various parts of the country, increased in strength and malignancy. The longer the drought held, the more fatal grew its ravages and the more cheerless the aspect of the whole land. Vegetation was parched to ashes. The dews no longer fell; the thirsty earth gaped under the merciless sun, and the trodden roads were piled with dust, so that every breath of wind which swept across them and every vehicle that passed along raised a blinding cloud. The skies seemed to have shut their chambers of mercy and to have no relenting toward the blighted earth. For long, long weeks, the heavens were watched for a cloud or some sign of mercy, but in vain. A hard metallic glare pervaded the whole arch, an impassable barrier to the blessings we so much craved. Meantime pain, disease, and death were stalking abroad. The pestilence claimed its victims in almost every house. In some the whole family was prostrated, and the sufferers were dependent on the kindness of their distant neighbors to minister to their wants. The fevers took their most malignant and fatal character in the "bottom lands." These, as the name indicates, are the low lands bordering the streams. On some of the larger watercourses they are very extensive, and on all they have a character which strongly distinguishes them from the prairies and barrens above. They are generally wooded. On most of those bordering the large rivers, the growth is extremely dense and heavy. Gigantic trees shoot up on the rich earth, made by the spring floods of every season, and weave their heavy branches above into a dense canopy which the sun can scarcely penetrate. On the black soil below, which is often ten, twelve, or fifteen feet in depth, and of the finest loam, vegetation riots in unbounded energy. Immense quantities are produced, the decay of which, with the heavy foliage of the trees, generates vast volumes of miasmata. The high bluffs then which border these teeming lands, together with the dense wood that covers them, prevent the circulation of the purer air from the uplands, and leave all the causes of disease to take their most concentrated forms among the unfortunate settlers. Most of the families living on these tracts were French and German settlers. The former are the remnants of the old trading companies, the latter more recent emigrants. There are few Americans among them. They live for the most part in cabins of the poorest description, and their general habits are little conducive to health. Here therefore, at this fated period, the pestilence found its readiest and most numerous victims. My husband sometimes rode through these regions, and frequently found houses in which every member of the family was sick; so that it was a blessing for a stranger to call and hand them a cup of water. In these districts individuals were found lying in all stages of disease. Some had never been seen by a physician; some were pronounced to have the yellow fever, and the few that recovered wore a ghastly sallow hue that was frightful to behold, as they crept about their death-stricken homes. One could ride miles through these dark woods, the steady sun when it poured through the leaves heating the still air almost to suffocation, and pass on his route many cabins apparently deserted; but on entering he found two or three, or perhaps a greater number of persons lying in the same dark room, tossing and raging in the various stages of consuming fever. It was frightful to hear of, and still more so to witness their condition.

But suffering and mortality were not confirmed to these gloomy districts. They spread throughout the entire country. Our little village was one of the last spots visited, but it paid its tribute in the loss of one of its most accomplished and excellent women, and the severe illness of many other citizens. On the eighteenth of September, the day of the great eclipse, two infants, twin daughters of our village teacher, were buried. I remember well the gloom of that afternoon. It was easy to conceive how in periods of affliction and calamity the benighted nations that had lived here before us should construe such an impressive phenomenon into an expression of anger by the Great Spirit. The prolonged and unnatural dark-

ness, and the alarm which prevails among the lower animals following the impression already produced upon the mind, might well
be considered as evidences of displeasure in the Power that rules
the elements. We trusted that some change would be wrought in
the atmosphere by this great event, that would break the dreadful
monotony of drought. There were but three or four wells in the
village that afforded any water, and the earth seemed actually consuming under the fiery orb, now for a brief space hidden from our
weary eyes. Not a drop of rain had fallen for near seven weeks,
and for a previous period of nearly twice that length the few showers
that had descended were barely sufficient to saturate the dust. But
our hopes were vain; the shadow passed from the sun, and he rode
out glaring and bright as ever in the relentless heavens. Gloom
and despair brooded over everything. Nature seemed about to light
her own funeral pile. People walked slowly about with countenances
darkened by their own griefs, or saddened with sympathy for their
neighbors. One met with nothing cheerful anywhere. I had on my
part no wish to have it otherwise. The wide-spread sadness har-
monized well with my feelings. The loss of my boy, and this loneliness, heightened by the previous death of my sister, made me
shrink from everything like joyousness in the natural or human
world. If my mind were won from its burthen for a moment by
books or conversation, it bowed the next, more painfully and ines-
capably than before. I could not get my own consent to resign
those whom all my griefs could never recall; and thus my days
wore away under the ceaseless gnawings of the bitterest and keenest
emotions. The unaffectedly good pastor of the church which we
attended, handed me from time to time many books, the perusal
of which he thought would tend to soothe feelings so deeply
wounded; but while I appreciated his kindness, and enjoyed a few
hours of comparative tranquillity over the pages of his choice, still
I found nothing of the peace and resignation which I had often
seen others manifest under similar afflictions. One afternoon when
I had exhausted the solace of tears over recollections of my lost
babe, the sublime consolations with which the Psalmist hushed his
griefs under a like affliction, occurred to my mind with unusual
force: "I shall go to him, but he shall not return to me." The
recollection of these words drew me to a more diligent and frequent
reading of the scriptures, a new set of faculties was called into
action, and the cloud began to pass away. From that time there
was a new element mingled with my grief—one which robbed it
of its fiercest power, softened its sterner lineaments, lighted its

darkest depths. I no longer brooded in despairing silence over my sorrows. I felt that there were infinite love and infinite pity in the divine Mind, and there was a solace which words can never describe in uttering them before Him. But the comfort which I found was no miraculous shining forth of anything external to myself; it was no everflowing fountain which poured itself out, independent of my own state of mind; such as many seem to have found, but simply a more exalted action of some powers which I had always possessed, and a partial subduing of others. The newly acquired supremacy of those which directed my thoughts heavenward, which made the departed, objects of benignant hope instead of black despair, could be overthrown. I found no power superior to my own mind, pulling down the one and setting up the other—it depended on myself. I found no perpetual source of joy flowing continually around me, but only one to which I could resort when I governed my feelings carefully, and sought it earnestly. But this was all that I desired, it was all that I could believe true—*it was sufficient.*

The pure and exquisitely beautiful sermons of our pastor, to which I had before listened with an intellectual pleasure merely, had now a higher import, a loftier mission to my mind. The sublime truths were interesting on other accounts than the chasteness and simplicity of the language in which they were presented. In truth I believed I had attained what I had always heard talked of as a great mystery, an incomprehensible blessing, viz., a religious state of mind. A blessing it certainly was to me. Its benignant aspect shone far over the future. It gave me strength and hopefulness, and while it lightened the present burthen, was itself a preparation for such as the future might bring.

Thus the heaviest afflictions on the one hand, and cheering hopes on the other, closed the second year of Life in the Prairie Land.

PART II

Prairie Land is tenanted by numerous varieties of native birds and animals. Among the former I have already mentioned the quail, the grouse, turkey, buzzard, and many others. Among the latter are many whose habits and characters contribute not a little to the interest which the country possesses for the lovers of humor or adventure. One of these is a little ground inhabitant of the prairies, bearing the uneuphonic cognomen of the "Gopher," and a passionate devotee of subterranean architecture. He is a small personage, not much exceeding in size the large wharf rat; wears a very compact coat of dark satiny fur, unequaled for fineness and beauty; a long tail, a sharp nose, and a pouch, or sack, outside each cheek, opening close to the corners of his mouth, in which he transports the refuse of his labors. He must have the most implicit faith in the strength of his genius; for he never suspends the cultivation of it for a day. If he is ejected from premises which he has improved, he never mourns his loss, nor institutes legal proceedings to recover damages, but, with unabated energy, seeks another site and commences anew. He is both sagacious and suspicious; and, in all his plans, manifests plainly a desire not to be unceremoniously intruded on. Thus, when he finds an eligible site, he proceeds, like all settlers in new countries, to break ground; but, having gone under the turf, he forthwith lays himself out to elude pursuit. Down he goes, crooking and bending his path, now straight, now obliquely, for five or six feet. It is not known that, at the end of this labyrinth, he applies his thumb to the extremity of his nasal organ, and looks contemptuously back; but it is presumable that he enjoys something of the feeling which leads to this gesture in biped builders; for he immediately turns toward the surface in another direction, and often extends his researches a fourth or a half mile within a few feet of it. At points, not many rods distant from each other, he emerges with his sacks filled with earth, empties their contents, and goes back to reload; but, from each of these points, he makes a winding departure as at first. Thus the little brown hillocks which he throws up, are only indications of his vicinity, but afford little clue to his immediate whereabouts. These deposits are often found

in great numbers together, forming a little village, in the subterranean streets of which it is not difficult to imagine many pleasant
incidents, when toil is relaxed, and the social feelings come into
play.

I remember one of these little towns, which must have contained
near three hundred little dark mounds on the space of an acre.
They looked very social and pleasant, and were calculated, withal,
to excite one's humor, when, on inquiring of a boy, in the midst
of them, for the town of ———, well known to eastern capitalists,
he answered, with a grin, "Why, this *hyur* is it, don't you see the
stakes?" Besides the Gopher settlement, there were two houses in
sight, one about a mile, the other half that distance from us, in
opposite directions.

The fox inhabits the prairie country, and is very much such a
fox there as elsewhere, levying contributions on domestic poultry-
yards, when it is expedient, and, in default of these, making the
most unscrupulous sallies against the grouse, quails, and other featured neighbors of his. He burrows in the copses which skirt the
plains, in the bluffs that border streams, and on the sides of the
most elevated swells in large prairies. Hunting him is a sport much
relished in the winter season.

The prairie dog formerly dwelt here, but he has retired with
the Indian, and is now scarcely found east of the Mississippi. He
was a gentle, gregarious, social tenant of this beautiful wilderness,
and seems, by some strange adhesion to the natives, to have fled
with them, while many other animals remained.

CHAPTER II

There are two species of native wolf found on the prairies. One
is the small red wolf, a comparatively harmless animal, rarely at-
tacking anything about the farm but sheep or small pigs. But he
is a noisy neighbor in the night. Congregated in large troops, they
trot off from one point to any other they desire to reach, and never,
for a single moment on the way, suspend the growling, barking,
yelping, and whining, in which they utter themselves in different
moods. I remember when I had lain on a sick bed for several days,
without sleep, to have fallen into a doze about midnight, and been
awakened by a band of these marauders passing under my window.
There must have been a large number of them, for the noise was
almost deafening while they passed the house. A party of maniacs,

of all ages and sexes, roaming the country, could scarcely have produced a greater variety and confusion of noises. It was an evil sound to steal upon one's slumbers, and, to my disturbed mind, boded no good. The next day we were informed that their wanderings had terminated in a sheep-fold, about a mile beyond us. The slaughter was complete, not one of the terrified innocents having escaped. This, however, was an uncommon occurrence. During a residence of four years I never heard of a similar one.

The large grey wolf is much more ferocious; when pressed by hunger, he not unfrequently attacks men. Many cases are related of travelers who have arrived pale and breathless at some cabin on the borders of a large prairie, their lives having been saved only by the speed of their horses. The ravening, famished wolf has hung upon their heels for miles and at last been foiled only to return with deeper rage and desperation to the solitary plain! Woe, then, to the unarmed traveler who next crosses his path! He sees his death warrant in the glaring eye and gaunt, foaming mouth.

In the early period of white settlements, the traveler was sometimes startled by coming upon the bleached bones and knotted scalp of some unfortunate, who had perished thus terribly. But these are now tales of the past. The supremacy of man is less disputed by these prowling marauders, as his dwellings multiply, and his means of invading their territory grow more formidable. Occasionally, however, when hunger makes them desperate, they compel the unarmed traveler to stake his life upon the speed of his horse, or, in default of this, upon the best defence he can make. I was informed by a gentleman that he was attacked so late as the summer of 1839, by a gang of these hungry fellows, in the midst of a prairie twenty-two miles in extent. One of his horses was sick, and very much emaciated, and he was without arms of any kind except a large club, which had been accidentally left in his waggon. He confessed that when he saw the hungry troop making toward him, and looked upon his feeble horse, and around on the empty waggon, he felt that there were many conditions more enviable than his. On they came, and for want of better tactics, directed all their forces against him. He was a large and very powerful man, and having previously made such preparations as the circumstances permitted, he gave his startled horses the rein, and seizing the club, addressed himself solely to defending the waggon. He dealt his blows with so much vigor and rapidity, that what with the progress made by the team, and the bruised heads and feet they bore down from each assault, they at length gave over, and parted company with him; but not without many looks and growls, which seemed to threaten dire vengeance, should they ever meet him in a more helpless state.

A most melancholy occurrence took place not far from us in the winter of '38-9, to which these lawless animals contributed; though how far could never be correctly ascertained. A poor fellow, laboring under temporary derangement, left his dwelling early one cold evening when the snow was two or three inches in depth, and still falling fast; and although the most diligent search was made for several days, no knowledge of him was obtained till the following spring, when on ploughing a neighboring corn-field, his bones were found scattered over it, peeled of most of their flesh, and exhibiting thrilling proof that after death, if not before, his limbs had been torn by these merciless animals.

In the early years of the settlement such painful events not unfrequently startled the inmates of the rude cabins which bordered the prairies. There were few other ferocious animals to disturb the quiet of the settlers. Occasionally a catamount or panther was found in the dark, wooded bottoms; but the treeless plains were never visited by them. There the wolf seems to have been undisputed monarch, and, like the hyena of the desert, when living prey was not at hand, he rifled the tomb of its sacred trust.

An incident of this kind, connected with the first settlement on one of the most beautiful prairies in the state, had a thrilling interest as it was communicated to me.

The great road from the northern to the southern extremities of the state passes, for the most part, over large prairies. These are sometimes divided by groves two or three miles in extent, sometimes by open, sparsely timbered tracts, called barrens, and sometimes by a mere thread of timber, towering above the swelling plain, showing a dark green line at the distance of miles, the first glimpse of which often elicits a cheerful "land ho" from travelers who are unaccustomed to these long voyages by *terra firma*. This road intersects at Peoria the Illinois river, with which it runs nearly parallel for sixty or seventy miles, at a distance varying from four to eight, ten, and fifteen miles from the stream. The wood which crowns the bluffs of the stream stretches back at frequent intervals in long lines, and fringes the plains over which the road passes. These groves are generally very beautiful. They are usually seen on the high swells of the prairies, their outlines clearly defined on the horizon, long before you reach them. Their edges are bordered with the plum, hazel, and other fruit-bearing trees, and shrubs, which are frequented by birds, hares, squirrels, et cet. The music, life and freshness of these woodlands, together with their utility to the husbandman, led the early settlers to select them as the sites of their new homes. There the cabin was laid up under the spreading boughs of the outermost trees; and there the hardy frontiersman placed his family, remote from every artificial means of comfort, "alone with nature," rich, beautiful, majestic, nature in the silent prairie land.

CHAPTER III

It was at one of these spots that the incident referred to took place. On the northern side of a prairie, eighteen miles in extent, two groves approach within a short distance of each other from the east and west. They lie on a lofty swell of land and are visible many miles away. The plain between these dark green promontories is smooth as the unruffled sea, and you fancy as you look upon its quiet outline, while the tree-tops toss, and swell against the clear blue sky, that the smallest object would be discernible. Presently a short dark line rises against the light, and as the coach toils over swell after swell, and brings you nearer the object, it grows distinct, permanent, and bold, and fastens itself with a strange pertinacity on the eye and mind. It concentrates your wandering thoughts, and you wonder what could have led to the construction of such an object on that spot. No dwelling or other tenement is visible, and the green wall of the western grove rises apparently a full mile from it. There it stands without proportion or symmetry, its harsh angles unrelieved by a single shrub, its silent walls brown with the storms of years. It is a tomb! Farther back in the grove, stands a house near which its silent tenant lived and died.

Long before these lands were vacated by the Indians, a settler came hither from the eastward, with his family. He was roving through these beautiful gardens in search of a spot whereon to make his home. One morning his white-topped waggon entered the southern border of this large prairie, and, all day, was seen by the wondering Indians at the grove, to rise and fall slowly among the green swells, coming nearer and nearer, till at nightfall it halted on the line where this solitary tomb now stands. Here the travelers encamped, and one who has visited the spot, will not wonder that when the patriarch had seen the next sun rise on the scene before him, he declared their journeyings ended! A site was selected in the grove for their cabin, the logs were felled, and laid up by the father and his sons, and a frontier home soon sent its smoke curling through the overhanging boughs. Their only neighbors were the rambling Indians who, in their excursions from the north and south, always halted at this grove. They had no domestic animals save the faithful cattle that had drawn them and a dog.

For many months after the cabin was built they depended on wild game and fruits for subsistence. The rifle of the father brought down abundant supplies of deer and grouse, and the smaller members of the family could trap the quail, gather berries and plums, and beat the hazel and nut trees.

The wife and mother wrought patiently for those she loved. Her busy hands kept a well ordered home during the day, and at night, they plied the needle to the wardrobe of her little household band. It was already scanty, and materials to replace the worn-out garments were far away, and would cost what she had not to give. When one was worn beyond the resuscitating powers of her needle, its place was supplied as well as might be, by the skins which they had taken from their game.

Sunrise and evening twilight found the father at his labors. He had no harvest that year, but if he would reap the next, much preparation must be made before the winter came. First, the turf was broken where he proposed to plant his corn, rails were next made and laid around it, some of the native hay was gathered and piled up at the corner of his cabin, and a little garden fenced and ploughed. When all these things were done, there yet remained the journey to the nearest settlement for winter goods and grains, and for the cow, which could not longer be dispensed with. When all was ready, the father and his eldest son started in the emigrant waggon, and were absent many days, during each of which the mother and her little children—protected, if danger came, only by the dog—looked anxiously out upon the great prairie, now embrowned by the frosts of autumn, and wondered when they would return. There were few travelers then in those uninhabited plains. Day after day passed, and no sign of life was visible on the plain, save the deer bounding among its crisp herbage, or the famished wolf, rushing madly against the winds which bore the scent of prey. The intense sunshine which flooded this swaying sea, was now softened by the hazy atmosphere peculiar to those plains in the autumn months, the flowers were all dead, the trees disrobed, and a wild, vast desolation, which penetrated the soul of the lone woman, seemed hovering over the face of her new home.

On the fifth day, a party of Sauk warriors, plumed and painted, entered her dwelling. Her heart beat quick, and her eye glanced wildly toward her little ones, as their swarthy figures darkened the door; but a moment restored her self-possession. She knew they were not enemies, and felt secure in her very helplessness. They had not lived much among the whites, and it requires some teaching to induce the savage to fall on a helpless person who is not his foe. With the few words and signs which she had acquired, she entered into conversation with them, and learned that they were on their way to give battle to the Kaskaskias and Peorias. Here was a new cause of solicitude; her husband's road lay through the battle-ground, and who could tell what savages, seeking blood, might do? or what would be his fate, should he fall between the hostile parties! Offering them such hospitality as her poor home afforded, and praying that it might purchase the safety of the absent, she signified her hopes and fears, and watched their retreating footsteps with a boding heart.

All day she bent her eyes to scan the plain, but nothing met her search save the forms of the retreating warriors, which grew dimmer with distance and the fading light, till at length they were wholly lost. With aching head and anxious heart she put her little ones to bed; and when they slept, she rose and looked anxiously out upon the night. Black broken clouds were driving across the heavens at a fearful rate, and the wind rushed through the naked trees, and howled around her chimney, like some evil spirit demanding sacrifice.

The only window of her cabin looks over the plain; and there she stands gazing as if the daylight rested on it, and she hoped each moment to see the long wished-for object heave in sight. Presently a strange light gleams on the blackened sky! What should it be? not lightning, for it rose instead of falling, and hung longer on the sight than the electric flash. But it is gone!—now again it comes, stronger, and looks as if the bright, fiery sun had lost his place, and without any precursor were rushing up the southern sky. Again it almost disappears; but the faint tinge is soon increased, and a broad glare bursts up which overwhelms that widowed heart. The dreadful truth pierces her very heart, and makes her whole frame tremble. The prairie is on fire! Oh God! what a conviction! She remembers now that they have talked of prairie fires, and promised themselves much pleasure in beholding them. But she never dreamed of the red demon as an enemy, and one to be encountered in this dreadful solitude.

Her heart sinks within her. There are no means to avert or escape
it. The only living things about her are the children and the faithful
dog. The former are sleeping quietly, and the latter sits at her feet
gazing in her face with a mute sympathy that brings tears to her
eyes. She does not need to look for the light now, for it has gained
so that she cannot escape its glare. The wind is bearing the fire
almost with its own speed across the immense savannah. She cannot
calculate the distance at which she first saw it, but if it were at the
extreme southern border, it must, with such a wind, reach her in
a few hours, nay, even less!

But what to do, where to go! She rushes to the door. Merciful
Heaven! It is all one sea of dry combustibles around her. Grass,
dry grass everywhere! she can find no refuge. The very tree-tops,
if she could gain them, with those she is bound to save or perish
with, would afford her no protection from such a sea of flame as
is roaring yonder! The wind increases, the elements seem to grow
madder as the flame approaches, and aggravate its fury. With every
blast, it towers and curls, and then, as if enraged at its own im-
potence, sinks a moment sullenly, to gather strength for a fresh
effort.

There is a large creek about four miles away, and on this the
lone woman hangs her last faint hope. The wind will not befriend
her, and she can only hope that the waters may arrest the flame.
Hapless woman! she little knew the strength of the devastating
demon that was let loose that night! A slender thread of water to
separate her from such a surging sea of flame! But if it did not
protect her! What then! If the last extremity came! what should she
do? She could have but few moments to deliberate, after the dreadful foe crossed this line. Bewildered, almost stupified, by the terrors
of her condition, she had not waked her children. She had contemplated their dreadful fate alone, almost in silence, and with
little action, after she opened the door and was overpowered by
the conviction that to leave the house was even more certain death
than to remain.

Now, when the time grew short, and the hot breath of her
relentless foe rushed fiercely around her, she addressed herself
rapidly to the care of her little ones; she woke them with much
difficulty, and with much more brought them to comprehend the
danger that awaited them. One lively boy enjoyed the spectacle,
and clapped his hands, and almost maddened his mother, by rushing
out to get a fairer view of the wonderful scene. But where was the
dog? the noble dog who was her only intelligent friend in this

fearful time? Her quick mind had counted on his protection, in case she should escape and were shelterless. But where was he? She stepped to the door; the light was now strong and revealed distinctly every object. He was nowhere to be seen! She made the wood ring with his name, and presently a low supplicating bark was borne to her ears on the hot wind.

The fire had crossed the creek, and was tearing its way, like an infuriated demon, up the plain. A few minutes must decide her fate—she fell on her knees, and commended herself and her helpless babes to the mercy of her God; and then rose, calm and collected for the event. She had not, hitherto, contemplated the wonderful scene apart from the dangers with which it was fraught; but now, for the first time, she was struck with its grandeur and sublimity. It was an unbroken line of flame, wide as the eye could reach, mounting, roaring, crackling, and sending up columns of black smoke which, as they rose, became rarer, and, rising still higher, were reilluminated so as to appear another devouring demon sweeping the heavens. Mercy and hope seemed alike cut off by its angry glare. The fiery wall shut out the world behind, except occasionally, when a blast cleft it, it opened upon a black chasm that looked like the funeral vault of nature.

Scarcely had she taken this brief survey, and noted the nearer approach of the flame, when the dog came bounding to her side, and, with the most earnest petitions, sought her attention without the door. She followed him a few steps, scarcely thinking what she did, but, finding nothing, and seeing him making rapidly for some distant point, she turned back, closed the door, and sat down before the window to watch the progress of the fire. In an instant he was there, pawing, whining, howling, and, by every means in his power, soliciting her attention. Before she could open the door to admit him he bounded through the window.

"Merciful God! what have you done! we shall all be consumed—there is no hope now!" He stood at her feet; the strong intelligence of his face fascinated her eye in spite of the danger. What could he mean? In an instant the sagacity of his instinct flashed upon her. To the ploughed field! Yes, there was hope, and there alone. She seized the two younger children in one arm, and almost lifting the other by her hand, she fled along the trodden path, the delighted dog going before, and manifesting his joy by every sign in his power. They gain the fence—the fire is at their heels, it almost blisters their unprotected faces! One or two more leaps, and the herbless ground is gained. The fire has nothing now to feed on, and almost faint with the sudden and certain safety, the exhausted mother drops on the ground among her helpless infants.

"Merciful Savior, what an escape!" In a few minutes the flames are besieging the house, the logs covered with dry bark are but a morsel in their fierce jaws, the hay-stack takes fire and communicates to the rest of the cabin, and while the great volume of the fire sweeps among the trees and over the plain, it leaves the heavier materials to be consumed more slowly. Long did the light of the burning home, therefore, blight the eye of the lone woman after the "prairie fire" had done its worst around her and gone, bearing ruin and devastation to the northern plains and groves. Worn out by the terrors of the night, she sank into the semblance of sleep, on the naked earth, among her babes, with her faithful protector crouched at her feet.

CHAPTER IV

She woke in the morning to the dread reality which had been briefly forgotten; but which now broke with stunning force upon her senses. Her children were chilled and hungry. The spot where late their pleasant hearthside shone was a heap of mouldering brands and blackened ashes, with which the morning winds were toying in merry pastime. There was neither food nor shelter! and when she rose to her feet and looked out upon the plain, its strange appearance startled her. It seemed more boundless than ever, and the blackness of desolation brooded over every foot of it. It was clean shorn of every blade of vegetation, and appeared, within the last few hours, to have been blighted with a curse from which the smiles of heaven could scarcely redeem it.

With faltering steps the unhappy woman gathered her little ones, and prepared to leave their cheerless bed. But whither should they go! there was no house within many miles. Beside her own little roof she had not seen another since they left the last settlement. To seek shelter or bread, therefore, from others was impossible. Her only resource was to search the wasted wood and plain for roots or nuts, or whatever might be left to support life, till her husband's return. The fire of her cabin would warm the shivering babes for one or two days at least, and if help came not then, she must trust herself to the mercies of a journey over the bleak desert.

Bending her steps, therefore, towards the smouldering ruins, she soothed and warmed her children, and set out with the generous dog to search the grove for food. It was a desperate pilgrimage: most of the nuts and fruits in the vicinity of the house, had been gathered and deposited in the loft for winter use; and of those that were left upon the ground, few had escaped the consuming flames of the previous night. Occasionally she found one sheltered by a decayed log or a heavy clump of grass, which the fire in its haste had not stopped to devour. But they were rare, and she had three mouths to feed beside her own! A scanty meal was, however, obtained, and she returned to the fire. The warmth relieved their sufferings more effectually than the coarse morsel they had eaten. The little ones wondered where the house was, but rejoiced in the great pile of burning logs, and after a little time, the mother had the happiness of seeing them forget their hunger in some merry games.

Long and intensely this day did her eyes dwell on the wide, black plain! She had no need to look so earnestly, for the most careless glance would have revealed the white cover of the waggon if it had been moving over the dark surface. Noon passed, and brought no signal of mercy. She could see the brown deer leaping timidly over the scorched waste, and the grouse wheeling his short, swift flight from place to place; but this was all. Another night of dreadful solitude! exposed to cold and hunger, and to the starved wolf! shelterless, weaponless—the dog their only defence.

During the day she had found a few of the ground-nuts, which grow quite abundantly in the edge of the grove; with these she fed her little ones; and parting with nearly all her clothing, wrapped them in the scant covering; and with pleasant words, while her heart was bursting, soothed them to sleep, and laid them on the charred turf to the windward of the smoking pile, while, with her noble dog, she sat down to watch their slumbers. At intervals, for several hours, the winds bore to her aching ears the short, querulous barking of the small prairie wolf, and once or twice her very blood curdled when the shrill, dismal howl, by which the large, grey wolf summons his neighbors for an attack, resounded over the bleak waste! The night was utterly black. Beyond the little circle, faintly lighted by the wasting embers, nothing could be discerned. Her eyes would not warn her of an enemy within three yards; and as often as she peered into the darkness at every new sound, the faithful dog would nestle to her side and lick her hand, and turn his intelligent eyes toward hers with an expression of sympathy and confidence that cheered her solitary vigil more than she could tell.

The cold winds howled around her thinly clad frame and chilled it to the core. The noises one by one died away, and, spite of the horrors of her condition, a drowsiness stole over her which she could scarcely resist. Her eyelids drooped, and her shivering body swayed slightly to and fro, when the smouldering ends of the logs tumbled into a new position, and sent upward a volume of shining, crackling sparks, which roused her sinking energies and braced her for another hour's watching. At last the darkness became profoundly silent! Save the steady pressure of the wind, not a sound was heard. The nocturnal wanderers seemed to have withdrawn to their haunts, and left nature to the undisputed reign of night. Chilled, and faint with fatigue and fasting, the lonely watcher could no longer preserve her wakefulness; she curled her shivering form close to the sleeping babes, and left the vigil to the faithful dog.

It was the stupor rather than sleep that locked her faculties till the cry for food recalled them. The fire was diminishing; the sun was up, but she looked coldly through a mass of leaden vapor that was crowing up the south-eastern sky. The whole heavens were curtained with the still, sullen mass which threatened every moment to descend in rain. A few hours before, she had thought her condition could scarcely be aggravated. But the impending storm was little less to be dreaded, in their feeble state, than the terrible foe which had exposed them to it. Her limbs were stiff and full of pain; her brain reeled, and her sight became dim, as she rose to her feet and prepared to search the grove once more for something to sustain life in her hungry children.

Her own desire for food was gone; she would have loathed the most tempting viands. But when the little ones hung upon her garments and begged for bread, she summoned her fainting limbs to one more effort; and, taking a direction which had not been tried before, she found, after a long and painful search, a few stalks of the ground-nut, which her feeble hands with difficulty removed from their firm hold upon the soil. The roots of these afforded a morsel wherewith to still the cries that pierced her heart. And when there was no farther hope, and her limbs tottered beneath her, and strange racking pains wrung her worn body, she hastened back to the spot which still seemed home, though nought of home was there, and felt, if her hour were come, it were better to lie down and perish by those consecrated ashes, than in the cheerless wood. A drizzling rain was falling when she reached the spot, and threatened to increase. It would be impossible to preserve the fire long; but pushing the brands together, she gathered her trembling little ones about her knees, and, between her periods of agony, sought to impress their memories with the terrible events that had befallen them. She endeavored to make the eldest boy comprehend that he might be the only narrator whom his father would find, should he ever return; and left many tender messages for him and for her first-born. With pallid, tearful face he promised to do as she desired; but urged her to tell him where she would be when his father came, and whether his little brothers were going with her, to leave him all alone.

The rain increased, and their drenched garments gave the chilling blast redoubled power. The embers hissed and blackened, and soon refused to warm the shaking group. Like the pangs of death grew the mother's agony!—as certain and relentless! And there, beside the reeking ruins of her home, the black earth beneath, and the pitiless storm above, there alone, her only attendants the helpless children and the dog, who sat at her head, and seemed almost to weep over her writhing form, the hapless woman gave birth to a little being, whose eyes never opened to the desolation of its natal hour!

Long did the mother lie unconscious alike of the terror-stricken cries of the children, and the moaning caresses of her dumb friend. The day was far advanced when her eyes opened on the dreadful scene. The cold rain was pouring steadily down, and twilight seemed to her faint eyes to be creeping over the earth. A pleasant sound was ringing in her ears, but it was either a dream, or its import had faded from her mind before it was fully grasped. She made an effort to rise, but fell senseless. Once again, her eyes opened, and this time it was no illusion. The eldest of her little watchers was shouting in her ear, "Mother, I see father's waggon"; and there indeed it was, close at hand before his untrained eye had discovered it. All day it had been toiling across the black prairie! The rain had softened the turf, and the wheels sank without cutting it; so that the last few miles had been inconceivably tedious. The mourning garb of the plain had struck the hearts of both father and son with indescribable terror. The former would have left his slow team and flown across it, but his son had charge of the cow, and this was impossible. More alarmed and excited as he advanced, he was still obliged to restrain his intense feelings, and accommodate his progress to the slow motion of the tired cattle. Night drew on before the desolation of his home was revealed to him. When within about a mile he should have discovered the house, but all was a level waste! Unable longer to endure the torture, he sprang forward, leaving the animals to follow as they chose. He flew, he shouted, and the dog bounded to meet the well-known voice. When the boy saw the waggon, the father had just left it, so that even as he repeated the joyful tidings, the stricken man stood over them, half-stupified by the effort to comprehend the nature and extent of his calamities.

A group of perishing children, an infant corpse, a dying wife! and all, all gone, wherewith to minister even the decent ceremonies of such a period. Oh, how bitterly his heart cursed the day when he trusted the treacherous beauty that invited him there. He raised the dying woman in his arms; the seal was on her glazing eye, and the faint fluttering at her wrist foretold the last and worst that could befall him! Slowly, word by word, she told her agonizing tale. He threw his garments over her, and wiped the rain-drops from her face, and drew her to his heart. But the cold dew returned, and told that storm or shelter would be soon the same to her! He prayed her forgiveness, and with wild, incoherent words, accused himself of her cruel murder. She vindicated him from these accusations with all her little strength, and with many messages for her absent son, and many prayers for her dear children and their father, she resigned her breath, just as the last light was fading from the western sky.

She had begged that her tomb might be made on the site of the burned cabin. And there, when he had watched two days and nights by her unsheltered corpse, and hewn a rough coffin to receive her and her untimely babe, she was deposited. The grave was a rude hollow, scooped with sticks and the hands of the widowed husband and his sons. The preparations were completed and the dead lowered on the afternoon of the second day. At midnight a troop of famished wolves attacked the holy spot, and but for the rifle of the husband, would have torn its sacred contents from their rude repose. The next day he felled the nearest trees, and laid them in the form of a vault on the spot. And this it is which greets the traveler's eye so many miles away on the untenanted prairie!

The grove has since retired and left the tomb alone! a bold and solitary mark on the high line of the horizon. The plain below is still unchanged. It is the same rich, green expanse in summer; the same bleak, howling waste in winter. It is now skirted with farms under the edge of the woodlands.

One cabin has sprung up in its midst, on the bank of the stream. But it is forsaken and dilapidated. Its door is gone, and the rough planks which made the floor have been used as fuel, by emigrants who have encamped near it. Its small cellar yawns dismally in the face of the curious traveler who looks within.

CHAPTER V

Such were some of the incidents of early life on the frontiers of prairie land! Yet the hardy settlers came and dotted the little groves with their cabins and inclosures; their domestic animals increased rapidly on these rich pastures; and in a few years from the time the first dwelling was built on the border of a prairie, considerable herds of cattle and large droves of horses might be seen frolicking and feeding on it. The early settlers were particularly fond of the latter animal. Living as they did, in the vicinity of abundant and delicious game, they cared comparatively little for the flesh of domestic animals. They used the ox less for draught too, than the agriculturists of the eastern states do. The turf of their fields once broken, they have little further use for them. Their motion is too slow to suit the quick and changing desires of the frontiersman. His work must be done quickly, and at brief periods. He is not the steady, patient laborer of twelve or fifteen hours. If his seed is to be put in the earth, he plants a few acres, then mounts his fleetest horse, and rides to the neighboring town to address his fellow citizens in behalf of his own or his friend's claim to some political office; or he takes his rifle and pursues the deer, or hunts the grouse or quail.

Thus swift horses are the most valuable stock of these people. Beauty, however, is rarely combined with fleetness, and the best are generally shortlived. This is attributed to the early period at which they are trained to service, to the random, uncertain character of their labors, and perhaps not less than either, to the exposures they endure for want of shelter and proper care.

For a western settler will live many years on his farm, without ever having a barn, or other outbuilding of any kind, except a very small corn crib, and sometimes a stable, the dimensions of which correspond better to those of a poultry house, than anything else. If barns are built, they come along after many years, under the head of admissible luxuries. The threshing is done in the open air upon a piece of ground made hard by repeated treading, in the vicinity where the grain is usually stacked. The horses and horned cattle run out all winter; and from the little care that is taken of them, look miserable, long before the spring herbage comes to their relief. The coats of the latter, particularly, stand up like the hairs of the caterpillar, and shake in the wind, making their poor owners look as if suffering under fever and ague.

———————

The country bordering on Rock River, in nearly its whole length, is one of the most beautiful that can be imagined. The stream itself is a clear and generally rapid current, running over ledges of lime rock or beds of fine gravel and sand. Its banks are beautifully diversified with grove and lawn, which sometimes form natural parks of many miles in extent. The trees of these lands are principally the white, black, and red oak, interspersed with the elm, hickory, and butternut in small numbers. There is rarely any undergrowth, unless it be of wild flowers, or fruit-bearing shrubs and vines. The blackberry is very abundant in some, and in others the mandrake is found in great profusion. The grass is of sparser growth among the trees than on the prairies, and the clean turf, spread beneath the lightly woven boughs, is a charming spectacle to the eye, and still more tempting to feet that love to stray amid beautiful solitude. When I visited this region, it was the heyday of nature. Midsummer among these cool copses, green lawns, and swift streams, is a joyous season, and if to these one adds a small cabin filled with the pleasantest friends, books and pictures, and surrounded with a few families of the choicest society, it will not be difficult to understand why I often wish that the eastern potentate could have made his ten days' experiment without his august retinue in the little town of C——. But no paradise is ever entered without some previous struggles which serve to heighten its enjoyments. Perhaps they could not be complete without these preparatory contrasts. Theologians so affirm, and the assertion is not destitute of a strong resemblance to truth, in my own experience on this occasion. Certain it is, that if the strength of the one is proportioned to the intensity of the other, I had a just claim to all the delights which surrounded me at C——. To reach them I had endured a solitary ride of three long summer days, (think of that, for a lady with a tongue!) over scorching plains on which not a drop of rain had fallen for many weeks. The feet of four horses and the wheels of a heavy coach consequently kept a dense cloud of dust afloat, which, although it may have seemed to the lookers-on very majestic, marching over the prairie, to lend a sort of halo to our progress, by no means contributed to the comfort either of the outward or inward person.

Our dining place on the first day was at the principal hotel in the flourishing town of Northampton. It (the town I mean, and the hotel may as well be included, for it is the only building in it) is nestled pleasantly among some hazels and scrub oaks, on a little elevation, which you approach by a winding road from below. The face of the hill is quite bold as you come up from the south; and on its brow are perched the remains of a windmill, which some speculating settler, not having the fear of Don Quixote before his eyes, had erected there, in the hope, which appears to have been vain, of realizing filthy lucre or corn meal from its labors. You ascend the hill, and, at the same instant, are quite astonished to find yourself before the piazza of a house, which a tall sign-post points out as the "Northampton Hotel."

If sign-boards were, like title-pages, any indication of the fare to which they direct, the table of this house would afford you fewer delicacies than most of its guests find upon it. The artist seems to have been a severe lover of the useful, and to have told his story in the plainest of all possible black letters, upon the dirtiest of all white surfaces. I did not notice whether any of the characters were inverted, or had turned their backs upon their neighbors, a thing not uncommon in that country of large freedom; but I think I am safe in saying, that the title-page of this house was not an illuminated one. The same cannot be said of the room to which the guests are ushered. There is nothing very striking in its furniture, finish, or proportions, on first entering; but its beauties grow upon the eye; and you experience some astonishment, on looking about, to find yourself in a sort of stereotyped picture gallery. I scarcely know to what school these efforts belong. That they are original does not admit of question, but whether the artist excelled in coloring or composition, whether his pictures are allegorical, historical, or merely representatives of nature in her ornithological, zoological, and floral creations, I must leave to *virtuosi* to determine. It was a problem with me, after I had spent a considerable part of two hours in examining them, and it still remains so. They are executed in red, green, and blue, on a plaster surface, and consist of a great variety of vines, curiously interwoven and knotted, on which are perched as various a collection of birds. I judge of the variety of the former from the different colors of the leaves only, for none of them seemed to be in flower. Some gloried in green stalks and blue leaves, while others donned the extraordinary altogether, and sported leaves "done in" Spanish brown, from stems "done in" blue; others combined all these colors, and, twined and grouped as they were, presented a lively and pleasing effect. There was but one point in the room where the artist condescended to enlighten his admirers; this was on the lower face of the stairway. Two heavy circular lines, the outer red, the inner blue, inclosed a large sanguinary figure, which more resembled the beeve's hearts, without the appendages, as they are exposed in market, than anything else in nature with which I am acquainted. On its upper surface were perched a pair of birds, apparently young eagles, in hot combat, for their ferocious talons were lacerating the heart, and their beaks interlocked, with such amazing fierceness, that if the hold of one had yielded, his antagonist must have been precipitated, in terrible disorder, to the ground. Eight letters were delineated between the concentric lines; they were at equal distances from each other, and a full period of most vivid green succeeded each. These letters were an immense puzzle. I read them from all points; from above, from below, from the sides, from the points forty-five degrees from the horizontal and vertical lines; but all to no purpose. I was about abandoning the enterprise in despair, and had taken my pencil to copy the curiousity, for the benefit of learned societies, both native and foreign, when I found that the letters L. O. V. E., written on a straight line, spelled a word with which I was tolerably familiar; and, a key once obtained, I was not long in unlocking the ring which contained the mystery. It was a beautiful solution, and the performance of it raised no trifling degree of complacency in my own mind, as well as respect in that of the host for my sagacity. He considered the Love Ring one of the best jokes that could be enjoyed at the expense of his guests, and laughed as heartily at each explanation of the mystical letters as if they were perfectly new and contained the essence of all wit.

I could start no reasonable supposition, explanatory of this artistical phenomenon, except that some impoverished Titian had wandered thither, and being unable to defray in money the expense of a sojourn, had at the instance of the thrifty landlord turned his genius to account upon the walls of the reception room.

The hostess meanwhile plied her vocation in the neatest of all kitchens, directly back of this room. Three or four sturdy children shared the apartment with her, and from time to time engaged in the discussion of various questions of authority and domestic policy, on which they appeared to have adopted opposite opinions. The warmth of their arguments occasionally brought the maternal palm somewhat smartly over the *meatus auditorius*, and led the parties to abandon their respective points; but always with a look which said plainly, "See if I don't give it you next time."

Opposite the hotel stood—and I presume still stands—the skeleton of a large house which had been erected some two years before, and had progressed in a most singular manner to a state of partial completion. It was partly roofed, partly inclosed at the sides, partly plastered; some of the floor was laid, one chimney almost finished, some of the windows were in; the cellar was partly excavated, one or two doors were swinging on their hinges; a picket fence extended two-thirds the length of the yard, and the climax was crowned by a gate that stood agape about midway between the extremities. The enterprising owner had abandoned it at this stage of its erection, and offered it for sale as "a large house in the beautiful and flourishing town of Northampton." I trust, for the credit of the place, it has found a purchaser.

CHAPTER VI

We left our artistical landlord, and the next stopping-place was twenty-two miles away. There the night was to be spent, in case any amicable arrangements to that effect could be made with the muskitos who had previous possession. The landlady too, as I had learned, was rather testy, and on my arrival, I found it even so. She had come originally from New York; but twenty-five years of frontier life had sharpened many points of a character originally salient, and the absolute dominion which she held over the comfort of those who sought her roof, the only one for twenty-seven miles of road, had made her capricious and imperious in the extreme. Nothing, she asseverated, could give her greater pleasure than to entertain a *lady* or *gentleman*; and who should know such better than she, who had come from the city of New York! Having learned therefore the cue, it was not difficult to stimulate the good woman's love of pleasing, so as to secure her most courteous hospitality. Her own room was tendered me, with a flowing bowl of water and an ample brown towel, for making a toilet, after the dusty ride. Just as this was completed, we were all summoned to the tea table, which was laid with a snowy cloth under an open shed attached to the rear of the house, and looking directly into the grove.

The sun was just setting, and the long shadows falling aslant the grass would have made a delightful accompaniment to our delicious supper, had not certain admonitory twinges about one's feet and ankles put sentiment to flight, and given warning of more serious troubles yet to come.

It was very warm; and how we were to exist during the night with the sleeping rooms closed so as to exclude these marauders, was a problem which I could solve on no other supposition than that muskito-bars surrounded our beds. To ascertain whether this item should enter into the anticipations of the evening, I put the proposition to our hostess in a general and abstract form, that where these insects were so numerous, it was a great luxury to sleep under the bars and listen to their wailings, while you were perfectly secure from attack. She assented heartily, and added that she wished all her beds were thus provided; but that, from one cause and another, she had delayed furnishing any but her own! This announcement effectually quieted all my hopes of rest for that night.

"How long have you lived here, madam?" I ventured to ask.

"Twenty-one years."

"And how long have you kept a public-house?"

"Ever since we came."

"And the muskitos have divided the spoils with you all that time?"

"Yes."

"How far is it to the nearest town?"

"Eight miles."

"How often do you go there?"

"Once or twice a week."

"How much does the muskito-bar cost a yard?"

"Two bits and a pic, or three bits."

I made no comment at the close of this conversation, and may add here, that at every step I felt as if I were walking over a mine that might spring at the next, and add a discordant bass to the muskito tenor that by this time had gathered its full strength for the night. The good woman, however, in respect, as Captain Dalgetty would say, I had resided in her favorite city and should probably return to it; and in respect, moreover, of the assurance of the driver, given aside, that I was "a right smart lady," for my husband had gone a very long journey to the west (though how this fact demonstrated his friendly assertion I could never clearly perceive), bore the questioning with the most obtuse good nature. I almost wished, when I saw how pleasantly she took it, and felt my face, neck, hands, and feet swelling and burning under the stings of the rapacious legions, that she had warmed a little. She remained cool, however, and offered me the choice of two rooms, one on the upper floor, under the western slope of the roof, which had been closed all day, and consequently afforded about as rational a prospect of repose on a July night as the engine-room of a steamboat. It contained three beds and not over a million of muskitos. Each of the former she pledged herself to have occupied by the females of the house, who would, she reasoned, share the depletion to which otherwise I alone should be doomed. The apartment beneath this contained one bed, a post-office, and, as nearly as I could guess after escaping from it, something more than ten times the number of muskitos that had tendered their services in the one above. The bed was curtained with thick chintz, from which she argued that muskitos could be expelled by the smoke of a few chips laid upon a shovel of coals, after which, nothing could be more easy than to fasten the curtains with pins, and so enjoy uninterrupted repose.

The circumstances on which she most congratulated me in this case was, that I could make the little apartment within so tight that the muskitos and even the air would be effectually excluded. The good lady, therefore, stood quite aghast, when at the close of her harangue I asked, with a kind of desperate resignation, to be lighted to the upper room!

Here I did service, turning, smiting, and groaning, until a rap at the door, just as the clock struck one, announced that some fellow-sufferer had grown desperate, and abandoned the attempt to sleep.

"Is the lady *hyur*," cried the voice at the door, in a tone by no means indicative of the tranquillity essential to rest on a summer night, "who is going north in the stage?"

"Yes."

"Well, it will be ready in fifteen minutes."

"But you were not to start till daylight."

" 'l I shouldn't, but I reckon we may as well be going, as to stay here and be bled to death by these ———— muskitos."

It would be superfluous to add that the closing substantive was preceded by one of the strongest compound adjectives which the language affords. In fifteen minutes, therefore, we were on our way from the residence of the New York landlady. I had almost forgotten to add that she had a husband—an intelligent, but very quiet, good-natured man, whom one would almost expect to find set down among the fixtures, if the premises were offered for sale. He had evidently preserved his thrift and industry, notwithstanding his early residence in the country; for his fields were well fenced, his crops luxuriant, and a fine growing orchard lay in front of the house.

At eight o'clock we arrived at the beautiful little village of Princeton. Here we breakfasted, at the first really filthy house I had seen on the route, and this was unequivocally so. There was no disguising the table-cloths, the soiled dishes, the buried floor, or the untouchable towell that was handed me to make my morning ablutions. The court was in session here; and among those summoned to the breakfast-table, I recognized several legal gentlemen from different parts of the state. Some of these had many inquiries to make in reference to the Oregon expedition; the answers to which made me known as connected with one of those who had accompanied it.

I afterwards experienced the benefit of this indirect introduction to the company, in the loquacity of the new driver, whose first greeting after we left the town was delivered from a face inverted beneath the right-hand corner of the coach roof, "I reckon now you'd be right glad to see your gentleman this morning."

As I was looking out in an opposite direction at the time, the familiarity of the address startled me rather suddenly from my contemplations; a fact which led him to "allow that it would not do for me to go such a journey, if I was as easy scar'd as that." On my assuring him that I was only a little surprised, and could not conceive how a lady should be alarmed while she enjoyed his protection; he said he "expected I was about right," and expressed a warm desire to see the man or men who would offer any harm to a passenger of his, more especially if that passenger were a lady. As no one appeared to brave this defiance, he resumed his upright position, and in a moment more the horses dashed off at full speed down the long "bluff" which borders the valley of the Bureau Creek. Occasionally in our rapid progress, I caught a glimpse of the precipice, on the brow of which the road winds; but on we went, sometimes hanging over it, at others, bounding against the bank on the opposite side. When we gained the level ground, the inverted face again appeared beneath the roof.

"I expect you're from the east?"

"Possibly."

"I allowed you was, 'cause no western woman would ever a rode down that bluff at that rate without screamin like thunder. I *druv* ten years in Kentucky, and four here, and I never carried a western woman that didn't holler like a painter every time I jolted her a little, or put the horses up faster than a trot."

"Then you prefer, I suppose, to have eastern ladies ride with you?"

"Yes, that's just what I do: if there's anything on airth I hate, it's hearin a woman scream." Having expressed his choice in these gentle terms, he returned to the perpendicular and drove on.

We soon mounted the opposite bluff, emerged from the beautiful grove which crowns it, and entered on the prairie, over which the remaining sixteen miles of this stage lay. It is a high swelling plain, large tracts of which were covered with the rosin weed, then in full flower; this plant is well known to the inhabitants of the prairies as affording a very pure white gum of a delicate flavor when chewed. Its leaves are very long, and about the width of a hand; they are cut in narrow scallops from the edge almost to the centre. They all spring from the root just where it rises above the turf, and the stalk shoots out from their centre to the height of four or six feet, and then it unfolds from one to three flowers of a bright yellow hue, very similar in form to the common elecampane of the eastern states. This plant used to be the Indians' compass and dial. It was now just beginning to deposit its gum in little, pure, transparent globules on the stalk, and my friend on the box proposed to halt a few moments, and give me an opportunity to test its excellence. Deferring my desire, however, to accept his proffered indulgence to the requisitions of the government, whose agent he was, I prevailed on him to proceed, expressing at the same time an intention to make the experiment at a more fitting time.

CHAPTER VII

One hour more brought us to the point of woodland where stood the next "stage-house." It had consisted originally of one small cabin of rough logs, which in due time increased to two. They stood in friendly contiguity, and were united by their roofs. In the shady passage between, at the time of our arrival, the hostess was seated, with an apron full of green peas, which she was ejecting from their lawful premises, with one of the most forbidding scowls I ever beheld on the face of woman. What could have happened? I was very thirsty, but who could ask even a cup of water from the owner of such a face? She kept her eyes studiously fixed upon her task, apparently determined to afford me no opportunity to express my wants, or exchange a word of conversation with her. I was quite chilled, and began to feel exceedingly uncomfortable at the prospect of the half-hour's stay which I had been informed would be made here. I revolved in my mind every possible form of address which could act as an emollient to her excited feelings, and at last was about to make a desperate onset, with my humble petition, when a couple of children came rushing around the corner of the lower cabin, full of glee and merriment. I knew not if she were their mother, but her face made them shrink back and hold their breath. It was evident they had some experience, and that, whatever the cause of the phenomenon before us, the person who presented it was not to be tampered with. I spoke softly to the elder of the two, a little girl of five years, and asked her to get me a bowl of water. She was gone a moment and crept back, whispering, "There ain't no water in the pail, but I've got the dipper, and I'll show you where the spring is." I followed her down a path that led to the foot of a little eminence on which the house stood, and having slaked my thirst, and gathered both curiosity and courage during my absence, I determined to make an assault on the icy fortifications of the pea-sheller. The whole affair began to wear rather a ludicrous aspect after my doubts about the drink were removed, and now, when I had no favor to solicit, I perceived that the countenance, instead of being that of a dangerous woman, was expressive only of vulgar and animal rage, which propriety had not taught her to suppress in the presence of strangers.

"Madam," said I, "are you the landlady of this house?"

"Yes, I am."

"Your situation here between two large unsettled prairies enables you to make a great many people comfortable?"

"Yes, but I don't allow it's my business to look after other folks' comfort, when they don't care anything about mine."

"That depends upon circumstances," I replied. "If you keep a public-house, you make it your business to attend to the comfort of people who visit it, and all well-bred persons will certainly return your kindness, by consulting yours as far as possible."

"Well, I don't want to keep tavern. Folks will stop here to suit themselves, I don't want 'em."

"But, my dear madam, you live in such a place that people must stop with you, or suffer all the inconveniences of traveling through an uninhabited country. One of the greatest comforts known among civilized people is that of finding a pleasant substitute for your own home, when abroad. You have traveled enough, surely, to estimate this yourself?"

"No! I never traveled only when we come hyur, and then we

camped and slep' in our waggons. If other folks 'ud stay at home, as I do, there wouldn't be no need of having every other house a tavern!" This was bordering on the personal.

"But, my dear madam, people cannot always stay at home. Suppose now, your husband were to leave you for a few days on business, and to be taken sick during his absence, and send for you; you would wish to go to him. But you could not encamp on the way, if you were alone, and then you would want to see kind faces where you stopped."

"I allow that's a different case," said she, eyeing me sharply. "Is your husband sick?"

"My husband is a very long way from home," I replied.

"Well, that's another thing. If I could know when folks stop *hyur*, that they was obleeged to go about the country on any such account, I shouldn't hate to wait on 'em so;—but I reckon there's very few that don't go to spec'late or see the country, as if there wasn't any about their own homes, or 'cause they're too lazy to do anything else but ride about."

Just at this moment the horn sounded, and I was obliged to bid the inhospitable woman a hasty good morning. She had risen from the task I found her engaged on, and was standing, pail in hand, ready for the spring.

"Good morning," said she, "when you come back this way, may be I'll be looking better than I am to-day. I had four gentlemen here last night, and it rained on their beds; they found fault with me, and I told 'em they might go farther and do better if they could. I didn't want 'em *hyur*. I had a right smart blow up with one of 'em. He told me we ought to be ashamed to live here five years, with a roof leaking, and I told him we'd live here ten years longer without mending it, if we chose, and he might go somewhere else for a dry bed if he wanted one; for he shouldn't have one here again! But I see John's team is at the fence. Good morning, ma'am. I hope you'll find your husband well." With these words she suffered me to depart, and went her own way.

About four miles on, we were stopped by a man emerging from a pleasant-looking cabin to deliver some message to the driver, who, I had forgotten to say, was a tall, sardonic-looking, half or quarter Indian, as silent as the other had been communicative. The man who hailed him, announced that the day was very warm; he nodded assent: that his horses sweated; another nod: that his wife was sick; he nodded again: that she had been sick several days; another nod: and didn't get any better; still another nod: and that he wanted to

send for some lemons. This time the assent was accompanied by
an abrupt offer to get them. "I reckon you may get three," said
the prudent husband, depositing a shilling in his palm. "Tell
——— to send me good ones." Another nod, and we drove off,
leaving the farmer gazing after us with his hand over his eyes, his
teeth entirely exposed, yet still wearing an expression of profound
admiration at the manner in which his silent friend executed a
right angle at the corner of his garden.

It was twenty miles from this house to the nearest settlement,
where medical advice or necessaries in sickness could be procured;
and several miles to the nearest house where common aid, in case
of accident or death, could be expected. This good man, however,
seemed as nonchalant while sending for his three lemons, as if he
had but to dispatch a boy across the street! So much indifference
do people acquire by living in the wilderness. He had come from
the east about eight years before.

CHAPTER VIII

At four o'clock we reached the southern bank of Rock River, at
a place called, indiscriminately, Dixon's Ferry, Dixon, and Dixonville. By the first of these names it has been known many years, as
corresponding on Rock River, to Fort Clark, now Peoria, on the
Illinois. There is much natural beauty about the upper part of the
town. The bank of the river is broken, and bold bluff of lime-rock
rises abruptly to a considerable height above the lower level, the
summit of which is wooded with open, beautiful barrens. The trees
hang on the brow of the ledge, and wave their arms pleasantly to
those below. A fine spring issues from the foot of the rock, but I
did not visit it. Opposite this portion of the town is a beautiful plot
of table-land, smooth as a summer lake, which its owner had converted into eastern capital and western promises, by consenting to
divide it into town lots. He had paid liberally for an engraved map,
on which the streets were adorned with trees, and the public grounds
with churches and other lofty edifices. Neither the trees nor
churches, however, seemed to have any very fair prospect of becoming distinguished elsewhere.

The old part of Dixonville, that around the ferry, is built upon
a bed of cream-colored sand, abounding in fleas. The banks of the
river are dotted with little copses and slightly broken. The northern
one rises into a high bluff, which, just below the ferry, crowds up

to the water's edge, and bears upon its face an occasional tree or shrub. On the southern side, the bluff bends away from the termination of the ledge, and sweeping inland, leaves a low track, the rear of which is broken by bushy gullies that come down from the height above, and terminate in the sand-bed before spoken of.

I was set down here, at another very filthy house. But that which so disgusted me on first entering, I soon found to be one of the least objectionable features of the establishment. The landlord was one of that class of people in whom all national and other distinctions are lost in the ineffaceable brand of villany that is stamped upon them. One would never pause to inquire whether he were American, English, Irish, or Dutch. You felt conscious of the presence of a villan; one of those universal prowlers, whose business it is to prey upon society, and who, when it will be most advantageous, prosecute their schemes alone, and when otherwise, surround themselves with a gang of ruffians, whose less disguised vices form a barrier between their leader and public indignation. He had a calm, imperturbable face, which, whenever he saw that his designs were detected, assumed an expression of the most profound meekness and resignation, as if its owner would say, I know your thoughts wrong me, but what then? I can bear even that!

I asked to be shown at once to a private room, and furnished with water and other things necessary to comfort, after a very warm and dusty ride. He escorted me to one adjoining the parlor. "But sir," said I, observing boots, hats, et cet., standing about, "this appears to be a gentleman's room."

"Yes, it is occupied by a gentleman, but he's out, and won't be here till night."

"Have you no room unoccupied?" I inquired. "Beside, there is no lock on the door!"

"You need not fear interruption," he replied; "I would give you the parlor, but we shall want to pass through there, and you can spend an hour here without any fear of being disturbed."

"Very well, sir. Be so good as to send me the water and towels immediately."

They were brought at the expiration of ten minutes, by a gross creature, who united the characters of mistress, housekeeper, and servant, to the miscreant landlord. Her whole person and manner were of the most disgusting description. She deposited her burthen, and then placing a hand on each side of her ungainly person, posted herself against the door, and commenced taking a deliberate survey of myself and my proceedings. I waited a moment, and finding that she intended to remain as long as her convenience or pleasure would permit, inquired if it formed any part of her orders to remain? "No; but didn't I want some help?"

"Not at all; the most effectual way of serving me will be to remove yourself as quickly as possible from my sight."

She disappeared, and I barricaded the door with trunks, chairs, and whatever else I could place against it. I had scarcely completed the task, when some person came rapidly up-stairs and through the hall, and seized the handle of the door with a violent push.

"Open this door," exclaimed a harsh voice, accompanying the words with another push, that made the fortifications tremble. I now added my own strength to the other securities, and informed the person that a lady and stranger was occupying the room for a very short period only, and that she presumed he would, as a gentleman, only require to be informed of this to be induced to leave her in peaceable possession; or, if anything were wrong, to seek the landlord, who had placed her there. To this he replied, that any person who was in his room must leave it in a shorter space of time than it would be proper to describe; and that he would see the landlord where it was supposed to be much hotter than it was there, before he would go after him on any such business. I now saw that I had done him great wrong, in supposing him accessible to any arguments that would touch a man or a gentleman, and, therefore, changed my ground.

"Sir," said I, "I shall not leave this room until I am ready, which will be a much longer time than you name. If you retire, and permit me, unmolested, to accomplish what I came here for, your room shall be vacated in fifteen minutes. If you remain there, I remain here; and I have, beside my personal strength, the aid of two very heavy trunks, and a rifle, placed against the door at about the height of a man's head. If you are not already acquainted with its contents, there is every chance that you will become so, if you open this door by violence." Muttering some terrific curses, he retreated down the stairs, and I proceeded to make my toilet, in a trepidation which shamefully belied my stout words. It was completed in a very short time, but even before it was done the door was again rudely assailed, and the inquiry made whether I "was not yet ready." I replied, that I should leave the room the first moment after I was ready, and that these visits, so far from facilitating my preparations, interrupted them entirely. Again the steps retreated, and, in a few moments, I removed the trunks and rifle, and walked into the parlor. At the same moment the wretch came up-stairs, and entered his room. He was a well-dressed, gentlemanly-looking person, and, strange to say, wore a wide crape band on his hat! He peered sharply into the parlor as he passed, remained in his room about the fourth of a minute without closing the door; and then disappeared down the stairs, and lounged away the evening about the bar-room and door of the house.

Everything I now saw convinced me that I was in a den of the foulest iniquity; but imagination, stimulated as it was by fear, did not conceive the half of what I afterward learnt to be true of the vile people who consorted there. This place is the Vicksburg of Illinois, and the enterprising proprietors of the mail line had chosen the headquarters of the gamblers, counterfeiters, horse thieves, et cet., as the most fitting place of entertainment for their passengers. I afterward learned that there was an excellent house kept in the upper part of the town, remote from the pestiferous atmosphere of these wretches, but, being a stranger, I had no opportunity of profiting by it. The people who live here are persons whose daily business is the stealing of horses, the manufacture of counterfeit money, et cet.; and such was their strength at the period spoken of, that although the better population of the place, of which I was informed there was a highly respectable body, held them in the abhorrence which their acts merited, they could make no demonstration against them without endangering their own and the lives of their families. Sometimes, exasperated beyond all forbearance by their enormities, the citizens were driven to some feeble measure of self-defence; and, at this time, there was a set of counterfeiter's tools under execution. But these movements generally ended in some tacit compromise, by which the villains were left to pursue their iniquity as before.

CHAPTER IX

One instance of the recklessness in crime, exhibited by the wretches referred to in the last chapter, was related to me. A settler, who had opened a prairie farm some miles below the town, became the owner of a very beautiful pair of horses. One morning they were both missing. He at once started in pursuit, went directly up to the town, and, a few miles on his way, discovered one of them lying dead by the road-side. It appeared that, for some reason, the robbers wanted but one, and, as the other followed his companion, they had shot him down to relieve themselves of his presence.

These, and many more incidents, evincing the most shocking depravity, were related to me after I had escaped.

But meantime my desire to reach the residence of my friends that night, increased every moment. I therefore sent for the landlord, and inquired the distance to C———. By the way I should observe that he added to the various callings already specified, some pretensions to the practice of medicine, and that I had accidentally heard him speak to one of his comrades in the passage, of having but recently returned from a visit to one of his patients, about four miles above the place for which I inquired. The name, however, when I mentioned it, seemed entirely new to him. He mused a moment, and said that really he could not tell. It might be between twenty and thirty miles down the river. There had been a little place settled down there somewhere, about a year before, perhaps he could find some gentleman about the house who could inform me.

"Let the distance be what it may," I said, "I wish to go there to-night."

"To-night! that is impossible. We could not send you there to-night on any terms. In the morning I may find it possible to take you, or procure an opportunity for you to go with some person that is traveling that way."

"As you are ignorant of the distance," I said, "you cannot name your charge until you ascertain it."

"No, though I think it would be reasonable to say five dollars."

I had paid but six dollars for the previous one hundred miles. "Do you know the distance to ———," naming the place which he had visited that day. "Not exactly, but I think it is about ———"

"You mean to say that you have never measured it with the chain, but having been there today, you could doubtless form a tolerably correct estimate."

He said that he had spoken of visiting a patient somewhere in the neighborhood of that place, it might be within half a dozen miles or so. I replied that "it was useless to attempt deception in so small and obvious a matter; that I would willingly pay an exorbitant charge to get from his house that moment; but as it was impossible, I should make up my mind to endure a night in it. Let me hear from you," I said, "at the earliest hour in the morning, in reference to my departure; and now, if you will oblige me by showing me the room I am to occupy to-night, I shall require nothing more."

"You are to sleep here," he replied, "there is no other room unoccupied."

"But this door has no lock, and if I am to judge of my security, from that which you promised in the first instance, I shall sit up all night."

Oh, there would not be the least necessity for anything of the kind. This was the parlor — it was never entered but by transient guests, and if any came, they could be shown to another room. He begged I would feel perfectly assured, and apologized in the humblest manner for the interruption I had experienced in the other room. The gentleman who occupied it had not seen him, and he did not know who might be in it or what they were doing. He regretted, et cet.

To this I replied, I should place no reliance on his promise, having found it worthy of none, but take good care to secure myself, and thus we parted.

It should be remarked here as evidence of a degree of civilized feeling among these ruffians, that they felt themselves wholly unworthy the presence of a virtuous woman, and never expected one to appear at table with them. It was not the custom of the house, so the female before referred to informed me, for ladies to appear at the first table.

"And pray where do ladies take their meals," I inquired, "when they are so unfortunate as to be obliged to eat here?"

"If they are in a hurry to go, we *tote* it up *hyur* to 'em; if they ain't, they wait and go to the second table!"

"And who sits at the second table?"

"Mr. ———— , the landlord, and I, and the drivers and so on."

A delightful circle, truly! I made no attempt to get a meal that day, though I had eaten nothing since early breakfast at P.

Making the best security I could, by placing the bedstead against the door, I prepared to retire.

The room was excessively warm, and had a stench which rendered it intolerable, except the window were thrown wide open. The bed itself would have been pronounced soiled by a jury of Irish landladies; I resolved, however, to make the best of the necessity which held me there, and addressed myself to rest with an earnestness which was well rewarded by seven hours of uninterrupted oblivion.

CHAPTER X

In the morning I learned that the good spirits had sent to my relief an excellent old New England farmer, who resided some miles below the place to which I was bound. He was in a tidy farm waggon, carpeted with an abundance of new mown hay, drawn by a pair of fleet horses; and more than all, he was an intelligent, honest, high-minded man, and a pleasant companion on the ride, which proved to be but twelve miles.

Before I saw him, however, the landlord informed me that he had made the necessary arrangements, and paid the charge, one dollar and fifty cents. He remarked that it was reasonable, though more than he should have charged for that distance, if he had been going alone, and directly past the place. I paid it, together with his own bill, which was about the same as one pays at the Astor House for the same length of time, and told him that I never paid money more freely for any purpose than for leaving his house; that I presumed, in fixing his first charge he had a just appreciation of my condition, and of the ransom which any person would pay to be released from it; and that, considering the relief which I should purchase by it, it was a very moderate sum.

Some remarks from my companion, on the way down, led me to inquire what he had received for my fare, and on his mentioning half the sum which I paid, I remarked that the fellow succeeded in robbing me of seventy-five cents at last!

"Only that!" said he, "you may consider yourself very fortunate; that is a small sum for him to let any stranger escape for"; he added, by way of vindicating himself, that if he had known it was a stranger whom he was to convey, he should have refused any compensation, but that the miscreant represented me as a woman belonging to the house, whose fare he was to pay, and, continued the indignant old gentleman, "I considered any price too low to induce me to take one of the gang into my waggon, but it is not safe to come to any open quarrel with them, so I told them I would take you for seventy-five cents!"

I hope the beautiful country has been purged of such a population before this. It was apprehended that the town would at some time be made the theatre of such a scene as was enacted at Vicksburg. I rejoiced heartily to escape from it, and still more to reach the hospitable and pleasant abode of my friend Mrs. P——. We arrived opposite the town, or rather the town site, a little after noon. The southern bank of the river is low and covered with very tall grass;

but it rises gradually as it retreats, and finally swells into a high, rolling prairie, which divides Rock River from Winnebago Swamp. The northern bank, on which the town is laid out, rises boldly up from the water's edge to the height of seventy feet, and is crowned with a few scattered trees. Two cabins on contiguous lots, fronting the river, and an unfinished framed house, which will, when the street is built, be several doors above them, were all the evidences of town life which I beheld when we stopped and hallooed for some one to row across the little canoe which lay moored under the opposite bank, for myself and baggage.

In due time the passage was effected; and after a scramble up the steep bank, I found my friends in one of the aforesaid cabins, and a snug, cheerful, social little home it was, as any the country afforded.

Here, also, were two other ladies visiting—one a magnificent woman, whose beauty had won her the title of Queen of the West; the other, her younger sister, a shrinking girl, just entering upon womanhood, with rare beauty of person and extraordinary delicacy of character. Here we were all good-natured, all friends, and all sufficiently accustomed to the unaccommodating necessities of western life, to made their exactions occasions of merriment, instead of chagrin, or ill-humor. A beautiful country was about us, we had horses to ride, a carriage at our service, a boat on the river, a swing between two tall trees on the bank, books, pictures, &c., in the house, and the most ample freedom to say what we would, range where we would, and draw amusement, pleasure, and instruction from any of these sources.

Our familiarity with these same necessities was no trifling advantage. When three guests were to be entertained in a little cabin having but one room, which answered the purposes of parlor, dining and sleeping room, and the smallest of all practicable kitchens, it will not be difficult for nice imaginations to conceive that there might arise certain points on which a strict adherence to etiquet by all parties might have kept us in *status quo* up to this period. For instance, if we could not have yielded in some cases, where guests in a larger mansion would think it impossible, we should never have gone to bed, or, once in bed, we should, by the same rigid construction of the rules, have remained there to the present day. There were five of us to sleep, three lady guests, our hostess, and her husband. There were two beds, and a most luxurious sofa.

The debate on the first night was, who should take the sofa. It was cool, capacious, elastic, in all respects but one the most desirable berth of the three. But this one, alas! It was fatal to all visions of dreamless sleep, on the cool hair-cloth. It was no constituent part of the sofa, nor of the pillows, nor of the linen. It did not enter into the composition or construction of anything in its vicinity. It was not, strictly speaking, a physical difficulty; neither was it, whether we consider its own nature, or the results of its operation on ourselves, in any sense a moral one. One might, at first, have pronounced it atmospherical; but this opinion fled, as did the patience of the sofa sleeper, before the tests to which he was doomed. It commenced with a sharp singing tone, which, continuing without the least inflection or variation, except that caused by the nearness or distance of the performer, grew, in a short time, decidedly monotonous. Thus it would have lulled one to sleep in the pleasantest manner, had it not, just as you were about dropping off into the land of dreams, suddenly changed, from a phenomenon in acoustics, to one in that peculiar branch of hydraulics termed "blood sucking." In this stage it was, beyond all question, unpleasant; one, two, three, four, or twenty songs ceased at once, and as many little hollow needles were instantly inserted into your hands, arms, or face; foreign branches fastened, *nolens volens*, upon your circulating system, and drawing off its current without the offer of an equivalent.

There are few persons so constituted as to endure, patiently, a succession of such Arab robberies during a whole night; and hence it was a question of some interest, who should take this post. Both beds were protected against these merciless despoilers by bars; but any permanent provision of this kind was impracticable upon the sofa. After due deliberation, it was resolved that I should make trial for that night. Accordingly, having gathered the veils of the company, with an ample array of darning needles and pins, and made the most effective outposts which such divided forces would admit of, I crept cautiously within, and congratulated myself upon the prospect of repose, sweetened by the war songs of baffled assailants; but, alas! how often are the grandest anticipations prostrated by the most trivial agents. My scheme and patience were alike blown to the winds by the entrance of one of these minute besiegers. He was soon followed by a ravenous troop, whose screams of exultation might, I thought, have awakened the sound sleepers of the beds. There was no remedy now but to begin again: mending would not do. So I removed the gossamer roof of my couch, and sat upright to deliberate on the best means of securing myself against these penetrating enemies.

It was all dark, and the deep, steady breathing of the four sleepers somewhat warmed my temper. I resolved, however, to make another effort, and, preparatory to its execution, rose and took a few turns around the room by way of getting philosophy in the ascendant. Another array of the veils, another insertion of the darning needles, another spreading of sheets, another cautious creeping under, so as not to disturb the arrangement, was very soon proved to be equally futile, by a second irruption of these Lilliputian vandals. Whose patience could be prolonged after this? whose fortitude could bear the painful effects of such a warfare? Scorning all such virtues, I determined, notwithstanding the heat, to adopt the only sure defence, that of wrapping head, face, arms, all but the mouth, in the sheet, and bid defiance to the exulting enemy. In this native vapor bath I napped away two or three hours, and, after one or two short walks, and one or two brief periods devoted to the widest destruction I could deal among my untiring foes, morning at last came.

The second night it was proposed that the sofa should be occupied by our host. I felt it my duty, notwithstanding the failure of the previous night, to express the opinion that the veils, et cet., might be made available in defence; and accordingly they were put in requisition. They certainly answered the purpose of permitting us ladies to get into a quiet sleep. It had not lasted long, however, when I was awoke by a dense cloud of smoke, which seemed to be increasing every moment. My first impression that the house was on fire, was almost instantly removed; for our host was stalking the room in the majesty of outraged patience, swinging a large iron kettle filled with smoking chips. This process is more briefly designated by its technical name of *"smudging."* It was performed on the present occasion with great vigor, and interlarded with frequent apostrophes to those whom it was intended to put to rout, and some passages of soliloquy that were very moving.

"Oh you brown stinging imps, I'll give you enough this time to lay you up a day or two, I promise you. I'm not playing with you now, you'll find, before this smudge is over—(Another furious swing and a smothered cough). Yes, these women would sleep if the smoke was so thick you could cut it; if I could sleep as they do, the muskitos might have carried me off into some tree-top and left me there—(A blow with the palm). You scoundrel, come here when my head is right over the kettle, will you?—I'll teach you to make *game* of me. By Jupiter, I'll smoke you till to-morrow night at this time, if that's what you want—(Another swing). Ladies, I don't think you'll sleep much longer, if you do, you've got better bellows than I have—(Another turn or two, swinging the kettle vehemently). There, you blood-thirsty rascals, how are you now, eh! all still? You won't sing any more to-night, I'll warrant you. Now I'll see if I can't sleep a little." So saying, he resumed his couch, apparently with every expectation of undisturbed repose for the remainder of the night. I was just losing the recollection of this amusing scene, when a violent blow with the flat hand again aroused me. "Here again, are you? Mars! what a set of vampires! If that smudge has not laid you up, there's no way to do it." By this time the smoke was very much diluted with the air circulating through the open doors and windows; the moon had burst through the clouds and lighted the whole scene within and without. There was a pause for a few moments, as if despair were gathering resolution, and then the suffering victim, enveloped in a sheet, rose and walked out of the door, muttering that he would try it at the waterside. He crossed the lawn, descended the bank of the river, and was absent some ten minutes, when he appeared again, having apparently made a fruitless search for a place of rest. His next resort was the unfinished house, but there it was no better; and again the sheeted form appeared like an uneasy spirit walking up and down.

The whole affair now grew so irresistibly ludicrous that it seemed sheer robbery to enjoy it longer alone. I awoke my companions therefore, and while I was endeavoring to convey some faint conception of the scene, lo, the ghostly demonstration strode again before our eyes. It was greeted with a simultaneous peal of laughter, but it passed on, and though our frequent bursts of merriment might have provoked the return of a less irascible spirit, it came not back. We were not a little astonished in the morning to see him appear looking refreshed and good-humored as any of us. Nor were we less amused when a day or two after we learned what resource he had finally availed himself of. Between the cabins stood a small sleigh with a box so high that it would have served for a prison van without a top. Into this, the persecuted man had climbed, and spreading his sheet over the top, sat bolt upright in one corner, bade defiance to the muskitos, and enjoyed for the remained of the night, as he asserted, the most luxurious repose.

Such scenes might have lost the power to amuse, but our "queen" was called away a few days after, and the sofa was at once vacated.

Yet many a hearty laugh afterward rang through the pleasant cabin at the memory of those nights. In sober truth these insects are a sad drawback to the enjoyment of the fine summer evenings which form one of the most delightful features of this region. The hours of sleep can be secured against them by the use of the bar before referred to; but they are a very serious interruption to the delights of the cool refreshing evenings which follow the sunny days of that open country.

It may not be amiss to remark here that the climate of the western states differs materially from that of the eastern in the coolness of the atmosphere after sunset. The solar rays acting all day on these large tracts of level moist ground draw into the upper regions of the air immense volumes of vapor which, after the former are withdrawn, condense and descend in a miniature shower. The dews are consequently very heavy, and the nights so cool that nothing like the oppressive heat of a July or August night in the Atlantic states is ever known.

CHAPTER XI

But let us look at the picture of this little town, or rather of the spot selected for it; for no town is yet there. We stand beneath a large tree, just in the rear of our cabin. This spot commands a pretty complete view of the "section" on which the enterprising proprietors confidently hope to see a goodly city rise. Below us, half or three quarters of a mile, the river bends northwardly, and just at the angle a considerable stream pours into it, which bears the name of Elkhorn. Its mouth is low and fringed with tall grass and bushes, and a few trees, which cut off the prospect in that direction. At a point a short distance from the mouth of this creek, rises a natural terrace of some twenty feet, which sweeps in a crescent form almost to our feet. The top of this terrace is crowned with wood, while the semicircular amphitheatre inclosed by it, is without a tree or shrub, and looks a fit arena for the proud savage, who but recently trod it. Its base rests upon the river, along the bank of which many dead are buried, their heads toward the water. Occasionally, as the earth crumbles away, the skulls roll out and tumble down, till they rest in a hollow or among the roots of bushes and trees which fringe the water. There is no under-growth in the wood which borders this amphitheatre, and the grass is shorter than that which grows on the prairies; so that you look across the surface, the tall straight trees seem to be set upon a smooth velvety turf, clean as a fairy temple. We are on the terrace at the upper termination, where it approaches the river after its graceful bend to embrace the little plain below. Above us the trees are more scattered, and can scarcely be called anything but stragglers, except at one spot in the open plain, two hundred yards perhaps from the river, where they assemble in an oblong hollow form, completely interweaving their arms over a lovely little bower. Directly in front of us there is a winding opening to the prairie beyond. Along this is now a pretty well wrought road. On the right is the common field or garden, in which all the settlers have their crops for this year. On the left deep in the grove is the residence of the worthy doctor. It has grown, by the addition of sundry wings and arms, from a simple cabin to quite a complicated cottage.

The view across the river is open: the prairie swells from the water's edge away for miles, rising gradually, and at last bears one solitary tree just on the line of vision. The stream itself is a clear, rapid current running over a rocky bed. It abounds in the finest fish, great numbers of which are easily taken by the spear after nightfall. The torchlights glancing about on the water make a pleasant feature in a night view from the high banks which overhang it. So much for the town site; now for the town and its inhabitants. It has been already stated that we have a next door. It is a cabin, and belongs to the original owner of the lands we have just described. When they were selected for a town site, he saw no good reason why he should not become a citizen, and so remained. He is a *native*, and the only one which the place can boast. But more than this, he is an extraordinary specimen even of his extraordinary genius. He is some forty-five years of age, was born and has always lived in the west; he possesses a mind of uncommon natural powers, which has been strengthened by his mode of life, and adds to this a great fund of reading. His ability to converse on books and other topics common in cultivated society, combined with that species of rudeness which a life so totally destitute of artificialities creates in the most elegant minds, makes him appear eccentric; but he is not really so. Place him, even at this age, in a city where he would be cut off from the free, wild influences of nature and subjected to the restraint of customs which men have agreed to pronounce elegant, and though he might never lose altogether the free bearing of a man who has communed much with nature and loved her, he would assume the conventional tastes of those with whom he mingled, and his eccentricity would wholly disappear.

His conversational powers are often displayed in remarks that would be brilliant in any circle, and he possesses a vast fund of knowledge, drawn from his fervent love and deep study of nature, which might well be the pride of more pretending minds than his. He is now a gentleman of leisure; the advantageous sale of his property enables him to spend his time as his tastes or pleasures lead him. He sometimes visits us, discusses poetry, science, and polite literature in general. One day he pronounced, in a very brief sentence, the most comprehensive and truthful criticism upon his three favorites, Shakspeare, Byron, and Burns, I ever heard.

It is painful to add, in qualification of so much that is admirable, that he has the vice which nobler minds have not escaped, that of intemperance. Though not an habitual drinker, he sometimes drains the cup too deeply, and then adieu to philosophy, poetry, and reason; he is one of the veriest infants of all the stricken family of the demon. His home is shared by a wife and one child, a boy of some four years.

In the unfinished house above, we shall find nothing but carpenters' benches, bits of boards, barrels of lime, &c., and as these three embrace the whole of the upper part of the town, we will step down the terrace and see what the amphitheatre contains. Here we find two tenements, one nearly in the centre, the other below. The latter is rather a queer affair, even for a new country, and would be pronounced decidedly so, where necessity was not the supreme law in architecture as well as other things. Its body, if it may be said to have one, is built of slabs in an upright position, and is roofed with the same material. It forms quite a spacious inclosure, the interior of which is partitioned with quilts and blankets into several rooms, each of which is thickly peopled. In this fold there are three or four families of "Buckeyes," who, of themselves, would make a respectable colony. They came hither from Ohio, early in the season, and are living in this slab house till they complete better dwellings. Their journey was performed in a boat built and owned by themselves, and propelled by horses. It is now lying just opposite the house, half out of water, its prow thrown up like the head of a dying alligator. It is constructed very much as our canal boats are, but seems a trifle higher. The families all bear one name, and are father and sons-in-law, or brothers and sons, I never clearly comprehended which.

When they concluded to leave the Buckeye state, they consulted together on the subject, and determined, in view of their large numbers, that it would be more economical, as well as more independent, to perform the journey in some conveyance of their own. Land carriage was out of the question, a flat boat would only float them to the mouth of the Ohio, a keel boat would be too laborious, and their last resource was to construct one which their horses could propel. This was accordingly done. The families and goods were shipped, and the strange craft launched upon "La belle Rivière." For many days she floated down its majestic waters, her silent way crossed occasionally by the resounding march of the high-pressure steamboats that crowd them. At night the prow was turned shoreward, and the little boat moored under some friendly tree, where a fire was kindled and supper served. The smaller members of the flock, who had been confined all day, could now range the wood, and make ample reparation to their ill-used muscles and lungs. By early daylight the refreshed animals were again put upon duty, and while the cool dews yet lay upon the silent valley, they moved onward.

I can imagine few things more delightful than this primitive, untrammeled progress over these majestic waters. When pleasure or convenience led them, they could go on shore; they could visit spots never before trodden by the white man, and sleep in the midst of silence never broken by sound of civilized life, save the snorting of the fiery steed that ploughs the water a brief moment and is gone. Vast, unbroken, majestic nature lay on either hand of them for many days. At last they reached the mouth of Rock River, and turned their little ark into its clear, bright waters. They landed at C——; lived in their boat till the slab house was built; and, in this improved condition, were waiting the still farther advancement of separate firesides within more substantial walls. Everything about this rude home wore an appearance of cleanliness and comfort that made even its plainness inviting. The paths were kept clean; the bits of board before the door were well swept, the children looked tidy, and the old grandmother, of whose fat, happy face, and clean-starched cap, I have yet a faint vision, seemed the *belle ideal* of a bold-hearted, strong-handed western woman, sinking into the well-earned repose of ripened years.

CHAPTER XII

In the house above this we shall find a specimen of a very different class of people, viz., a Massachusetts sea captain. There he stands; a man of fifty years; a little above the middle height, with a slender person, and a slight stoop which takes something from his stature. His black hair just frosted, and his small, keen, black eye dancing and twinkling beneath the dark brow, like the heat lightning of a cloudy July night. His dress is very neat, his motions quick, and his searching face always clad in smiles. He speaks much to the point, when he chooses, without a wandering or superfluous word; and when he does not choose, will baffle a whole corps of lawyers. His smile is a genuine bubbling-up of sunlight, which bursts and is gone, to be replaced by another as fleeting. He is a great lover of sunshine, and enjoys in a high degree the ability to produce it for himself. The early part of his life was spent on the sea, but circumstances led him a few years since to unite with a colony and emigrate with his large family to the west. His genius seems never to have fully expanded itself until it reached the prairies. Not even the briny element he so much loved brought out all his resources so entirely. There, while sailing from port to port, his mind was comparatively unemployed. A severe storm might occasionally call upon his strength, or make it necessary for him to assure his passengers that the weather was delightful, and the ocean never in a finer state; but there was little room for the play of those faculties which find a rich and endless field for speculation and thrift on the teeming prairies. Here he could calculate the amount of income which every foot of land would yield; he could select town sites, lay out the lots and sell them too, while he was riding along on his ordinary business; he could construct imaginary bridges where sloughs were any detriment to a fine "location," and make the most envious neighbor confess that it was better than if the land were all smooth. If his horse was fastened in one of these places, and the countenances of his companions darkened, his admiration of everything about him rose to the highest pitch, and he appealed to them with a smiling earnestness which could not be resisted, to say if it were not the finest country ever beheld by man! Even while he was struggling through the quagmire, burthened with some helpless member of his family, he would asseverate in the most cheerful tones, and with a smile which nothing could repress, that the country was incomparable; that the very sloughs themselves, with their deep beds of black soil and water pools, were one of its best features; that nothing would be easier than to construct ridges "athwart" them, when they would be a delight instead of the trifling inconvenience which some might think they now were.

He had already aided in building up one of the pleasantest little towns in the central part of the state, had erected a good house for himself, occupied it about three years, and then, yielding to his love of fresh enterprise, joined this colony, sold his home, and come into this newer region to begin again. He has selected a beautiful farm skirting the river adjacent to the town, on which he is about building, but his mind is now all absorbed with schemes for making the town grow into a large village. Of the success of these he entertains no doubt.

The only other *character* in this embryo city, is our host. He is a son of New England, and has spent a considerable fortune, which was left him in early life, for the pleasure of beginning anew on his own strength. He wandered through the western states a few years ago, when many places that are now blooming with cultivation were waste and solitary; he built a double cabin in the edge of a large grove south of the Illinois river, furnished it with a fine library, and other cherished household goods, and returned one morning in January from a ball, to find it burned to the ground with everything it contained. He subsequently opened several farms, and after many years of bacheloring in the new country, became possessed with the idea that the presence of the absent one was indispensable to his happiness. Acting on this conviction, he left the prairies after the autumn frosts had fallen, and returned with the flowers the next spring, bringing a fair girl who had consented to leave the Granite State and share his prairie home. This is our accomplished and lady-like hostess, a highly educated, intelligent, affectionate, and truthful woman; one who would have adorned the most polished circles. She is now the mistress of this little rude cabin, but her culture and worth, so far from being thrown away in this inelegant home, make her shine the brighter; as genuine diamonds do in plain setting. She is a fair-haired, blue-eyed blonde, graceful in every movement, and only prevented by the extreme slenderness so universally courted among American females, from possessing an exquisitely symmetrical figure.

CHAPTER XIII

Such is the place, and such are the people, among whom many pleasant days were spent. Our everyday pursuits and amusements were varied occasionally by a ride to the store and post-office, about five miles up the river. There were some charming views on this road; the river at some points lay spread out before us in full width, dotted with its emerald islands, and notched with the rich woodtops that bordered it, and at others it retreated from the view so as to leave only a liquid thread here and there visible amid the waving green which embedded it.

In one of these rides we were overtaken by a shower. It came with a violent wind, and consequently fell at an angle of about sixty degrees, so that if we had turned our gig and stood still, it would have protected us perfectly. But in the plenitude of our wisdom, we decided to seek refuge in a house about three quarters of a mile distant, in the precise direction of the storm. We therefore faced the wind and rain, urged our noble old Bucephalus to his utmost speed, and after a most ludicrous flight of some minutes, bounding and springing over the knotted turf, arrived, drenched, and starchless, at the door, just as the rain ceased.

One of our favorite out-door amusements was riding on horseback; another, sailing in our pleasure-boat; another, swinging on the bank of the river in front of the new house; another, gathering mandrakes in the grove. Within, we had Shakspeare, Byron, Burns, Bryant, and others, in the poetical line; some variety of scientific, philosophical, and sentimental reading; Hogarth and Dickens in the witty, and some fine copies of Italian and Swiss scenery, by way of preserving our love of the picturesque and rugged in nature. With all these resources, and a country more charming than language can describe, it would have been unpardonable not to be happy. We were not so guilty.

One of our aquatic excursions was undertaken for the purpose of spending an afternoon with Mrs. C., a widow lady, who with her six sons and only daughter resided about two miles up the river, on the opposite side. They had emigrated from one of the principal cities of New England, and were altogether among the most intelligent and valuable families in society I ever met. Their little dwelling stood about a quarter of a mile from the river, and was approached by a hard-trodden, narrow path, through grass rising on each side almost to the head of an ordinary sized man. When you emerged within a few rods of the door, the scene that opened before you was unexpectedly pleasant. The house stood in a little open glade, on a rising ground which commanded a fine view of the adjacent prairie and groves, and admitted one or two glimpses of the river, buried among the trees and tossing grass. An arm of timber from the waterside stretched up within a few rods in the rear, and another a little farther off in front of the house. The building itself had been constructed something more than a hundred miles from the spot where it now stood, had been taken apart, moved on waggons, and set up again on this spot. Its various pieces were nicely jointed and fitted together, so as to answer admirably for a summer-house. How it would serve when Boreas came down with his frost burthen, admitted of some question.

Mrs. C. was a woman who possessed the highest order of mental elegance, viz., that which is native and unaffected by outward circumstances. The hospitality of her plain little home was charming as it could have been if sumptuous viands had been served on costly plates, and luxury had waited on every indolent desire. Elegant without art, wise without pedantry, amiable without vanity, she was the model of all that is lovely in woman. Her sons had inherited much of her excellence and talent, and were universally beloved. We left her little cottage at dark, and embarked for home. The day had been very warm; the lightning was flickering around the southwestern horizon before we started, and there was every probability that we might be overtaken by a shower before we reached our landing place. There was little wind at first, but it presently increased, and bore upward flying masses of black cloud, which obscured the little light given us by the stars, and left us in darkness, only deepened by the frequent lightning-flashes. Our little sails, filled by these gusts, bore us merrily through the rippling waters till they ceased, and left us to float with the current until another came. The banks of the river were involved in profound darkness, except when the cloud-lamp burst up for a moment, but the broken surface of the water reflected innumerable fragments of light, so faint as to be perceptible only to an earnest and searching eye. When you caught them, the water seemed to grow more and more luminous, till another flash came and destroyed the beautiful illusion.

Our company were merry, notwithstanding the anticipated shower, and, striking up the "Bonnie Boat," made the silent woods echo with its cheering strains. It was a delicious night to be abroad on the water; and our spirits were so much exhilarated by the scene, that we should have rather rejoiced than grieved had we been visited by the shower. We reached our landing place, however, just as the first large drops began to plash in the water and patter among the leaves. It was ten o'clock: the muskitos had sought shelter and would be harmless while the rain continued to fall. We opened our doors and windows, therefore, and the cool air came in laden with the fragrance of reviving nature; a delightful precursor of the sweet sleep which was to follow.

CHAPTER XIV

The country north of this section of the river is one of the most beautiful that can be imagined. Its high rolling prairies are dotted with groves through which clear rapid streams wind and babble like those of the eastern states'. It was at this period principally held by the first settlers. A few late emigrants from the Atlantic side were creeping in, however, and making claims, as they are called, on some choice spots; but the "Suckers" still held the dominion.

This process of making claims is a somewhat curious matter, and not unfrequently leads to serious disturbance among the settlers. It is governed by different laws in various neighborhoods. In some it merely consists in erecting a house or something like it, in which the claimant or his agent shall reside for a certain length of time; in others he is, in addition to this, required to break and plant a piece of ground, and in still others, the latter is alone sufficient. So that you may sometimes ride through a piece of corn, growing on the open prairie with no house or other sign of cultivation or ownership in sight. These claims, if made according to the governing customs, are generally as much respected when the land is thrown into market as a deed conveying the fee simple. But if the law of the neighborhood has been evaded in part, or if there be rival claimants, each of whom have set their marks upon a single tract, it leads to serious and often fatal strifes. The emigrant, however, has in all these the advantage over the first settlers. For as the numbers of the former increase, the latter retires before them as the Indian has retired before him. He forms the second wave that pours itself into the bosom of this wilderness. When the *Yankee* homes thicken about him, and farms are opened within two, three, and four miles, he begins to feel straightened, oppressed; he wants more room, and resolves to sell to the first Yankee that offers to buy. He does not wait long; and a bargain being concluded, he stows his *plunder* underneath the cover of the large waggon, harnesses his four horses before it, hangs his "bucket" beneath and his "feed-box" behind, starts his two cows on in advance, sets his eldest boy on the right-hand wheel horse, with a single rein in his hand, and commences his journey westward, shaking the dust of the Yankee settlements from his feet. He has often no place in view, but journeys on, always toward the setting sun, for he knows that freedom such as he seeks has retreated thither. He travels on, day

after day, and grows more complacent as he gets further off. Sometimes they sleep in the cabins by the way side, and at others in the
waggon and again on the ground. The females always do their own
cooking either by the camp fire, or on the hearths where they stop.
They never complain if the journey continues for weeks, but relieve
its tedium by walking, driving the cows, &c. I have met many
hundreds of these moving caravans, and scarcely ever saw an unhappy or anxious face among them. They love the large liberty of
the wide prairie, they love its sunlight, its waving grass, its flowers,
its lone trees, its groves, its silent streams. They love the anticipation
of making a new home on the brow of the remote wilderness, and
living there, with half the careless ease of the Indian and more
than his happiness. Their minds exult in the boldness and freedom
of those enterprises which demand little practical detail. The dangers which hung over their early years have cultivated in them a
certain boldness and love of adventure which find no proper field
but on the wild frontier. The richness of the soil has obviated the
necessity of severe labor, and they have consequently grown up
with habits of indolence and a want of practical talent, found in
no other free states of the Union. Advancement in the useful or
ornamental arts is a thing almost unknown among them. The son
is content to spend his days in the rude and comfortless cabin that
sheltered his sire; he rides in the same heavy, uncouth vehicle; he
never bestows any increased care upon his crops; even though his
eastern neighbor on the next farm doubles his harvest by it.

His aspirations are equally stationary in the more important particular of educating his children. He "reckons" they should know
how to write their names, and "allows it's a right smart thing to
be able to read when you want to." He "expects" his sons may
make stump speeches if they live; but he don't "calculate that books
and the sciences will do as much for a man in these matters as a
handy use of the rifle, and a free range of the prairies." As for
teaching, "that's one thing he allows the Yankees are just fit for";
he does not hesitate to confess, that they are a "power smarter"
at that than the western boys. But they can't hold a rifle nor ride
at wolf hunt with 'em; and he reckons, after all, these are the great
tests of merit.

With all these peculiarities, and this ignorance of what is esteemed
essential in cultivated society, these people have strong intellects,
bold and vigorous ideas, and possess a vast fund of knowledge,
drawn from sources with which a more artificial society is too little
acquainted. They have an order of eloquence peculiar to them-

selves, rough, bold, and strong, and glowing with illustrations drawn from nature as they know her, and from other sources familiar to their minds. I have often listened to them with delight, as well as amusement. They are not so witty as they are accredited to be; but their thoughts and figures, so different from those we are accustomed to hear, take us by surprise, and produce an emotion of contrast so strong as to excite irresistible laughter. Their illustrations are not drawn from the lore of Greece and Rome, but from the infinitely truer teachings of nature, amid which they live. If they have not the artificial elegance which the mighty minds and associated events of centuries have given to the former, they have a higher intrinsic value, and tell more effectually on their assemblages than would all the mythology of heathendom.

CHAPTER XV

The hospitality of the people of the west is exhaustless. Such as their homes are, the stranger is ever welcome to them, and to what they contain. The single room is as freely shared as if it were twenty, instead of one. The abundant table is never too small for all that are within hearing when it is laid. You may feel embarrassed at the narrow physical limits within which all this is confined, but your feelings are never perceived or appreciated by your entertainers. You rise in the morning and are conducted to the well or spring, or a bench beside the door, to perform your ablutions (necessarily scanty under such circumstances); your host, meanwhile, descanting on some "*baar*" or "wolf hunt," on the approaching or past harvest; on the last or the coming election, on the merits of a horse, or the "chance of mast" for fattening pork, the sickness of the last season, the necessity of burning the prairies to prevent it, &c.

Within, the good wife has meantime commenced her preparations for your morning meal. The first step in this, as in all other meals, is to place her large, two gallon coffee-kettle at the fire. Next she lays the covers of two small iron ovens upon the blazing logs, removes some coals to the hearth with her large wooden shovel, and introducing its blazing edge to the ashes in the corner, ascends the ladder with a tin or earthen vessel. Presently she reppears with meal for her *dodger*. This is made by wetting the meal with cold water, and mixing it with a little salt to the consistency of a thick batter. It is then taken in the hand and deposited in three or more oblong cakes in the angle of the skillet; the cover is put over, a few coals thrown upon it, and so much of breakfast is in progress. If you are a southern or eastern guest, or particularly respected for any cause, the next step is to make a mixture of wheaten flour, cold water, lard, and salt, and cut it into small cakes, which are deposited in the other skillet. Then come the meats, which, with the corn dodger and coffee, are the essentials of all meals among these people. Morning, noon, and night sees from one to three varieties of this article on every well-spread table. All this time the coffee is maintained in the most vigorous ebullition. The table is laid at intervals, the dodgers and "hot cakes" watched, and when all is done, the coffee is drawn back and settled with an egg; the ashes are turned from the covers; the cakes taken up on plates; the meats dished; the hearth brushed; and some few little matters of taste about the room regulated; and then you are invited to the table. The coffee, it must be confessed, is execrable, and can only be disposed of by the aid of the rich cream, which is not often spared. The hot cakes, as might be expected, are solid and of a deep leaden hue; the dodger is incomparable; the quails delicious; the grouse or deer equally so; but the bacon insufferable. This is pretty nearly your bill of fare for the day. You have fruits or sweetmeats and pudding added at dinner; and fresh baked cake at tea. But at each meal you have all the meats of the first, with one variety, replaced sometimes by the domestic fowl, and sometimes by fresh baked pork. All the food of each meal is cooked at the time it is to be eaten; and the first step of this long process is to place the "coffee-kettle" where it shall come to the boiling point as speedily as possible. The western people have an unconquerable aversion to food that is not served hot and fresh from the cooking vessel. They would look with contempt upon the most sumptuous hospitality of eastern tables, if one of the staple dishes had been cooked on the previous day. No bread is ever found in their houses; they make a large loaf in their iron ovens which is fermented by what they call *salt-rising*; but it must be eaten warm, and is then only tolerable to an eastern palate.

As might be expected from this excessive use of coffee in its worst form, from the great amount of animal food, and some other causes belonging to the climate which these greatly aggravate, they, for the most part, wear complexions of a faint yellowish brown. Their skin has little appearance of life, and looks more like a soiled lemon-colored glove than the membrane of mingled red and white which of right belongs to them.

CHAPTER XVI

The morals of these people partake strongly of the characteristics already named. They are too magnanimous to be often mean, too free from avarice to be often dishonest. A little fraud or shrewd trick played upon a Yankee they consider a commendable evidence of superior sagacity; a thing to be exulted in rather than repented of. Their passion in trade is for the never-sufficiently-to-be-prized horse, and a considerable part of their petty litigation grows out of this class of transactions. Indolence is one of their worst vices; for it leads to many others. This, however, I am bound to say, is confined to the male sex. The females cannot be indolent if they would, and this for a number of reasons; one of which is, that the females of all newly settled countries have many kinds of labor to perform of which they are relieved in older regions by the greater perfection of machinery and architecture, and the presence of a larger proportion of their own sex. Another is, that the western country is visited by great numbers of single men; strangers, who are dependent for all the domestic offices on the women of the region or neighborhood in which they stop. This has been a very important item in the labors of these females for the last fifteen years. But the male population may be pronounced unequivocally indolent. On a bright day they mount their horses and throng the little towns in the vicinity of their homes, drinking and trading horses till late in the evening. It is not extraordinary to see two or more of them come to blows before these festival days end.

They are prompt to redress an injury by legal process when the law affords it; when not, by personal strength. It is, however, due to them to say, that they are equally prompt to make reparation when it is demanded in an *honorable* manner. They have little love or charity for the vices that stain artificial society. Duelling is rarely defended, licentiousness is little known, and theft is scarcely conceived of among them.

Respect for the Sabbath and for religious observances generally, is not very widely spread. Few churches are sustained, and but little expenditure incurred for the support of religious institutions. The prevailing faiths or forms of worship are the Methodist and Campbellite. There are others of course, but these are by far the most numerous. Without attempting any invidious distinction between these beliefs, it will certainly be adhering to truth to say that the latter are generally the more intelligent people, the former the more honest. The pulpit oratory of both is quite peculiar. I heard many of their "Circuit riders," and several of the settled clergy of the Methodist church, and am bound to say, that before I had this experience I should have considered any true description ironical or libelous. Among them all there were but one or two that deserve to be designated by any other name than that of the most arrant ranters. Their efforts bore no comparison with those of the stump orators and disputants of debating clubs, lyceums, &c., which you may hear every week in the small towns settled by western people. Like most empty speakers, these preachers have an abundance of furious action, a bellowing utterance, and a tone which renders it extremely difficult for the possessor of a cultivated ear to preserve both gravity and patience through one of their interminable harangues.

The primitive style of their meetings, and the motley and heterogeneous appearance of the people who assemble, makes them one of the most striking novelties to the curious observer of Western life and manners.

The Circuit rider embraces in his field of labors from thirty to one hundred miles of country. His meetings are called in schoolhouses and churches, when held in towns or thickly populated neighborhoods, and in the cabins of the settlers in more primitive regions. His audience are seated on boards, the ends of which rest upon chairs, or, where these are not to be had, on blocks of wood of convenient height. One chair is always reserved for the speaker, in which he sits until the congregation is assembled. He then rises, takes his position behind it, drops his flag handkerchief upon its back, and reads a hymn, repeating each couplet, the better to aid the memory of the singers, most of whom are without books. Thus commence the exercises of the occasion. The singing is followed by a long incongruous prayer. After this, the text is announced, and the sermonizer launches at once, without preface, into the utterance of some of the many things which he intends to communicate.

I remember becoming wearied with one of these harangues, which was more vapid than usual, and finding great relief in a study of the motley group around me. There were mothers present, with infants of all ages, from four weeks upwards. One of these, about four months old, was curiously clad. It wore a dress of coarse brown English merino, sleeves short, and ruffled at the elbow, with plain footing about a nail in width. I inferred that it had been originally white, not from any evidences then visible, but from the fact that I never saw it colored in the shops. On the head of this child was a calico cap of the coarsest texture and colors, trimmed profusely with an orange and green ribbon of some antiquity. My next neighbor on the other hand was dividing her attention between the *sarmont* and an infant of some six weeks, dressed so grotesquely as to be irresistible. A light cloak of blue cotton material partially covered a dress of green and black calico of the largest stamp; the head was covered with a cap of the finest cambric linen, exquisitely wrought, and trimmed with a faded black lutestring ribbon, about two inches and a half in width. The mother wore one of the ancient scoop bonnets, natural hose, a calico dress, and a cape of different color and figure. Directly in front, sat a young lady, the belle of the settlement, and withal not a little of a coquet, as I afterwards learned. She was clad in a dress which had once been printed, but yielding to the pressing solicitations of the rubbing-board, had parted with its colors, and was now passing for white. Each of its large threads was distinctly visible. Her neck was dressed in a very coquettish style, with a bright red bandanna handkerchief drawn tight over the shoulders, and fastened with a pin, and a long pink ribbon, which flowed nearly to her cowhide boots. Her hands were naked and empty; a *tasty* calico apron being made to do duty in place of a pocket-handkerchief. Her head was covered with the soiled remnant of an ancient green calash, the bridle of which enabled her to play off many effective glances upon the stricken *"fellers"* in her vicinity. Such ludicrous varieties of dress were inexhaustible, and afforded a rich field of observation while the orator was floundering through his subject; which on this occasion was an argument on the immortality of the soul. He had not approached this abstruse question without feeling its importance, and making due preparation. His mind had evidently been refreshed by the recent perusal of some elementary treatise on the science of astronomy, which has been supposed by other great minds to afford some evidence on this and kindred questions. How this evidence was borne did not very plainly appear from this discourse; the principal use made of his knowledge being to propound to his audience the questions found at the bottom of the page; and after a due pause, to answer them himself. Half an hour's exercise of this kind, abounding in the grossest and most ridiculous blunders, convinced the gaping assemblage that Brother A—— was not only "a powerful smart man, but one of mighty larnin."

It was safe then to return to the original question, which every one had forgotten, but which, at the end of the lesson, he seemed fortunately to remember. After some well-rounded sentences in his loudest key to prepare their minds for the tremendous question, he said, drawing himself up with a dignity and complacency which no words can convey, "Now, my friends—What is the Soul?"

A most impressive pause followed this interesting interrogatory. Every mind, save those of the dashing coquet and her rival admirers, was bent on it; the house was awfully silent for the moment; but the answer enunciated in a measured tone and manner, "My brethren, soul and body is enonemous terms," carried my gravity by storm and let down the rapt audience with such a sudden substitution of plain fact for sublime inquiry, that there was an instantaneous shuffling of feet, drawing up of bent forms, and exchanging of smiles, which said, "That is it, but we could not have said it so well."

When this sermon was over, an elderly sister, who had exulted at every sentence, asked my opinion of it. To the reply that I thought Mr. A—— possessed a fine voice, she rejoined—"Ah! he's a powerful smart man. We thought Brother ———," naming his predecessor, "was as good as anybody could be, but Brother A—— is a heap ahead of him. Where on airth he ever gets larnin to answer the questions he's always askin, I can't see; I reckon he must read a power of books."

But notwithstanding the ignorance of these men and the often ludicrous character of their discourses, their presence and services are of great value to the communities among whom they minister. That most of them are honest men, there is no doubt. The arduous and slavish character of their duties, compared with the exceeding small salaries which they receive, are testimonies in favor of their integrity, which no candid mind can reject. Nor can the value of their ministration, indifferent as it is, be doubted. Among the people whom they teach, religion is a simpler and more genuine emotion than in other states of society, where its rites and appliances constitute so much that is the subject of thought, envy, prejudice, and opposition. They have little of the vanity that poisons more refined christianity. The stirring housewife sets her little cabin in order for the meeting, and her neighbors prepare to come in with far purer and more intense religious emotions, than the plumed and jeweled dame arrays herself to visit the splendid edifice thronged with the votaries of fashion and wealth. There is sublimity and beauty in the stern simplicity of these gatherings—the rough cabin but one small remove from the handiwork of nature, whose broad and silent kingdom is spread around—the honest sympathetic faces and hard hands that clasp each other with no feigned warmth, that commend their bond of union more strongly than magnificent piles, and pealing bells, and sounding organs. Theirs is the simplest action of the religious faculties. The solemn story of the Cross and the teachings of Him who suffered on it, bring them together to worship, adore, and love Him. The motives to a false profession of religion are also fewer here than in a more complicated state of society. The vices of this condition are not such as would be either concealed or aided by the cloak of hypocrisy. They become professedly religious because they are, or at least think themselves, actually so; not because it will enable them to cheat in trade with greater impunity, or rob their neighbors' widows and orphans, on the strength of long prayers and a stereotype solemnity of faces. Religion is regarded by them as a source of happiness merely, not of gain or standing, or as a license for fraud.

However simple and imperfect, then, the ministration of their wandering clergy, it must command the respect and complacent regard of every honest and reflecting mind. Its fruits are the budding and blossoming of Faith, Hope, and Love in the wilderness. Religious institutions and observances have greater beauty and force here, where man is restrained by few motives external to himself, than where he is under the numerous obligations and restraints of a more artificial condition. These bold, daring people are brought into the church from a freedom and responsibility to themselves alone, scarcely more circumscribed than those enjoyed by the savage; and the strength and harmony of the christian code are beautifully demonstrated by the submission of such a character to their guidances. There is besides a fitness in the relative condition of the minister and his people which renders him in every respect an object of their highest regard, and secures to his teachings the most unbounded reverence. His ignorance is never discovered by them. His blunders, when he ventures beyond his usual aim to exhort or denounce, instead of exciting indignation, disgust, or mirth, only stamp him as a man of wonderful learning. There is no discrepancy between their expectations and his abilities; and his position, therefore, becomes ridiculous only to better cultivated minds. These he does not profess to instruct. He is not sent for their benefit; if they participate in what he has to dispense it is their own choice; and the liberality with which he offers it should certainly secure him against ridicule. As the Yankees increase in the settlement where he officiates, he willingly retires and leaves them a minister of their own choosing. It must not be understood that the description I have given has no exceptions. There are men officiating as servants of Christ in these wild regions who possess an eloquence and strength that would render them eminent anywhere; men whose oratory is clothed with the richest imagery, whose every figure is a flash from the glowing altar of nature, whose fervid emotion and lofty sentiment kindle and elevate the soul.

CHAPTER XVII

As my departure was now a fixed event, we began to cast about for a choice between several little excursions in the neighborhood, which yet remained to be performed. "You must go to the store with me once more;" said Mrs. P., "and to the council-house and burying-ground above Captain S.'s farm; and take another evening ride on horseback; and—do whatever else is possible."

No objection being made to these propositions, they were allowed to stand as the order of proceeding for the remaining five days. The next afternoon was devoted to the shopping. Tom was driven to the door at dinner time, and left at our service. As soon as the house was set in order, and dresses changed, a duty which, among western houskeepers, belongs to the afternoon instead of the morning, we took our seats and drove off over the beautiful road already mentioned as lying along the river.

Our shopping was rather incongruous, consisting of the entire variety usually collected in a country store, viz.: dry-goods, groceries, hardware, crockery, and glass-ware, et cet. Little Nell must have two frocks and an apron, and Hamlet a cravat. There must be half a dozen new tumblers, two butter plates and six bowls, a tin pepper-box for the kitchen, a new water-pail, some darning and tape needles, three or four deep dishes for pumpkin pies, a jug of molasses, a paper of ginger, a pound of tea, seven of coffee, a few nails, and a stone pot for the winter butter. These were put up in the smallest possible compass, and even then it required no little ingenuity on the part of the polite and energetic shopkeeper to demonstrate that we could get them all home in the gig. They were, however, stowed in, and then it required as much care to finish the demonstration by keeping them there; but we succeeded, by picking up one or two parcels when they fell, carrying the glass and crockery in our laps, and bracing the pail filled with promiscuous articles between our feet.

Our next and only remaining excursion was to the burial-ground and council-house of the Sauks, on the bank of the river, about a mile and a half above the town. The trail to this lay immediately on the margin of that beautiful section of the river before spoken of. Unbroken views of the entire stream, followed by glimpses, smiling through waving tree-tops or swelling grass, continually presented themselves. The trail lay along the very verge of the high bank, save where the latter bent from a straight line. It was deep-worn, and showed that many a swarthy foot had trodden its narrow bed. Occasionally, under a clump of bushes or the overhanging boughs of larger trees, were two or three graves, their rude outlines nearly effaced by the storms that had beaten upon them and the leveling hand of time. Where the soil had crumbled from the face of the high bank, a ghastly skull, rolled from its dreamless slumber, lay half way down the descent, arrested in its fall by the roots of shrubs or trees.

The council-house is simply a circular area some eighty feet in diameter, artificially elevated by a terrace, perhaps four feet in height. Its surface is strown with bones, the remains of feasts that have been celebrated here. It is in a beautiful spot. A fine growth of young trees secludes it from the river, so that those who are upon land may be perfectly acquainted with the movements of friends or enemies on the water without being seen themselves. More interesting to me were the graves thickly strown along the verge of the bank. Some had fallen in and partially revealed the skeletons sitting upright, their decayed canoes, which had rudely served in place of coffins, crumbling and dissolving about them into the earth whence they had sprung. I know not that this particular spot has been the theatre of great events in the history of the people who have now disappeared forever from it, but I know that its rare beauty, in the still autumn day when we visited it, seemed to me fitted to foster the wild melancholy which so deeply tinctured the character of its decayed sovereigns. Yet many a tide of excitement had swept over this lovely spot, if it had not burst and spent its rage there. A few miles above was the principal seat of the Black Hawk war, the last faint struggle of the red men of the north to retain their ancient realms. A few miles below was the village of the Prophet—the man who communed with the Great Spirit, and interpreted to His children His will concerning them. Along this very spot had wandered excited warriors, cunning "medicine men," and wondering women, in all the variety of emotion inspired by their several conditions. Rage, hatred, love, and sorrow had been born and buried here, deep in the bosom of past centuries; while the solitude and grandeur of the wilderness was unbroken by sound or sight of civilization. The strength and freedom of the past were in sad contrast with the weakness and humiliation of the present. Formerly thousands of proud and fearless men ruled these beautiful wilds. Now how different! I had seen, a few days before, the miserable, degraded remnant of their race that still lingered in these pleasant haunts. Drunken, poor, clothed in tatters, begging of those who dwelt in their former home the fire that had consumed their souls—nay, offering to barter their wives and children for it; they were a painful spectacle—a sadder ruin than the crumbling temples and broken idols of Eastern lands.

The war which a few years before had swept over these plains, had been the last struggle of a chieftain and hero, vainly seeking to infuse into his perishing people a spirit that would lead them to contend against a mighty race. But the eloquence that warmed their hearts did not restore their brave dead, nor increase the number of their living warriors. A little band of *savages* against a nation of armed men! a handful of withered leaves upon the tempest! They could have but one path before them; and they have trodden it. Westward it led them, and now their ancient council-houses are deserted; their hunting-grounds bloom under the hand of the agriculturist; their tombs crumble and sink away beneath the plow; the smoke of their lodges no longer curls on the breath of morning; their hunting-dances are no more seen at evening! All that remains of them tells of a race that has dwindled from power and the strong majesty of freedom, to humility and wasting feebleness.

The story of the Indian is a melancholy one. I have often pondered upon it, with a sympathy that would not be hushed by the voice of reason; though it proclaimed that they had fulfilled their mission, and must pass away. A fair land abounding in all that would contribute to the highest condition of civilized life, was the lawful estate of civilized man; and when he came to claim it, it was not the office of the savage to dispute his right. I mourn not so much the fate of the Indian, as the indecent, the fraudulent precipitancy with which it was consummated by our selfishness. We had room and time enough to have waited more patiently, while Nature was finishing in her own way the plan she had begun. And assuredly, while we congratulate ourselves upon the wide extent of our territory, our complacency must be somewhat qualified by the reflection that, in our haste to possess it, we have rudely expelled the original owners from homes which they loved and venerated; that we have chosen our own time to bid them disappear from a heritage around which the very fibres of their hearts were twined in love and reverence for the dead who were sleeping there, and for the living beauty and majesty that overspread it.

We need not clothe their departure in poetical garb, to make it touch the heart of flesh. The Indian, with all his pride and independence of character, with all his energy and daring, with all his veneration for the ashes of his dead, all his keen sense of the great, the free, and the beautiful in nature, all his fond pride in the magnificent hunting grounds where he had been born, and where he hoped his dust might rest, when his spirit should be set free in that scarcely more beautiful region pictured by his imagination; the Indian standing in the attitude of one who bids farewell to all these, and is about to flee before the superior craft and strength of enemies whom he despises, and yet cannot resist, seems to say, "All this have I loved, and still love; all this did my forefathers, before they slept, give to be mine forever; yet now the Great Spirit asks it for his pale-faced children, and will not be denied. The arms of our warriors are palsied before them; the bow refuses to send its arrows to their heart; they outnumber us like the sands upon the shore of the great blue waters, or the leaves of the summer forest! a destiny is awaiting us which we cannot avert! It bids us depart, and come hither no more. I hear it in the winds. It speaks to me from the depths of the storm, and whispers in the sunshine! It tells me that this shall no more play around my lodge; that I must meet death far hence, and be content to tell my children of the former glory of the red man."

One must feel that these leave-takings were fearful events in the life of a being all impulsive and unreasoning as the Indian was. How the fierce heart must have wrung and resisted, while it panted for the wasted strength that once would have secured revenge! And then how must it have refused to quail and retreat before a power unfathomable, undefinable indeed, but one whose representatives yet commanded no respect, inspired no dread!

CHAPTER XVIII

During the season following that in which the events described in the last chapters occurred, I visited various parts of the state. Some of my journeys were made alone—others, in company with a brother. They were always attended with great fatigue, but often with a novelty, either in the manner of accomplishing them, in the events that befel us, or the characters that fell in our way, which amply repaid the inconvenience.

Once I remember, at two o'clock on a bitterly cold morning, we found ourselves with six other persons, exclusive of two on the outside, crowded into a coach originally calculated for six. Our progress on this occasion, beside being extremely uncomfortable, was attended with no little danger, the weather having suddenly changed during the night, and sheeted the whole country with ice. The coach, consequently, stood at all angles to the horses, and seemed every moment to become possessed with a sudden fancy for exploring road-side slopes, or the foot of any little swell we chanced to pass. The horses, too, were in all positions; now up— now down—now half-way between both; and on each recovering, seemed more alarmed and uncertain than before. Under the excitement occasioned by all this variety, it will readily be credited that we did not suffer greatly from the intense cold or the keen winds, biting as they were. The morning dawned and found us in a deep wood, from which we emerged just as the sun showed his fiery disk in the stern, cold sky. There was an immense stretch of prairie before us, a great part of which had been burned late in the autumn; and now its black bosom was covered with one entire coat of the frost-mail.

One rarely sees a more impressive spectacle than was produced by the flood of strong red light that was poured over this immense mirror. The naked summits of the swells, black as ink by contrast with the surrounding brilliancy, looked like so many sable monsters stretched upon the plain. These, and the color of the charred surface, perfectly visible through the transparent ice where the light did not fall upon it, and the myriad hues of red and green, purple and gold, which the inequalities and our uneasy motion caused to be reflected to the eye, made one of the most gorgeous displays conceivable. Fiercely, therefore, as the winds swept around us, no objection was made to throwing up the curtains, that we might have free view of this wonderful spectacle.

"It will soon pass away," said a gentleman, whose head, covered with a woolen net cap, had for the last two hours been dancing in very inconvenient continguity to the shoulder of my companion.

"There will be another change in the weather, gentlemen; and before night we shall have little ice to complain of, or I'm no prophet," he muttered, after a pause; his head resuming its old motion, and his eyes fast closed again. It seemed suddenly to become a matter of great interest with each of the seven persons inside, to ascertain whether the alternative suggested were afterward to become a matter-of-fact or not; for all eyes were instantly turned upon him. Apparently they brought their owners to very different conclusions: some turned away with entire indifference, as if it were of the least possible consequence that such a prophecy had been uttered; others looked again to the cold glaring sky, and stretched their heads from the coach, as if to catch the wind anew and form an estimate of its character; while others shrunk deprecatingly into their wrappers or buffalo robes, and seemed to say, "Heaven send it may be so!"

These few words of conversation, and the strong light, roused the ninth inside passenger from his slumbers, and caused him to raise his head and look deliberately about, to the no small astonishment of those who had not seen him before. He was not, what the reader will anticipate, a baby, about to announce, in the usual way, that his slumbers were at an end, and that other people's must consequently terminate too; but a noble, great pointer dog, with large liver-colored ears, fine in texture as a French glove, lying over his white clean face. He had been nestled at my feet all night, keeping them as warm as if I had been at a bright fireside, or in my own bed. He became a favorite at once, but not so his master, who was a young man in a flashy dress, with the swaggering air of one who says, "If you talk of men who have seen the world, look at me."

About an hour after daybreak we stopped to breakfast, on fried quail, bacon, leaden biscuit, dodger, and the most abominable coffee, if one might judge from its color and odor, and the rapidity with which the company followed my example of a glass of cold water. Our meal over, we journeyed on; the prophetic gentleman settling himself comfortably in the back corner, repeated his prophecy, in a tone clearly intended to be one of defiance to any who should be so presumptuous as to dispute him. No one seeming disposed to do it, however, he fell off into his old state, which led the owner of the pointer to remark, that "if he went on that way all day, the weather might change as many times as it liked, and he would not be the wiser for it."

Notwithstanding the keenness of the winds, which swept over the great prairie, the warmth of the sun soon melted the ice from its surface; and the cold abating, by slow degrees we found ourselves, at dinner time, thirty miles forward on our route, and little troubled with ice indeed; for the wheels were rolling in the soft black soil, thawed to the depth of two or three inches.

The morning had worn away in the discussion of politics, the future prospects of "the west," the condition of the banking system, and the Internal Improvement bill. On all these topics there was the usual diversity of opinion,—one gentleman holding it to have been demonstrated, that the party then in power was the most intelligent, patriotic, wise, and pure body of men who had ever been entrusted with the destinies of the state; another, with the same sources of knowledge, holding, with equal pertinacity, a directly opposite opinion. All agreed, however, that "the west" was a great country; but one thought its greatness would be materially enhanced, and the wheels of its prosperity thrown forward a century at least, by carrying out the liberal system of internal improvement already projected; while another pronounced it the last evidence of folly which the people had to expect from their legislators. One regarded the destruction of banks as equivalent to the total extinction of all the sources of wealth in the nation! Earthquakes, floods, tempests, conflagrations, were nothing in comparison with it. Another thought it the measure, of all others, best calculated to secure the prosperity, welfare, integrity, almost the salvation of the people.

And thus they talked. My four-footed friend occasionally looked up and snuffed the air, while these discussions were going on, but he evidently felt that the interest of the scene was a poor compensation for the effort he was obliged to make, in struggling through the forest of limbs that hemmed him in below. When darkness came on we were within a few miles of the capital of the state. The winds blew warm from the south, the mud had deepened, the sky was overcast, and there was every promise of rain before the following morning. Our prophet had congratulated himself many times on the certainty with which he had foretold the coming storm; and though, in this case, the "shadow cast before" had been a severe attack of rheumatism, nearly disabling him, yet he evidently would rather that its severity should be redoubled, than that his sagacity should prove to have been at fault.

We reached the city long after nightfall. Except in a few public places, it was pitchy dark. The black streets received no light from the clouded heavens; and looked themselves, like a more dense continuation of the same darkness that reigned in mid air! The stage drove to a large and well kept hotel, the name of which I now forget, where we stopped for the night.

After supper I was ushered into a drawing-room, where three or four highly dressed ladies, and as many gentlemen, were sitting at cards and backgammon. They were evidently playing to wear away the evening, not from love of the games. In the intervals of the games, they carried on a desultory conversation; and more inane or pointless efforts of the kind, it has seldom fallen to my lot to hear. The ladies were engrossed with "the perfectly beautiful style" of something that had lately made its appearance in the fashionable world; and the sole theme of their thought and speech was how it would become them, or certain persons of their acquaintance; where it could be had and what was its expense.

When all possible changes had been rung upon these various branches of the momentous subject and all varieties of opinion expressed, one took up a Jeremiad over the loss of her piano! She was "immeasurably grieved that pa should have thought it expedient to come west without it." Not that she was very fond of music (a confession, by the way, which was entirely superfluous, considering that her auditors were possessed of eyes), for she was not, but it was an accomplishment that she prized very highly, and she was certain that now, when she was so far removed from everything that could confer the smallest happiness on a refined mind, she should feel the loss much more painfully. In short she felt quite positive that when they came to be settled in their new home, she should be very wretched in consequence of this loss; to say nothing of the thousand other elegancies which she had been compelled to resign in coming to this dreadful country. Her companions listened with an expression of respectful sympathy for her sorrows, and she was evidently fast working herself into the belief, that a more unhappy and self-sacrificing female did not live, when the door opened, and an elderly lady of fine mien and most intelligent countenance walked into the room.

She took a vacant chair near me, and, after listening a moment to the foolish lamentation still pouring forth at the table, turned and addressed herself to me in a few commonplace remarks. I replied, and very soon found myself in earnest conversation with one of the most intellectual and affable women I had ever met. She was a stranger like myself, but her observations on the country, the character of its inhabitants, and the effect which life in it was calculated to exert upon different classes of persons, evinced a mind gifted with strong powers of perception, keen discrimination, and exalted feeling.

"I have never," said she, "been more entirely convinced of the empty and worthless character of our plans of female education at the east, than when I have seen the subjects of them transplanted to this beautiful country. They unfit females for everything like a natural or useful life. All things must be artificial about them. In truth they become, while passing through these systems, as nearly artificial themselves as a work of the Creator can. Instead of preparing them for any of the duties and pleasures of life, they go far toward destroying whatever natural capacity for these may have been originally possessed. The more finished and prolonged the process, the more complete is the destruction of all power or wish to be useful, or to reap enjoyment from any but the most false and unnatural state of society."

"You are severe," I replied, "nor can I deny the justness of your remarks, lamentable as is the truth they contain."

"Yes; lamentable indeed, when one considers the vast interests periled by it, and the ruin, dishonesty, and faithlessness which grow out of it. I never see a young female pining over the empty sorrows created by these artificial wants, but I think with pity on the stern and real griefs which wait to follow in their time—the sore trials sure to be multiplied by a thousand-fold in consequence of this very condition of her mind—and tremble for the weak purpose and fainting integrity with which she must meet them. And what is worst of all," she added, after a moment's pause, "I fear there is in the present state of society little rational ground for hoping that it will be better."

"I must be permitted to differ with you there," I replied. "I entertain strong hope that a remedy will soon be sought for this very evil."

"Your youth will account for that," said she, with a smile. "When you have lived as many years as I have, and seen men persist in the wrong course when the right seemed plain as the path of the sun, you will have less confidence in signs that promise reform. If by that time you have lived much in society, and reflected on its interests, you will have seen that the reform of a wide-spread evil like this, is slow as the growth of mountains."

"I grant it is slow, painfully slow, to those who see its need. But every moral movement, be it individual or associated, is governed by laws; and once in progress, much hope is to be entertained that if it be not consummated itself, it may lead to others that will equally effect the object. The first step toward the remedy of any evil, is that we become convinced it is such. This conviction is, I think, taking pretty general hold on society, in reference to the present mode of educating females. And as more rational views of the duties and obligations of woman get abroad, may we not expect that a better preparation for them will be demanded?"

"To a certain extent, but I have less confidence in the efficiency of reformatory doctrine, and the force of new truth over old prejudices and long indulged habits, than your remarks betray in yourself. Nevertheless, I am willing, nay, anxious to hope, could I but find that whereon to ground my hope. Go among the educated classes of females who have come hither from the east, and you will see and hear that which will wonderfully depress your sanguine expectations of reform. Daughters pining over the absence of the finery in which they were wont to decorate themselves, and interested in nothing so much as what will restore them to their former outward estate; mothers grieving that their daughters are cut off from the opportunities of education in fashionable schools; from French, Italian, embroidery, and music; mourning over the loss they will sustain in these things, when the volume of nature, filled to overflowing with whatever is best calculated to stimulate intellect, strengthen the nobler feelings, in short, develop the true and the strong in man or woman, is displayed all around them. I blush at such folly in my sex."

"And grieve, I can well believe," said I, "for the sufferings which, folly as it is, it inevitably creates."

"Yes, I cannot choose but do so," was the reply; "though my pity is sometimes, I fear, qualified with too much indignation."

As I was about to lead the conversation in another channel, the door opened, and my brother, accompanied by one of our fellow passengers, came in. They had evidently just come from the enjoyment of some rare joke, in which they seemed to think I might participate. It was a personal adventure that had just befallen a gentleman who had rode with us during the day. He was a stranger in the country, one of the corps editorial of the empire state, on a tour of observation through the prairies. He had sat all day muffled in his buffalo wrapper, scarcely speaking, but apparently having a keen eye and ear for whatever was passing. On arriving in the city and learning that the stage-coach would leave before daylight the following morning, he expressed a wish to see something of the place, and sallied forth, despite the storm and darkness, and the remonstrances of his companions, to look about. He had gone but a few yards from the door when by some mischance he fell prostrate in the black mud, not even saving his face from the unworthy contact. His sudden reppearance in such melancholy plight, and his determination, facetiously expressed, to go to bed and see no more of the city, after having left a pretty bold impression upon it, was very heartily enjoyed by his friends.

CHAPTER XIX

At four o'clock we were again under weigh, with the rain pouring in torrents through the black morning upon the blacker earth. Daybreak found us at the breakfasting place, the first post from Springfield. The house was one of the better class of cabins, and had about it some marks of age and cultivation, such as fruit trees, and a few currant bushes. The room which we entered at once by the outer door, contained a great log fire, blazing finely, a few chairs, a table, sundry chests, a Yankee clock, giving the most exaggerated report of time conceivable, two rifles suspended by wooden hooks from the beams overhead, a variety of overcoats, et cet., upon the walls, and two beds, both tenanted.

The entrance of eleven persons, two or three of whom, the unfortunate outsides, were dripping and smoking from the storm, and all cold and hungry, was a circumstance so unfavorable to the prolongation of slumber, that the four sleepers proceeded forthwith to vacate their beds, and make ready for the events that might follow our arrival. In a very brief space of time they joined the circle at the fire, and as it might be supposed, the newcomers were more conversant with whatever was going on abroad then they who had slept peaceably all night, proceeded to question one and another on their several places of departure and destination, how long they had been on the road, how the traveling was, whether the storm was likely to continue all day, and if not, when it would cease. All these inquiries being duly answered, and sufficient time having been taken to collect themselves, after being so suddenly awakened, they proceeded to complete their toilets. The instruments wherewithal it was accomplished, were a small iron skillet, on a bench beside the back door, certain parti-colored pocket hand-kerchiefs—their own personal property, and a small wooden comb, a part of the personal estate of the oldest member of the party.

When the processes of washing, drying and combing were severally completed, they reëntered, seated themselves at a little distance from the fire, and one of them drawing from his pocket a book, proceeded to read inaudibly, the others maintaining, meantime, a profound and studied silence. The peculiarity of the affair was explained in a moment by one of our company whispering "Mormons."

The landlady looked aghast when she saw the number of guests for whom she had to prepare breakfast, but she nevertheless stirred about with a right hearty zeal, setting on her quail, chicken, pig, dodger, and biscuit. The table was ready in a short time, and our cloaks, overcoats, &c, being cast upon the unmade beds, we gathered about it. The scarcity of chairs threatened at first to be a very serious inconvenience; but what with mustering one or two small ones, and as many with broken limbs from the kitchen, and moving a large chest to one side of the table, we were all at length seated; though at such unequal heights as almost caused the smile, with which each regarded the rest, to break into a broad laugh. The good woman—and a really good and gentle woman she was, notwithstanding her rude, poorly furnished cabin, and coarse attire—made many apologies, and seemed quite overwhelmed to find herself the entertainer of so many strangers.

"It was a new thing," she said; "they were not prepared for it; the passengers had always breakfasted at the next house till the day before, when some difficulty having occurred, she had been applied to for accommodation. If it continued, they could be better prepared in a few days to make travelers comfortable." There was so much willingness in her manner, and such apparent truth in her apologies, that we all felt disposed to receive them with the utmost kindness. Just as she had delivered them, a waggish lawyer, seated on the opposite side of the table, in one of the small chairs, his head just visible above the board, looked up and asked, "How long have you lived here, madam?" and when she replied "Seventeen years, sir," looked down at his low seat with an expression so suggestive of the disparity between the length of time and what it had produced, that several incipient bursts of laughter were just faintly heard, but suppressed to be indulged on a more fitting occasion.

"I don't know," he added, when, the meal over, we were seating ourselves in the coach; "I may err in judgment, but it seems to me that chairs ought to have grown taller than that, in seventeen years!"

All day the rain poured dismally down, and our progress was very slow. Before nightfall, however, we reached the town at which we were to part from our fellow passengers, and go on in an "extra." We had yet sixty miles to accomplish, and hoped by making forty the first day, to reach our place of destination before the second night.

These same "extras" at the west are sometimes curious specimens of their genus. Ours, in this instance, was a farm waggon with slender bars of wood fastened along inside the box as substitutes for springs. They answered the purpose, however, exceedingly well. The roads were now so heavy—and as we proceeded northward, where the rain had not extended, were covered with so deep a coat of snow—that we advanced much less speedily than we had hoped. Having obtained directions we set out about two o'clock to cross a considerable prairie, beyond which was a grove, and still beyond, a house, at which it was proposed to spend the night. We went on slowly, toiling over the snowy plain, not a little perplexed frequently with the number and obscurity of the diverging tracks, and finally altogether at a loss to know whether we had followed the right one or not. But if wrong there was no remedy till we should meet some traveler or reach a house, of either of which there was no sign whatever. Immense flocks of crows screamed and cawed from the low shrubs and woods skirting the plain, or wheeled with a kind of chilled and dismal motion through the cold air above our heads! Darkness began to creep on, and still no sign of life or human habitation! Chilled and weary, our situation became at last extremely uncomfortable. The miles seemed lengthened to leagues, and our uncertainty much increased whatever else was disagreeable in the prospect before us. At last we reached the grove which we seemed to have been an age in approaching. We entered, and the road still led on with nothing more to cheer us than the plain had offered, except a partial protection from the bleak winds; and even this was more than counterbalanced by the increased darkness.

At last, however, just as the night began to conceal the road from view, we found ourselves upon the high bluff of a small stream with a mill below, and a little cabin faintly visible on the opposite height. To our great joy we had reached the spot where we proposed to take up quarters for the night. The long hill was descended, the stream forded, and the opposite summit at last gained. When we arrived at the house, there was still just light enough to render visible two huge emigrant waggons standing near the door.

"These immense waggons and the small house augur ill for our prospects of rest here," said my brother. "Nevertheless, we will try."

The driver halted, and was about alighting to make inquiry, when a man appeared at the door. "Friend," said the last speaker, "can we find rest with you to-night? We are cold and very weary."

The man cast his eye at us, for a moment, as if to assure himself of the right number, then at the waggons, and then, turning quite around, took a deliberate survey of the height and general dimensions of the cabin. This done, he once more faced us, and rolling his quid of tobacco in his cheek once or twice, replied, "Wall, I reckon you'd find it considerable snug in thar," making a backward motion with his head, to signify that he meant in the house. "Thar's my family, besides the man that's runnin the mill, and a right smart one it is"; (whether this was a compliment to the family, the mill, or the man who was running it, we were left to conjecture); "then you see thar's the movers that come in these *hyur*," — pointing to the waggons — "and another man, a sort of lawyer, I reckon, that come on that beast, and allowed he couldn't git any further, nohow, 'kase he'd had a shake gitting through the grove."

Of course we had seen our fate long before this statement of difficulties was completed, but it would not do to leave the man while making it, and moreover, we were desirous of getting some information as to the road and prospects for entertainment beyond.

"The road," said he in reply, "I reckon you'll find right bad; thar hain't been much rain lately but thar's a right smart of snow, and it's about half melted now. That makes wheelin heavy."

"How far is it to the next house?"

"We call it a smart three *mild* and a half — it's good that; nearer four."

"Is it probable we can stop there?"

"Wall, that's just what I can't tell you, nohow. The old man has got a nice place thar, but his woman ain't always so accommodatin as she mought be."

The driver had drawn his reins and the horses advanced a step or two, when he called out, "You hain't got such a thing as a bed in the waggon, I reckon?"

"You are right," replied K——"we have not."

"I just allowed, if you had, you mought find a place in thar to spread it down; the nights is so dark and cold, that's all."

CHAPTER XX

Plunging once more into the blackness that had now almost become palpable, we journeyed on, floundering through mud pools and patches of half-melted snow, shivering, hungering, sometimes groaning and sometimes laughing, till at last a feeble light was descried in the distance, and visions of a bright fire and warm supper began to float in our despairing minds. We were favored with the most liberal of all opportunities to indulge these pleasant anticipations, for the approach to this cheering beacon threatened to be interminable.

" 'A good four *mild*,' indeed!" said the driver; "he might well say that. It's nearer six. In a night like this, it would measure seven, with any chain and compass I ever saw. But they say all things have an end, and I s'pose this ride will, by and by; I wish it would come sooner, that's all."

It did come at length. We stopped opposite the light, for the outline of the house was perfectly lost in the thick darkness and fog. A loud halloo brought the "old man" to the door.

"Can we stop with you to-night, friend?" said K——. "There are three of us—my sister, and a driver, beside myself."

"I reckon," was the laconic reply.

We were just rising on our benumbed feet to avail ourselves of the privilege thus equivocally granted, when he darted suddenly back, and returning after an instant, said, "My woman ain't willin to it."

A parley now commenced, not exactly in derogation of the "woman's" prerogative to say so, if she chose, but inquiring into her reasons, and faintly suggesting whether it was quite kind to refuse strangers, already so much fatigued, and in such a night. She presented herself to answer in person, and seemed, at last, to compassionate our condition somewhat, for she inquired again, how many we were, and being told, asked if any two could sleep together.

"O yes," was K——'s reply, "the driver and I could occupy the same bed, if you have not enough for all. We shall none of us be over nice in such a night as this, after having ridden forty miles."

"Then you'll want," said the churlish woman, "two beds, and—"

"Supper," suggested the driver, in an under tone.

"And some supper," added my brother.

"I reckon you may as well go on to the next place," she replied, half closing the door, and looking out from behind it, " 'tain't but a mild and a half, and they often take folks there." So saying she latched the door and cut off all chance of remonstrance.

"That is no western woman," said I, indignantly, as we drove slowly away. "So churlish and narrow a heart as that was never born on the prairies!"

Now again we were toiling slowly onward. A mile and a half! It

was, doubtless, true; but even if double that, there was no alternative but to go patiently toward it. Dwelling with many bitter
denunciations on the inhospitable and even rude rejection we had
last met, estimating the distance we had traveled since morning,
and weighing the possibility of being compelled to go on all night,
we were quite busily employed, till the feeble light from the next
house glimmered on our discouraged senses. It seemed a long way
from the road. Two or three sharp halloos, however, brought some
one to the door, and again the question was put, "Can you accommodate three persons with supper and beds to-night?"

"I expect," replied a man's voice; "I'll see my woman, an' tell
you."

"Heaven grant that the woman may be more propitious this
time!" I exclaimed. In a few seconds he appeared again at the door,
with a cheerful "Yes," and an invitation to "come in!" We rose to
comply with this welcome request. My brother had already alighted,
and I had placed one foot on the side of the waggon, preparatory
to launching into the unfathomable darkness below, when the driver
suddenly cried out, "Stop a minute, till I see if he's got a stable.
—I say, friend," addressing himself to the kind host, who was now
approaching with a lantern to light our way, "have you a good
warm stable? My horses are very tired and warm."

"Yes, I've got as good a stable, I calculate, as any man in these
parts."

My foot became entangled in my cloak, or I should have been
on the ground in another instant, when he added, "'Tain't just
hyur, it's up to t'other place."

"And where is the other place?" said the driver.

My heart misgave me!

"Oh, it's just up *hyur*, about three quarters of a *mild* through
the grove."

"Three quarters of a mile! Pray, madam, be seated again, and
you too, sir; we must try once more, if you please. Much obliged
to you, sir," he continued, speaking for the party, "for your kindness, but I can't think of walking three mile to-night, and I can't
go to bed without seeing my horses once after they are put up. I
would rather drive them all night."

The settler, whose benevolent visage was now faintly discernible
by the light which he held over his head, regarded the speaker
with some astonishment, and then replied, with a facetious sort of
grin, that we should have been welcome if we'd "had a heap more!"

"It's five *mild* to the next house," he added, "and I reckon you'll hardly find 'em up when you get there; but they'es right clever, and won't make much account of gittin up if they can take you."

We jogged on. The kind, cheerful aspect and demeanor of this man somewhat changed the complexion of our feelings, and though it was later than when we left the last house, and the distance to the next nearly five times as great, we had derived a courage and spirit for the task that made it seem comparatively easy.

The ludicrous aspect, also, of the affair, began now to present itself, and, what with the recollection of similar adventures, and the comments which this drew forth, we grew very pleasant, and had many a hearty laugh long before the five miles were accomplished. Suddenly, the chance of passing the house, in the profound darkness, it being too late for the quiet settlers to have a light still burning, checked our mirth, and made us peer into the surrounding gloom with a business-like feeling, quite in contrast with the careless abandonment we had just been exhibiting.

"Do you watch one side of the road," said K—— "and I will the other; and if you see something that looks a shade blacker than all the rest of creation, call out."

Nothing could be more favorable to the indulgence of fancy, and the seeing of sights, than to be set on such a watch as this. Darkness is ever more densely peopled than light, and with such strange objects, too! But when you look into a good dense mass of it, expressly to see something, your senses all sharpened and awake for that purpose, what an unlimited license your fancy has! The way which had hitherto been solitary, became at once crowded. Cities, churches with towers and tall spires, shooting into the clouds; fantastic clumps of trees; farm-houses, large and generous-looking, like those of the east; coaches with four horses; single waggons and foot passengers; herds feeding in the adjoining fields; great overhanging piles of rock; rivers and wooded hills, rose up and spread about us as if by magic. It was wonderful! Many times I was on the eve of calling out, but a little sharper look convinced me that the object I was regarding was not the cabin, but something very different, mere foggy space!

At last! could I be mistaken? No! that was surely a light gleaming before us, and there must be the home of the settler! But what did they with a light at that hour? It was certainly ten o'clock, and only some extraordinary emergency could keep them astir so late. We were beset with fears. Sickness, a previous arrival, company, something which would conflict with our prospects, was certainly afoot.

We reached the door, and called again. A man stepped quickly out, and, as he did so, revealed a great blazing fire and a clean-swept wide hearth, that redoubled the gloom and cold of the outer world. "Can we get lodging here, friend?" was the anxious inquiry. His first reply expressed a doubt; his second a stronger one; and his third the almost positive certainty that we must again go on. But we had been rejected too often to yield this last hope without some argument. Would he tell us the reason?—some other beside mere convenience; for, as to that, we could sleep almost anywhere, and go without supper or get it ourselves. We would be no trouble, if he would let us come under his roof and rest from our long and cold journey.

"I should be right glad to 'commodate you," he said, in reply, "but—" and he hesitated.

"But what, friend?" said my brother, somewhat petulantly; for, by this time, our patience was pretty well exhausted.

"Why, the fact is," said the perplexed man, "my wife is not well; there's a couple of the neighborin women hyur, and my oldest boy has gone for the doctor now."

"Spoken like a man at last," said K——, unable to suppress the laugh which the honest man's confused and awkward manner provoked. "Drive on; we will not force ourselves upon your kindness under such circumstances, if we find no shelter till morning. But how far is it to C——?"

"Four mild, and you'd better not stop till you get thar. The roads is tolerable good now, and you'll find poor 'commodation any whar this side."

"Thank you." And for the fifth time we were on the way.

"The fates are against us to-night, certainly," said K——, "I never knew the jades so perverse before. I shouldn't wonder now, if there were no rest for us till we got to the end of our route. How far is it, driver, from this place ahead to ——?"

"Fifteen miles, I believe, sir, and I've been thinking that perhaps we may as well go on."

"We'll try our fortunes once more at C——, and if they are not better we may perhaps think best to do so."

CHAPTER XXI

The roads proved, as the settler had told us they were, much better than those we had passed, and we soon found ourselves before a wooden hotel, in the principal street of the village. A bright fire was shining through the uncurtained windows, and a group of men were sitting and standing about it, smoking and apparently enjoying the highest degree of comfort. We alighted, determined to stop here at all hazards. I followed K—— into the room, and we seated ourselves on chairs that were vacated for us at the fire. The apartment was redolent of tobacco smoke and the fumes of brandy. In one corner was a little triangular box containing sundry bottles, glasses, cigar boxes, &c.; in the opposite one a flight of stairs leading to the room above. The company, with the exception of three or four strangers like ourselves, seemed to consist principally of the villagers. They were complimenting each other in various potations of brandy, whiskey, and other similar beverages, betting on horses and candidates for the county offices, and discussing a notable wolf hunt that had recently taken place, at which a fine horse had broken a leg. A few were more rationally talking over the different methods of agriculture adopted in the neighborhood, and speculating on the probable results of each. With one or two exceptions they were all western men, and, I suppose, they presented very much the appearance which this class of persons always do in such meetings. They seemed in the bar-room a totally different order of beings from the same men at home. I was pained with the contrast.

We were seated but a few minutes when the door of an adjoining room opened, a little weazen-faced man looked in, and after glancing at us, called out in the strangest of all voices to some one in the apartment beyond, to "make a fire in the ladies' parlor!" I was quite astonished. The idea of a ladies' parlor was so remote from my anticipations! Nothing could be more welcome, however, for the noise and bluster of the drinkers increased and rendered the place anything but agreeable.

"If there is any other room with a fire," I whispered to my brother, "pray let me go to it." He followed the man with the wonderful voice, who returned with him in a moment and told me if I would just step into the kitchen till the fire was made in the ladies' parlor, I would find myself quite comfortable. "Certainly," I replied, "let me go to your kitchen." I followed him across a naked dining-room into an apartment apparently boundless; its walls, if indeed it had any, being wholly shrouded in darkness. Three or four filthy, ragged servants were crouching and chattering over an immense cooking-stove, on the top of which stood a tallow candle, the only source of light and heat in the room. There was no floor, save the black earth trodden into numerous little hard hills and hollows; there was but one chair visible, and judging from the general aspect of the place, I dared not sit upon this. The landlord had opened the door, motioned me in, and retreated with the light so that I had no alternative but to stand there in the black, cheerless room, till some one came to relieve me. I did not wait long till he returned, and saying that the fire was burning above, desired me to follow him. I did so, and returning to the bar-room was ushered up the open flight of stairs, through two sleeping-rooms, into a third containing a curtained bed, a Franklin stove in its centre, a large rocking-chair robbed on one arm and otherwise mutilated, some half-dozen wooden chairs of various colors and fashion, and a volume of dense blue smoke that quite took my breath.

A lamp was standing, as it appeared to me, in a very precarious position on the stove; but there was nothing else on which to place it. The door closed immediately after I entered the room, and I was again alone.

Chilled as I had been with the long ride, I was still trembling with cold, and thought only of getting to the fire. I could be indifferent to everything else if there were a generous fire in the stove. I walked round in the front. A few blocks and ends of boards were lying flat upon the hearth, with here and there a remnant of a shaving between them. There were no tongs, no andirons, no fire—not a spark visible. Both the large windows in front were wide open to permit the smoke to pass out, the stove-pipe apparently having no connexion whatever with this office. I took hold of the large chair, and found my glove whitened with the dust and ashes lying upon it! This was the last blow that by forbearance could endure. Walking straight to the bed, I took one of the yellow pillow-cases and rubbed every part of the chair with which my clothes could come in contact, and then seated myself to wait the reppearance of the man who had brought me thither. In a few minutes he came, accompanied by my brother. The face of the latter was glowing from the warm fire he had just left.

"What!" he exclaimed, "have you no fire here? What does this mean, sir? You told me she had a good fire and was very comfortable. Do you call this comfort?" slamming the windows down with a force that made them rattle.

"Dear me, sir," said the landlord, making a violent stir among the blocks on the hearth, "I told them to make a fire, and I supposed they had."

"Supposed they had!" replied the other impatiently; "would it not be as well, if your people are no more to be trusted than this, to look a little after the comfort of guests yourself?"

"I try to sir," replied the little man, meekly, "but I can't be everywhere at once."

"Well, in any case attend to ladies, when they come in from such long cold rides as my sister has had; never leave one again in such a den as this, without fire or light, and filled with smoke."

"There, that will do now," the shavings having been coaxed by the application of the lamp and a world of blowing, into a feeble blaze.

"Give us some hard wood, that will create a little heat, and then see if we can have a warm supper."

"None for me," said I, "I shall sleep better without it; let me but get warm and I will retire."

"We can give you a good supper, ma'am," said the obsequious host, rubbing his hands and bowing.

"Well, where? Your kitchen gives poor promise of that," I replied. "Give me a good fire and show me a sleeping-chamber, and I will ask no more."

"Really, ma'am, I wish—"

"Will you get us some wood," interrupted K——, "and leave us to our own choice in other matters!"

"Certainly, sir!" and he departed.

The next morning we were off at a brisk hour, and breakfasted with the neat hospitable family of an intelligent Illinoian, about five miles from C——. The warm, cheerful cabin, well lighted by a couple of windows, the bright fire, the clean floor, the generous table, and the frank hospitality of both host and hostess, were in lively contrast with the disappointment, churlishness, and imposition we had encountered the previous day.

A little after noon we found ourselves at our place of destination, where the comforts of a hotel, rarely surpassed in the east or west, amply compensated for the hardships and toil we had endured in reaching it.

CHAPTER XXII

The opening of the following spring found me domiciliated for a time with one of the pleasantest families in the beautiful city of Alton. I say beautiful, because it was never otherwise to me. When I first reached it from the north, where winter was still protracting his reign, the foliage of spring was just bursting its brief bounds. The days were bright and sunny, and such were welcome after my tedious pilgrimages in the more rigorous north.

The position of Alton is one of much beauty. It stands at one of the most charming points on the upper Mississippi; having its clear, dark waters broken by two beautiful, wooded islands near the opposite shore, and commanding from the bluffs a fine view of the junction of the Missouri with the former stream. Immediately above the city, terminates a line of limestone bluffs, bold and towering, which wall in the Mississippi for near fifty miles. Immediately below, commences the celebrated "American bottom," which extends almost unbroken to the mouth of the Ohio. The town is divided into upper, middle, and lower Alton. The last-named lies along the waterside, and is the principal place of business. Middle Town extends back on the heights, and contains some very picturesque and beautiful spots; and Upper Town still farther back, and down the river, has some points that, transferred to canvas, would bear comparison with the boasted scenery of the old world.

A considerable proportion of the houses in these three divisions are built of stone; the great abundance of it on the river rendering it as cheap as any other material. The grounds are sufficiently old to be ornamented with well-grown trees, shrubberies, &c.; and in the season when the heights and broken swells are covered with verdure, few more beautiful spots are to be found in the country. In the immediate vicinity of Lower and Middle Town, indeed within their yet unsettled precincts, there is great variety of scenery. High, rolling ridges, divided by deep valleys or round basins, as perfect in finish as if constructed by rules of art, diversify the whole surface. The heights are for the most part covered with the hazel, low shrub oak, and forest trees. The level grounds between, are clad with a smooth green turf, set during the spring and summer with a great variety of wild flowers. In the vicinity of the town are many beautiful groves and tracts of barrens; and farther back, are small prairies, divided and bordered by clumps of trees and clean open woodlands.

Many a charming ride and walk had we through these natural parks, when they were in their perfection of beauty. When the early showers were over, and the clouds had passed away, we used to ramble into the groves or barrens and return after an hour or two with great clusters of the phlox, painted cap, moccasin flower and geranium, bright and fresh from their pleasant homes by stream and tree, to adorn and perfume ours. While we were gathering them, the quail was running to and fro on the clean turf, and whistling to the merry breeze; the robin was singing in the tree top, and the brown thrasher performing his seriocomic solo, a little farther off on the lower branches. The winds ran wild among the trees, shaking their long arms and making their lengthening shadows dance upon the bright sward with a gay motion; as if the very genius of mirth were disporting itself in the universal jubilee.

Oh, glorious were those days! and beautiful the life which they inspired in the members of our little circle! I have been in many places where nature had lavished her charms as freely; I have visited such alone, and with others, but I scarcely ever found that harmony between heart and heart that gave society the power to enhance the emotions which nature inspired. One is almost certain to feel that it is better to be alone or with one kindred spirit. We must deny ourselves the social to enjoy the natural. Because the former is false, and inharmonious! Some selfish passion, some carking care, some worldly anxiety possesses one heart or more of those you would have free, and strikes a jarring chord in your own. The flowers are less exquisite, the sunshine less bright, the breezes less inspiring from that moment. Thus much of what should be enjoyed is lost. The dew is first brushed from the flower, then its exquisite colors are dimmed, then it is crushed and at length wholly lost. The plain of life is a dismal waste, on which one sees neither verdure nor bloom. But with us it was different. Of the few who knelt together around this festive shrine of nature, we could have spared no one without pain. All were free, all harmonious! The chaste and elevated joy which nature afforded was not frittered away in pitiful efforts to appear other than we were, nor in any of the thousand petty cares and strifes which so degrade the spirit; but seized on as a boon from heaven, and enjoyed with right hearty zest and freedom. In such a social atmosphere, and surrounded with such objects, one feels that to be is a blessing, and wonders that life could ever have been irksome. The toils and vexations with which man seeks to enlarge himself before his fellows sink into their true insignificance. We suffer none of them to mislead us at such a season. We laugh at them, and say in our hearts, "See, what are all that you can bring, compared to these birds, these flowers and trees, and running streams, and winds, and storms, and sunshine! These are what God has provided for my enjoyment. But ye are born of men, toiling, struggling men, whose spirits travail all their lives, and bring forth monsters to brood upon their death-beds. Away, we will none of ye! The earth is a fair heritage; and blessings on its Author, it is ours."

Even the cares and anxieties for the absent were sweetened by the all-prevailing calmness and joy of the season. Beautiful indeed was life during that brief period.

CHAPTER XXIII

Indeed we almost lived out of doors. What with rides, walks, visits, calls on the few who made up our free circle, we were very much abroad. We could not have been too much so. A pleasant proposition was made one evening to forsake the abodes of men for a whole day and betake ourselves to the woods. It met with unanimous approval. We would all go, and take the children. It should be an informal turn out; nobody should take any care beyond putting a loaf of bread and a few other plain refreshments into a basket. We would meet at the "White Cottage," and without any preconcerted arrangement drive into the woods, seeking pleasant places. An entry made in my diary after our return, will show how wise we were, and how foolish was the Ethiopian monarch, when he commanded *preparation to be made* for ten days' perfect happiness!

"We started at eleven in high spirits for our picnic ground; which, by the way, was not selected. Indeed, the direction we proposed to take was but vaguely conjectured by most of us. As many as could be conveniently stowed in Mr. A———'s large farm waggon were thus disposed of, and the rest followed in smaller vehicles, but all making a merry band, hailing each other from the foremost to the hindmost, and exchanging many gay challenges to marvelous feats when we should reach our stopping-place.

"Before we started, every appearance of rain, with which we had been theatened in the early morning, had vanished, and the sky, softly and beautifully blue, when seen, was skimmed over with light, feathery clouds, screening us in the most friendly manner from the otherwise too ardent rays of the sun. The morning was breezy and fresh in the green, open wood, and the bright phlox, and dazzling painted cap, and tender geranium danced and sparkled gaily, as the winds went by, like careless children who had nothing to do but revel in the life and beauty about them.

"We rode five miles. Our way, for the most part, wound along the summit of swells that divided cool, shadowy ravines, and then descended the height to the shore of the Mississippi. Here we left our carriages, took each a portion of the necessary articles, and commenced the ascent of another bluff, Mr. ——— and myself preceding our friends a little, as a committee of selection. We climbed the hill for half a mile, and as we rose, that rose before us; now a little opening shaded by overhanging oaks presented itself, and now we were bending beneath their sweeping branches. Gradually as we ascended, the prospect widened, until at length, when the summit was fairly attained, a prospect burst upon us magnificent beyond description! 'Eureka!' exclaimed Mr. A——, and we both felt that further search would be vain.

"On the very pinnacle of the bluff, the east side of which was thickly wooded and the west opening upon the river, we found a little shaded nook, just large enough to admit our number. Here, after the vines and light undergrowth had been cleared away, we spread our white napkins, table cloths, &c., and laid out our simple refreshments. Two or three loaves of bread, a bottle of cream, some golden butter, a trio of cold chickens, and a loaf of plain family cake of the largest size, constituted the whole. A committee was now appointed, and sent out with authority to search the neighboring hills and hollows for water. Their protracted investigations had begun to give rise to some anxiety in the more youthful members of our party, when they returned with a brimming pail of the purest and coldest water. The thanks of the company having been tendered them, in a neat speech by one of the gentlemen, we proceeded to seat ourselves, in true oriental style, around the cloth.

"Stories, songs, and hymns followed the lunch, and when these were no more called for, one or two chess boards were routed from their repose at the bottom of the baskets, and put on duty by some, while others strolled out to enjoy the prospect. I was among the latter; and rarely indeed had nature invited more irresistibly, than in the pomp and glory about me. Behind lay the still wood, into the green depths of which the younger members of our party had strayed, in search of flowers, and whatever else of rare and beautiful might be found. Before, and far below us the Mississippi rolled its majestic waters, now sleeping as placidly in the misty sunlight, as if they had never tumbled and rushed in angry floods, terrifying the hearts of beholders. Away in the distance, where they shone and flashed like molten silver, clusters of green islands sat upon their bosom, the farther ones still, as if chiseled in emerald, the nearer ones alive with their tossing foliage. This river had been to our childish minds an almost fabled creation. A far away land had given us birth; a far away clime had lighted our early years. We had read of the great rivers, and almost suspended our breath in wonder at their magnitude; but never dreamed that our eyes would be favored to look upon them. And now one was sweeping its silent way two hundred feet below us, and the other rolling its turbid waters onward through the dense forest, only a mile from the opposite shore! It seemed the realization of an impressive dream! To the left, on the Illinois side, bold rocky bluffs overhung the waters in which they had been mirrored for centuries. To the right, the horizon stretched away in the faint sunlight, until the eye was pained with the endeavor to define it, and the Mississippi might be seen at intervals, like a silver thread, shimmering through the green extent. A light haze rested on the distant hills, mellowing and softening the landscape with that peculiar tinting which only the hand of nature can impart. Nothing could be imagined more magnificent than the entire view, while in our immediate vicinity the bluffs were alternately piled into high conical hills and hollowed into deep ravines, laden with vegetation, which, tossed by the winds, lent a peculiar grace and changefulness to the landscape. Beneath us a precipice, two hundred feet in height, overhung the water — its face hollowed in so deeply, that it was only by a somewhat dangerous experiment that one of the gentlemen, laying himself flat upon its summit and looking over, could see its entire depth! On its very brow a deep-worn, narrow track told of the wanderings of the Indian! Many a light-hearted troop had filed along that dizzy height, conscious of perfect security, while our tamer blood curdled in our veins if one of us approached its brink!

"As we sat and gazed from these heights, my thoughts reverted to the early time, when the light canoe skimmed those majestic waters; when, from the surrounding heights, the council fires of a mystery-loving and sanguinary race flashed against the evening sky, and lithe and dusky forms trod with free step the unsoiled turf! Now all that had made the life of those scenes had departed! Only the mortal evidences that they had been, remained. Rude graves, that had closed long years before over those who shared them, were piled around us on the summits of the hills. On one of these a solitary wild rose-bud had unfolded its delicate petals: but a blight had fallen upon it, as on the mysterious race whose existence it shadowed forth! The bright and glowing green had faded, while it was yet spring, into the sickly yellow. The spirit of the departed had breathed over it in sadness; no kind hand was near to cherish it, or remove the cankering rust; and the fair rose was already numbered among the fallen.

"A beautiful tale, told that blighted bud, of a race that had passed away—of a people free as the waters beneath, and swift as the winds playing around, who had trodden the very spot where we were seated; who had gazed upon the varying landscape, the bright river, and the far hills, with feelings we could never know— who had scaled the beetling cliff, and mocked the eagle in his flight; whose war-shout rang through the wild wood, and over the water; and whose songs, once heard there, were now for ever hushed!

"With emotions chastened and elevated by the scene upon which we had looked, and the recollections with which it was fraught, we ressembled after our devious ramblings. Conversation, music, and anecdotes succeeded, till the shadows began to lengthen on the hill side. Just as the second lunch was spread, the white signal of a steamer, far down the river, became visible, curling and fading on the sunny breeze. Mere speck as she appeared at first, she was pronounced by the gentlemen, on her near approach, to be a boat of the largest size. When directly opposite us, her distance was still so great, that the large black letters on the wheelhouse looked like a fine line drawn across it. She ran close under the opposite shore, and, as the white wreaths rose from her iron throat, and faded away among the green boughs, and her hoarse breath sounded faintly over the waters, she formed a pleasing feature in a landscape which had been hitherto made up exclusively of natural objects.

"We had little relish for our second meal. The sense of mere existence had been such a joy and blessing all the day, that the common pleasures of life had lost their power to engage our faculties. We were merry, but our merriment was not that which flashes in fitful gleams from the troubled heart, or breaks forth for a moment to subside on the recurrence of care into a deeper gravity than before. It was founded on the deep, full, inward joy which we had been all the day drawing from the pure and beautiful world around us. And when the frequent bursts of laughter, provoked by the wit of the moment, subsided, they were followed by no reproving or half-repentant visages, but an expression which showed that we were ready to enjoy the next as heartily. The deep old wood resounded with our mirth.

"Another report from the water committee was called for, which those gentlemen very ingeniously relieved themselves from making, by introducing, with a very pompous preamble, a resolution that we 'were not dry.' It was passed by acclamation, and followed by one as formally introduced, unanimously applauding the acumen, research, ability, and scientific profundity evinced by this discovery. When the sun began to peep under the arch of our leafy bower,

we commenced preparations for our return. The napkins, fragments, et cet., were repacked, and, when all was ready, we seated
ourselves on the turf for a parting song. 'Rosin the Beau' was first
sung, in full choir, and followed by the beautiful hymn, 'God is
good.' We then bade adieu to the fairy spot, and, taking up the
line of march in true Indian style, we descended the bluff, slaked
our thirst at a delicious spring that gushed from the bank into a
rocky basin below, and then stowing ourselves into the waggons,
were soon on our way homeward, by the same road, now bright
and checkered with the shadows of evening.

"It was a delightful close to a happy day. I believe, as we retraced
our steps, we each felt that it was good to have spent it in communion with nature and our own hearts, under her divine influences. As we were recounting our advantures and enjoyments in
presence of a person who had not been of our party, he remarked
that as every sweet had its bitter, he waited to learn what ours
would be. But we had none. The very elements had conspired with
the fair earth and our own spirits to make it an occasion of unalloyed
happiness. At half-past ten we retired, just enough fatigued to
appreciate the luxury of a quiet bed."

CHAPTER XXIV

It will readily be credited that one could not leave a place and
society like those I have attempted to picture, without many regrets;
but the happiest seasons are sometimes the briefest, and one may
not hesitate when duty calls. With the ripening summer I turned
my footsteps northward, and a few days after the picnic found me
in the village which had formerly been our home. It had changed
little in outward aspect since I last saw it. But one little knows,
when revisiting places which are familiar and seem to the eye
unchanged, what events may have happened to those who have
never left it, to make olden haunts and long-trodden paths the
entrance to a world all strange and new. It may be one of joy which
fills the heart, or grief which crushes it. The streets may be the
same, the houses, the gardens, the groves, the fields—nay, the very
persons who dwell among them, unchanged, as to their identity;
and yet one may have entered a world of happiness while pursuing
his daily ways among these things, while another has reached the
opposite goal. While the heart of the one is rejoicing in its new-
found possessions, and seeing brighter flowers, and warmer sun-

shine, and gladder skies, the other beholds all nature clad in funeral garb. The winds that breathe around him tell of sorrow, the sunshine brings no gaiety—all that was wont to awaken joy and rejoicing is changed. And yet they are the same!

I had not been long absent from our village; yet events, clothed with power to work all these miracles, had befallen many of its citizens. One tragical occurrence, that wrapped the whole community in gloom, had fallen with such a crushing weight upon the heart of a wife and mother, as seemed to defy all attempts to heal and raise up the broken spirit. A husband and father, whom I have before introduced to the reader, had left his home on a bright winter morning for a few hours' sporting, and never returned to it! His last words, as he left the door, had been a playful invitation to his wife to prepare some favorite dish for his supper, for which he promised her a reward that death never suffered him to pay.

As night drew on and brought him not to the fireside and table where his beloved presence was awaited, the expectant wife grew restless at the long delay, and often stood beside the window overlooking the prairie, whence he was to approach. Twilight came and deepened into night; the evening wore away, and supper was at last partaken without him. The mother, having expressed some wonder that he did not return, had been assured by her sons that he had gone to the house of a neighbor, about four miles away, where he was wont to stop occasionally in his excursions.

At last the family retired. The heart of the wife was not altogether quiet, but that, she reasoned, was because it was so uncommon for him to be from home. The mere sense of loneliness, not her fears, she was certain, prevented her sleeping well. The night was long, very long, in truth, but then he would doubtless walk home to breakfast. The morning was mild, and she thought with an inward smile how pleasant it would be to him, who so loved the activity of the outer world, to walk those four miles, breathing the pure air, enjoying uninterrupted communion with his own thoughts, and, above all, anticipating a social breakfast at his own home with those to whom his presence always gave delight.

She rose early to prepare the morning meal; there was not need of this, for the long walk would make him late; but then it was pleasanter to be up and occupied, than lying in bed when she could not sleep; and beside, he might rise early and be there before she expected, and then she should be prepared for him. So she had a bright fire blazing a welcome that would greet him a long way off, in case he should approach before daylight, and her preparations for breakfast went cheerfully and pleasantly forward.

Pausing in the door once or twice, she heard at a distance the howling of wolves, that struck her ear unpleasantly, and made her rather hope that he would not start very early, lest he might encounter some of them. When they grew louder and quite dismayed her woman's heart, she thought with much comfort that there was no probability of his leaving the house early; he would be fatigued with the chase of the previous day and would rest well, knowing that they would be perfectly easy about him. Then she wondered that she should have been so foolish as to think he would be there early—still she could not help listening whenever a sound from without met her ear, and once or twice she started to the door with a bright smile on her face, for she was almost certain she heard his footsteps in the path. But when she got there, the night was black and silent as ever; the low moaning of the wind, or the dismal howling she had heard, being the only sounds she could distinguish.

Daylight seemed long coming; but then she had risen early, and being alone must expect this. At last a few faint streaks began to be visible in the east; then she summoned her sons that they might have their cattle fed, and be ready for breakfast, so as not to keep him waiting a moment; for the long walk would have sharpened his appetite.

So the usual stir of the morning commenced. And very pleasant it seemed to her to have things going on in their accustomed way. The stepping in and out as the light gained, the milking and setting the pail on the table, the straining and placing it on the shelf where it belonged; the fading of the candle, and the assurance which the broader light without gave her, that he would soon be there; the necessity arising from this, of bidding her sons hasten to be ready, was all very cheerful and agreeable.

Finally everything was attended to without, and the young men came in to wait breakfast. Here all was ready too, and broad day was on the prairies—a little greyer yet, perhaps, than it would be half an hour hence; but she could see a long way down the plain.

There was no one yet in sight; but the grove was only a mile off; he might be in that yet, or he might when she chanced to look out, be in one of the many little hollows that cut the prairie. But she wished now more than ever, that he would come, for the waiting, when there was nothing to do, was more tedious than before. The daylight too made it more wearisome than when it had been dark. As it wore on and the sun came up—the sun, that, bright and clear as it was, ought to have cheered her, she could not but confess to her inmost soul a chilly sinking of her hopes.

For now the day was going on as it always did, and yet he came not. While it was dark there had been a sort of excited life in her feeings which the full day almost extinguished.

At last she proposed faintly, hoping that her sons would dissent from it, that they should wait breakfast no longer; she half suggested in a slow, hesitating tone that perhaps their father would not be there till late, and they would want to be at work. Then it occurred to one of them that he would stop to breakfast where he had spent the night. He had taken his game there with him, and as his hostess had been an inmate of their family for some time previous to her marriage, and knew so well how to prepare his favorite grouse, and delighted so in doing it for him too, of course he would take breakfast with her, and afterward walk home. What more probable than this? Foolish woman! she thought, why had it not occurred to her before? She wondered at her thoughtlessness. But it was for-tunate for them, she said with her own sweet, patient smile, for the favorite dish of their father was theirs also, and if she had not expected him to breakfast, she should hardly have risen early enough to prepare it. She had forgotten that she could not sleep!

They ate breakfast. She was a little nervous, and started once or twice when something like footsteps were heard about the door; but she laughed faintly each time, saying how foolish it was, for he would not be home till ten o'clock. When the meal was over she set her house in order, and thought, if it came on to snow, as the grey gathering clouds seemed to promise, how pleasant their fireside would be when they were all there, and the storm was beating without. Her sons left her to attend to their morning cares, and she fell into her ordinary state of mind, feeling quite as she did every day, when they were all out engaged in their various duties.

The short morning wore away, and it was time to prepare dinner. She was quite surprised when she noted the hour—he had not come yet, and a faint gleam of the feeling that had, she must confess it now, dismayed her so in the morning, returned. But then it was probable he had stopped on the way for game, and, perhaps, even now, would be there before her meal was ready. So she went busily to work, and, as her labors proceeded, she glanced occasionally from the window to see if he were near. No! he was not yet; and then she bethought herself, with a suddenness that blanched her whole face, that she had not heard his gun all the morning! She almost opened the door with the intention of communicating this to her sons, as a new and unthought-of evidence that they ought to be alarmed. But then she could hardly persuade herself to do it. They might laugh, and say it was not strange; or wonder that she would suffer herself to be anxious; but she was still more deterred, though she hardly confessed this to herself, by her reluctance to give form or expression to her feelings.

Noon came, but she did not call them to dinner; they had better dine half an hour later, and be all together. Beside, their breakfast was late, and she did not feel the least appetite! Half-past twelve— one—and still no return! Now the phantom fears that had hovered in her mind, would no longer be denied their hold. She was no longer afraid to speak, and act, as she had been half prompted to do all the day. With her better defined apprehensions for him, she acquired more courage over her own emotions. She called her sons, and requested the younger, after he had eaten his dinner, to ride down to Fanny's and see if his father were unwell, or what detained him. She spoke only thus; for, with all the calmness she had acquired, she found it impossible to name the alternative that was lurking in her bosom.

And now came another long period, during which she must compose her feelings; though it was not so easy as it had been in the morning: there was more expectation now; and its termination was clearly before her mind. Her sons would return soon, and then—

He came. She had seen him a long way off over the naked plain, and felt her blood rush tumultuously about her heart, when she saw him alone! But a moment's reflection taught her that this was folly; for, of course, his father would not be with him; and then she wondered she had not thought to send another horse down! But why did he ride so fast? He was, perhaps, hastening to relieve her fears; or—and once again she made a vain endeavor to supply the remainder of the sentence. He came on fast and faster yet! His horse was almost running! She could see that his face was pale! And then she turned from the window, and placed one or two chairs in order that had been left standing—took up a work basket that was upon the table; wound some thread on a spool; and laid it down again. The same instant the swift feet stopped at the gate; the rider dismounted, and, rushing in, pale and breathless, exclaimed, "Father has not been there at all!" Then, seeing he had been too abrupt (though he had only uttered words that had been on his lips every step of the way home), he attempted, by some broken speech, to soften the terrible truth. He might have been led farther from home than he intended, in pursuit of some rare bird; or he had met with some acquaintance and gone down to D——, a neighboring town some ten miles distant, or—but here his bewildered tongue refused to furnish another word in aid of his attempt; and, when he looked mournfully at his mother, he found she had not comprehended a word of what he had last said. She was looking at him with a stony, unmeaning gaze, as if she had a dim perception of his being there, and, uttering something which she ought to understand, but did not. He spoke to her in terms of affection, and, after a little, she recovered, and looking slowly about her, said, "Go find thy brother, and then, perhaps, thee had better ride up to the village, and—inquire," she added, in a tone below her breath.

He had not been at the village, neither had any one seen him, but all thought, or, said at least, that perhaps he would be home that night. It was probable he would. If he did not they must go out over the country next morning in search of him. Meantime a few anxious individuals mounted that night and rode out in various directions, but neither heard, nor saw anything to report. Thus the day closed!

Night came on. Night which so much changes the aspect of the whole world; which furnishes new images to the mind, and new energies to the physical powers; which brings a cessation of care, and a release from the burthens we have borne through the busy day.

But it brought no change to her! She could not look so far over the prairie as before the darkness came on, —the prairie over which she had looked for many, many hours before; though her eyes scarcely turned from the great waste since she sat down. There was but one object, indeed, that could have stirred the sense, now blind to all others, and that came not.

I said that night brought no change; and it did not. There she sat, sometimes speaking, when her sons, or one of the kind friends who had come in to be with her, addressed her; but her lips only spoke. At length they persuaded her to seek some rest. She retired, but lying down it was just the same. The position and place might change, but these had no relation to her stricken soul. The connexion between the material and the immaterial seemed to have been suddenly severed; and the latter to be existing in a time long past. The body might suffer changes, might grow old, or be diseased. But until the spirit had released its hold upon that point of time, it could take no cognizance of these.

Morning came and then hundreds of horsemen might be seen, far and near, scouring the plain, looking carefully through the groves and copses, searching by the banks of streams and logs, and then raising themselves up, and looking all abroad, and then at each other, with countenances that rendered speech superfluous.

Another night came and went, and no trace of the absent man could be found. They had looked for shreds of clothing, for the hat, the gun, anything that could give the faintest clue to the awful mystery; but nature refused all evidence, and left them to conjectures made only more painful by every disappointment. They had thought the accidental discharge of his gun might have disabled him, and they should find him somewhere awaiting the arrival of help. A more terrible supposition was, that in this state he might have been fallen upon by wolves! but no traces of any such fearful catastrophe could anywhere be found. He might have fallen into the stream, but all search that was practicable in its then frozen state was made — to no purpose. Other days and nights passed, but all ended as they had begun; the search was fruitless, and at last was gradually abandoned. What more could the utmost kindness do? His fate, from the hour when he left the house with the gay challenge on his lips, was involved in impenetrable mystery. Hope, even wonder almost died in the lapse of time. But what were her feelings? She had returned at last to a full consciousness of what had befallen her! She had passed from the doubts, fears, hopes, and dread of the long search, to the terrible certainty that she was widowed! But how? That was the most painful of all. Had she smoothed his dying pillow, had she heard his last kind words, it were bliss compared to her present torture! The most fearful conjectures thronged her agonized mind. Death, in his most terrible aspect, seizing on the helpless victim, was ever before her! Ravening wolves, overwhelming floods, bearing away their prey despite the fearful struggles for life; or, more terrible still, the slow death by starvation, in some possible nook that had escaped the eyes of those who sought to find her lost husband! Oh! who shall ever conceive the agony of that period, when to know that she was a widow was a small part of the burthen that pressed upon her heart, and made its agony almost palpable! She had friends with her, kind, gentle, loving friends, who would have counted no effort too great, could it have assuaged her grief. But what were these? They could tell her nothing. They could not answer one of the many questions which her heart never ceased to make everywhere and at all times.

Weeks wore away, and though the inquiry ceased to be first on the lip when neighbors met, and was followed, when made, with less earnest conjectures, still it was alive there, pressing its cankering tooth to the very core of her being.

The rude winds of winter at last began to be followed, at intervals, by the softer breath of spring. Nature began to dissolve her icy fetters on plain and stream. The season of birds and flowers, and universal beauty, which he had so loved, was approaching; the season when their happy home was even happier; when all its pleasant places were pleasanter. What would they be now?

On the stream which he had contemplated crossing, four or five miles below his house, was a mill. It stood in a pleasant spot—for woods and waters are ever pleasant in the prairie land—and when the winter ice had disappeared, and the fresh burthen of the early spring rushed along within its banks, it was cheering to see it come dashing past the mill, leaping the dam and bearing along decayed logs, bits of board and fantastic branches, rearing, plunging, resisting, and anon hurrying along more madly than the waters themselves.

Here one sunny March day stood a lad, watching the frolic and haste of the stream as it curled and foamed along, when suddenly the leaping current deposited on the verge of the dam, a large object which, at the first glance, he took to be a log! Then the water streaming from some dependent fragments, made him look again with somewhat of earnest curiosity! He approached to get a nearer view! and then ran as for life to the house! In a few moments graver persons appeared; took the long-lost body; laid it reverently in a fit place; and made preparation for the legal and decent ceremonies of the occasion. Though cruelly disfigured and changed, it could not be mistaken. The strongly marked head and face would have been recognized anywhere.

And now once more it returned to the home, almost as much changed as itself. They dared not let the widow see it at first, and as she was ever patient and gentle in her grief as well as her happiness, she did not murmur or attempt to oppose their wishes. At length, on the second day, when her mind was calmer than it had been, and she had learned to think of him as they described him in a few words, the gentlest they could use, as bloated, dark, bruised! when they had separated from her mind the idea of what he had been and brought it by the tenderest means to what he was; they led her to his bier.

There he lay, all that she had so loved in her early youth and sober womanhood, the father of her sons, the noble friend and protector of her past life, the tender nurse, and sympathizing friend of her sick years, her reliance when misfortune or sorrow came, her shield, her strong and patient friend in the adverse trials that had transplanted them from affluence in the east to toil and comparative poverty in the west!

She looked at him, and the blended emotions that had harrowed and torn her bosom since the day of their parting, were now all resolved into one simple and overwhelming tide of grief. There was no longer doubt, nor fear, nor hope—all had died when she looked on the mute witness that lay before her. And a mighty grief, that seemed to strike with iron fangs into her very heart, took possession of her.

They buried him, and she returned to her home! And there, when I saw her several months after, she went meekly about, discharging her daily cares and duties to her sons, and when she thought no human eye was upon her, permitting, as the only relief her feelings could have, without being painful to others, tears to stream silently down her pale, suffering face. I never looked upon grief so touching.

And this mother and her two sons were all that remained of the family we left on a former page in such happy and beautiful relation to each other, and the world around them.

CHAPTER XXV

The return of my husband was now *the event* to which I looked forward. Sixteen months of perilous wanderings in the wilderness, and upon the ocean, were now drawing to a close. His arrival had been joyfully heralded by letters from California, and last of all, by the public prints, announcing that it had been in his power to save the lives, and restore the liberties of several of his countrymen and Englishmen, prisoners to the authorities of that misgoverned, but beautiful country. The period of waiting was prolonged much beyond what I had anticipated. Days ran into weeks, and summer was drawing to a close, and still he came not. At last the third anniversary of our departed boy's birth, among the last days of August, brought him. It was early one morning, just after breakfast, that he came into my friend's house, following one of the villagers whom he had met in the street, and who could not forbear playing the startling office of usher on the occasion.

I pass over all that followed, the thousand interesting things to be heard and communicated; the welcomes and congratulations of friends, and come to the time but a few weeks forward, when we were preparing to leave prairie land and sever all the sacred ties that bound us to those who were sleeping in its quiet bosom, and those who still trod its beautiful surface, full of life and hope.

We visited Prairie Lodge and the resting-place of those who had been laid in the quiet graves near it, two long years before. At that distance of time, I could look calmly upon those hallowed spots, regarding them as what they really were—one, the tomb of a woman who had lived, loved, and suffered—the other, the tiny couch of an infant, whose tender bud of being scarce opened ere it closed again, to bloom in a more genial world. They were now objects of faith and hope, not of harrowing grief; and it was not altogether painful to linger over them, and train the evergreens and other plants which I had placed there long before. The foliage of the surrounding trees and shrubs had already faded from the high vigor and pomp of summer into the sober and gentle beauty of autumn—the season Mary had so much loved. A few short weeks, and the leaves would no more rustle to the gentle winds, the birds would no more dance in the boughs above, the mellow sunshine would no longer stream through the trembling canopy that softened its stronger glare into a tone harmonious with the hallowed character of the spot. All were departing; and we were going too; a few days would see us bid farewell to the country in which we had enjoyed and suffered so much; which still contained so much of life and death, to enchain our affections, and draw from our hearts in after times strong longings to behold it once more.

It was late in autumn when we bade adieu to the little village in which our home had been, and to the few faithful and beloved friends it contained. Yet late as it was, nature was still clothed with the full majesty of her departing grandeur. As we rode slowly over the high rolling prairies of the north toward our point of embarkation, I thought I had never seen the country more magnificent. It seemed inviting us to return. Distant fires, scarcely kept alive by the gentle winds, crept lazily over the great brown meadows, curtaining them from the flood of sunlight that filled the upper air, and just veiling the line of the horizon, so that it seemed an interminable distance away from us, and from all mortal care and toil—a quiet and holy region, where, indeed, earth and heaven might meet without exalting the loveliness and peace of the one, or lessening those of the other. Never was prairie land more beautiful to us, than in her farewell smiles. Never were our hearts more deeply touched by her charms, than in those days when we were passing away from them all.

The surface of the river, till our steamer broke it into foam, was smooth as the skies it reflected, and even then its agitated waters fell off, as soon as we had passed away, into a soft undulating motion, that died upon the sleeping shore, as if the repose of nature were too deep to be broken by man. Trees, half disrobed of their trembling leaves and bathed in sunshine, swayed softly to and fro, their long arms reflected from the still waters with a distinctness that suggested the idea of another creation slumbering beneath!

Myriads of wild fowl sat upon the tranquil stream, chattering in low tones, and lazily disporting themselves in the genial element. They had been arrested in their migratory flight by the wondrous beauty and softness of those days, and now lingered in the still waters, their dreamy rest broken occasionally by the panting steamer, and the more cruel gun of the sportsman on the shore. At long intervals, these merciless sounds boomed over the surface, and sent thousands of geese, brant, and ducks screaming into the air, till the silent woods and long line of water reëchoed to the cry. These were the only painful features of the scene. Nature would have been altogether lovely and gentle in her repose; but man was there, with his selfishness and cruelty, to mar it!

Our route lay through the theatre of many of the most interesting scenes and events in the history of the race that has now almost disappeared from these lands—the classic ground of the west! Legends of mighty deeds, such as make the boast of prouder nations, fierce hatreds, undying loves, such as troubadours delighted to sing of the knights of olden times, float over all these beautiful realms.

There is the "Starved Rock;" its frowning sides overhanging the quiet waters—its half-naked surface strown with the bones of brave men, tender women, and helpless children! The storms of near a century have bleached and wasted them into crumbling fragments; for here, so long ago, a band of warriors retreating with their wives and little ones, took refuge from their more powerful enemies, thinking to make their defence good on the small area, which could only be approached by one narrow passage connecting it with the mainland. Here they spent many days, defying their besiegers, and laughing at their efforts to drive them from their shelter. Food they had in plenty, and water ran at the foot of their fort, two hundred and fifty feet below them, which they raised in buckets attached to bark ropes. One afternoon, however, a bucket was let down, but when the Indian would draw it up, it was strangely light! Twice or thrice, after shooting it a few feet, he returned it to the stream, wondering that it did not dip! At length, weary at being thus foiled, he drew it hastily to the top of the rock. Consternation seized every bosom! The rope had been severed, and the bucket was gone! The experiment was repeated at another and another point with the same result! Where now was their hope? The base of their rocky fortress was surrounded by the canoes of their enemies! If they remained, a death more terrible than the tomahawks and scalping knives of their foes could inflict was before them. Yet, with their small numbers, and their wives and children there, it were madness to venture a sally. A council was held, at which it was determined by the warriors to await some relaxation on the part of their be-siegers, or some interposition of the Great Spirit in their behalf. Days passed in this fearful condition. Mothers with their nursing infants were famishing of thirst. Their babes were starving for the food which their exhausted systems could no longer furnish! Strong warriors began to look aghast, and tremble, as they walked about! The Great Spirit was angry with them; for clouds, charged with the blessing they so much craved, floated over them, and poured out their delicious treasures on the senseless plains and woods around, but never there. The clear river lay stretched for miles before them, its waters glancing in the sun, or maddening their thirst more fearfully when clouds darkened its checkered surface, making them look still more cool and inviting. Nay, it ran at their very feet. When the gusty night-wind swept over it, they could hear the waters faintly plash and chime below, and could almost in their madness have precipitated themselves into them, from the fearful height, to revel for one brief moment in their abundance. Sometimes, at the deepest hour of night, a vessel would descend the rock, stealthily and slowly, that no untoward contact might arouse their cruel watchers, if haply they slumbered. But vain and infuriating the hope and effort. It resulted only in the loss of the vessel, and the more dreadful aggravation of their sufferings. The terrible watch was never relaxed for a moment of the day or night, and the stern sufferer, at every failure, could hear the exulting laugh and the fierce congratulation of those who had caused it. Then they would heighten his agonies by toying idly with the water, making it splash and leap till the victim could almost see the light bubbles dancing on its cool dark surface. Some of the feeble women and the children died. But they could not be buried. Their bodies were laid decently away on the verge of the rock, and then the friends sat down to wait till they should follow!

Oh! what days and nights were those. Manacles on the limbs of the free, proud warrior, the lighted deathfire, the flashing tomahawk would have been his paradise, could he but have thrown himself upon them. To sit in miserable inaction all the day, he who was like the wind in swiftness and love of motion; to endure the raging torments of thirst and hunger (for the latter had at length been added to their sufferings); to see his wives and his young warriors sinking and dying around him; to make trial after trial for their relief, each ending in failure, more exasperating than before — was one of those fearful conditions of human being, which occur but once in the history of ages, and form in the annals of nations the proverbial evidences of bravery and fortitude, to which countless ages turn back with pride and exultation.

At length, when the exquisite torture could be no longer borne, and the prospect of an ignominious death by slow degrees was the only certainty before them, they determined on a sally. Seizing an hour, when those stationed on the landward side would least expect a movement after their long repose, and causing their women and children to render redoubled vigilance necessary at the base of the rock, they armed themselves, and, strong in the fury which their fearful suffering had provoked, issued silently from the retreat and fell upon their foes.

The contest that followed was bitter as Indian hatred and cruelty could make it. It resulted in the total route and destruction of the Illinois. From that day they were no more seen in council-house or battle field. Their name became extinct or was borne only by a few miserable wanderers from tribe to tribe. Their bones were left to crumble on the field, and their enfeebled women and children slain within the fortress, whence they watched the fatal struggle.

Such is the legend of the "Starved Rock!" It is now, in these tamer days, a curious and interesting object to visitors. Surrounded on three sides by the waters of the Illinois, it rears its frowning summit two hundred and fifty feet above them. The sides are smooth in many places and overhang the base, looking into the dark mirror below, as tranquilly as if they had never formed an impassable barrier between mortal agony and all that earth could afford to relieve it. The summit of the rock is crowned with vegetation; rich grasses and a light growth of young trees render its surface a more agreeable resting-place now than when the wretched Indian pined and famished there in the noonday sun. From its top it commands a view of the river for many miles, broken only here and there, by interposing trees or the gigantic vegetation that crowds its banks. One can imagine the unfortunate savage standing on it and looking out upon those waters which his light canoe had so often parted around him, with a desperation and agony that only the strong pride of his race could prevent him from uttering in tones of inexpressible anguish. To me it was a thrilling and fearful spot.*

But here is Mont Joliet with its fair proportioned valley, and swift running stream—the theatre where the good French père planted the first cross ever reared in these sublime solitudes. The tale is longer than I can tell, but it is a beautiful one—beautiful in its exhibition of exalted virtue, and its connexion with this lovely spot. It is one of the most glowing of those old legends that enrich the past. The past in the prairie land! What romance, what mystery, what uncounted volumes of thrilling interest sleep in its mighty bosom! Into these majestic solitudes, ages ago, came the wandering trapper and the solitary, self-sacrificing missionary. Here they lived, alone and humbly, among the proud sovereigns of the land. Their rude cabins were constructed beneath the forests that bordered the streams, and there, upon the margin of the still waters, the former sprung his trap, and the latter, clad in his long, coarse gown, the symbol of his faith and calling pendent at his girdle, preached, for the first time in these vast domains of nature, the doctrines of the Cross.

Seasons came and went; tender spring, glowing summer, ripening autumn, stern winter; and in them all was wondrous beauty or impressive majesty! From fort to solitary fort they floated on streams, thousands of miles in length, winding their lazy ways through a country unparalleled in fertility, beauty, and grandeur. Forests, magnificent in their richness, sublime in their loveliness, hung upon

* This rock is about six miles below Ottawa, on the east side of the Illinois. It projects far into the stream, and is connected with the mainland by a narrow passage which could be defended by a few men against thousands. Thither a band of the Illinois retreated, after a severe engagement at the north, when pursued by their more powerful and numerous enemies, the Pottowatamies, and then occurred the painful scene described above.

the margins of these rivers, their dense foliage peopled with myriads of gay, glancing birds, their dark mazes occasionally threaded by the startling catamount and panther! Passed these! and plains, not less impressive in their vastness, stretched out before the eyes of the *voyageur*, dotted with countless herds of the buffalo, the elk, the deer, and the antelope, feeding upon their peaceful bosoms. The gaunt wolf, stealing silently among them, hiding by day, and sending his dismal howl into the silent hours of night, added a striking feature to the strange joyousness of such wanderings.

Nor were these journeys less impressive when undertaken by land. Their way from post to post lay in the narrow trail which the Indian had trod from time immemorial. Day after day they wandered over these plains, and night after night slept upon their bosoms, beneath soft skies and gentle winds. Sunset and twilight, such as Italy would boast, ushered in their slumbers; and the grouse, with his mournful matin song, aroused them with the dawn, and sent them on their way with hearts swelling in unison with the world-wide peace and joy of nature!

What marvel, if they never wearied with telling the wonders of their new home! What marvel, if they spread its fame to far lands, and were content to die, away in its deep solitudes? What marvel was all this? Streams, whose course was equal to a quarter of the diameter of the globe, were stretched around them; storms, whose fearful wrath made the firm earth tremble, gathered and burst over them; sunshine and winds, birds and animals, flowers and fruits, such as only the fairest regions of the old world would return to unsparing labor, were here spread over half a continent! What marvel, if, amid these, they felt that language was too poor for their emotions, that fable could not exaggerate them?

Amid this magnificence they lived—alone with the "untutored Indian," sole lord and sovereign of it all. And wild and free was their life, with its abundance—its great untried resources—its boundless variety. One may well conceive that, with minds such as they possessed, it was the realization of their highest ideal. But it was destined to vanish! The second era of civilization dawned over these majestic realms, and its light dispelled their dream.

While the streams were yet unvexed by the impetuous steamer, and the beaver and otter dwelt unscared in their early homes; while the forest tracts were yet dark with the unbroken foliage, and wide plains, over which ages were destined to roll before plow or spade should mar their beauty, lay spread around them; came softly, one by one, the white-topped waggons of the early emigrants. They had left the dense forests of Ohio and Pennsylvania, the undulating hills of Kentucky, and the old homes of Virginia, for the new and more hopeful country which adventurers assured them lay beyond. Before them the Indian would retreat, and his white friend must follow. The bond that linked him to his kind was between him and the red man. He had lived in his lodge, shared his hospitality, smoked his pipe, united in his hunts, scalped his enemies, and cemented still more strongly their bond of union, by marrying his daughters. What had he in common with the cultivator of the soil, though wearing a skin of the same color? What had he not in common with those who retired to make way for him?

Here nature would be herself no longer. All her former aspect would fade away beneath the despoiling hand that labor would lay upon her charms; and they must flee to other regions where the spoilers had not come; their old haunts by stream and woodside were forsaken; the smoke no longer ascended from their solitary forts and villages; the rank grass overgrew their well worn trails, and the solitude of their familiar places was deepened by every object which showed that man had been there and departed.

Slowly, and with many regrets and painful yearnings toward the land which time and association had so much endeared, they wended their way to the yet unbroken realms between them and the setting sun.

Scarcely less a distinct race than these, were their successors. Their former lives — exposed as some of them had been by contiguity to savage neighbors, reared as others were in dependence upon slave labor, and accustomed as all were to the plain subsistence afforded by only partial industry — had begotten in them a love of ease, an unrestrained freedom which the new country was well calculated to foster.

To labor with the steady perseverance which anticipates its reward — to toil for the grain which, slow in accumulating, smiles only on the later years of life, was not their mission. Why should freemen do this, when nature was inviting them by such pomp and fascination, to come abroad with her, and enjoy every passing hour. The first settler could not live far from her; a rude cabin and a single field were all that he could brook of separation; more than these were burthensome to the spirit, and reduced freemen to slaves; more was unnecessary in his new condition. We have already beheld him living thus, content as if palaces rose around him. But a dark shadow soon fell upon his home. Files of earnest men, with hard hands and severe, calculating faces, pressed toward it from the east. Tales of its beauty, its grandeur, its freedom, its wondrous fertility, have reached their far firesides and rocky fields; and they are pressing forward to see if such things really are. When their eyes rest upon the glorious plains and gigantic forests, they exclaim, "This was no dream! Here is all that we looked for, and more than can be described! We will build our homes here."

They sat down beside the second son of nature. They fenced the plain adjacent to his field; they built a cabin, more finished than his; its smoke was continually ascending before him; their axe was heard in the neighboring grove, and the brave old trees, that had tossed their arms in the storms of ages, fell and were piled into lofty barns, that were visible wherever he went. If he chased the deer or hunted the grouse, or was returning from a visit to a neighboring settlement, there they stood, the first objects that greeted his vision; a blight upon the fair scene whose free aspect he had never thus marred. They struck his sight unpleasantly. He liked not these crowded ways of living, nor the busy sounds that floated with the morning light from his neighbor's home, nor his earnest toil in field and wood, nor his large crops, nor anything, in short, pertaining to his toilsome life. The country was less pleasant than it used to be, when there were no buildings, no fences, no living things in sight but his own and nature's.

He begins now to contemplate the possibility of following those who fled before him, and even while he is doing it, comes his neighbor's friend or brother, and proposes to bargain with him for his cabin and field! Now indeed, it is time for him to betake himself to a land of liberty. When the Yankees, not content with curtailing his freedom, his very breath of life—not content with crowding around him, and making a prison of his home, come and ask for that home itself—there is no longer any alternative. Everything admonishes him that the time of his departure has come! He therefore gathers his few worldly goods, and these, except his horses and rifle, are more than he wishes they were, and turns from his deserted hearthside to seek a more congenial spot, where industry and trade have not yet despoiled the fair earth, or crowded it with busy, thriving homes.

And now in his place succeeds a permanent population. His old haunts and pleasant ways are trodden by men, who, while they cast a careless eye upon the flying deer, count the resources of every acre which he scorns.

Broad farms open as by magic on the blooming plain; stately houses take the place of the solitary cabin; and industry, that counts her gains, has stretched her transforming arm over all the fair land. The wild, the free, the mysterious, are fading beneath her touch. But a power is growing up where they vanish, before whose might a continent may tremble. Who shall define the limits of its growth? Who shall conceive what intelligence and moral purpose may do, when they seize upon resources such as these, wherewith to consummate their energies.

Lands, boundless in extent, exhaustless in fertility, lying under every variety of climate from the tropical to the arctic; accessible in all their parts by continuous water-courses of magnitude unparalleled on the globe, containing so much to stimulate the nobler faculties and gratify the senses; so much that is calculated to induce a high state of physical development and fine perceptions of the beautiful, the grand, and the true; lands whose primeval glory, when it shall have become ancient, will form the theme of the poet and glow on the page of the historian; though too feebly sung and written to convey to future ages what the present feels. It must be the theatre of a life larger than human prophecy can foretell!

When the tide of intelligence shall have swept from the green barrier on the east, to the bald, heaven-reared wall that stretches along the west, and from the northern lakes to the gulf; when the remote tributaries of the great streams shall have become the commercial channels of the vast regions which they drain; and territories equal in extent to empires renowned in history, and surpassing the gardens of the old world in fertility, shall be overspread by a free brotherhood, united as to the great purposes of life, and pursuing them under a liberal and fostering policy—then will be presented the phenomenon of a life, of which we can have now but a faint conception. The pent-up, famishing legions of Europe may find room and abundance here, when they shall have burst the fetters that bind them there! And here may future tyrants behold how great, and good, and strong, is man when left to govern himself; free from want, from oppression, from ignorance, from fear!

But we are departing from prairie land! The bright waters of Lake Michigan dance around our steamer. Blue and dim in the distance, fades the mellow-tinted shore, its long faint outline trembling in the golden haze of the Indian summer! Farewell! land of majestic rivers and flowering plains—of fearful storms and genial sunshine—of strong life and glowing beauty! Glorious in thy youth—great in thy maturity—mighty in thy age—thou shalt yet rival the eastern lands of heroism and song, in the worship and affection of man! Thy free plains and far-reaching streams shall be the theatre of a power and intelligence never yet witnessed! Thy countless acres shall glow with checkered beauty and hum with busy life, when the generations of those who love thee now, sleep in thy peaceful bosom! Land of the silent past and stirring future, farewell!

THE END

The University of Illinois Press
is a founding member of the
Association of American University Presses.

_____

University of Illinois Press
1325 South Oak Street
Champaign, IL 61820-6903
www.press.uillinois.edu